Prais

"Once in a great while a book emerges so authentic in voice and messaging that we are compelled to rethink every religious belief or scientific theory we've ever contemplated about the origins of the human race. In The Origin Story, award-winning author Dr. Allison Brown, in partnership with her husband Will Brown, share provocative, inspirational messages about the seeding of humanity and its future from the 12 Collectives who represent our galactic ancestors, and validate that humanity has never been alone nor could it ever be separate from the One Infinite Creator. With this book, the couple's skills as a channel for the Source Field elevate them among this generation's most beloved and trusted psychics, healers, and channels — names such as Dolores Cannon, Neale Donald Walsch, Carla Rueckert, Jim McCarty, and Paul Selig."

— TRACY CROW, PRESIDENT AND CEO AT MILSPEAK FOUNDATION

THE ORIGIN STORY

ALSO BY DR. ALLISON BROWN

The Journey Within

Love Notes from the Animal Kingdom

(Co-author) The Ancestors Within

THE ORIGIN STORY

REDISCOVERING OUR GALACTIC ANCESTORS

DR. ALLISON BROWN

PALM AND LOTUS PUBLISHING

Published by Palm and Lotus Publishing

www.palmandlotus.com

ISBN: 979-8-9851252-2-1

CONTENTS

Foreword   xiii
Author's Note   xv
Introduction   xix

1. ANDROMEDANS   1
   Reset Versus Ascension   5
   DNA   7
   Humans and The Milky Way Galaxy   8
   The Andromedan Galaxy   12
   Emotion   14
   The Andromedans' Existence   16
   The Andromedans' Appearance   17
   The Andromedans' Unique Role   20

2. AGARTHANS   22
   Galactic War and Planetary Reset   25
   The Galaxy and the Universe   26
   Humanity's Ascension   27
   Hybridization and the Terra Beings   28
   Traversing Between the Surface and Inner Earth   30
   The Agarthans' Existence   32
   The Agarthans' Appearance   33
   The Agarthans' Unique Role   35
   A Message for Humanity   37

3. ORIONS   39
   The Reset Process   43
   Humanity's Partial Reset   46
   Humanity's Ascension Timeline   47
   Ascension is a Collaborative Effort   50
   Earth's Future and The Event   52
   The Original Plan for Earth and Humanity   54
   Understanding the Galaxy and the Universe   57
   Energetic Dominance   58
   The Orions' Perspective on the Galactic Wars   59
   The Orion Planetary System   62

Disclosure   64
Connecting with the Orions   65

4. SIRIANS   67
The Search for Meaning   70
God and Our Galactic Connection   73
Hybridization   73
Galactic Beings Taking On a Human Body   74
The Human Soul and Frequency   76
The Sirians' Appearance   77
The Sirians' Existence   78
Connecting with the Sirians   80

5. VENUSIANS   82
Multiple Levels of Reality   84
Multiple Levels of Source   85
Source Upgrades   86
The Venusians' Existence and Appearance   89
Impact of the Galactic Wars on Venus   91
Hybridization and Relationship to the Hathors   92
Valiant Thor   93
Connecting with the Venusians   95

6. LYRANS   97
Humans in Relationship with Other Beings   101
Interacting with "Nefarious" Beings   104
Interbreeding and Manipulation   107
Hybridization and the Galactic Wars   109
Lyrans as Overseers   111
Ascension and The Event   113
The Human Veil that Shields the All   115
The Lyrans' Appearance   117
The Lyrans' Unique Role   118

7. PLEIADIANS   122
Separation and Duality   125
Technical Aspects of Ascension   127
Families and Ascension   130
Our Solar System   132
The Pleiadians' Perspective on the Galactic Wars   132
Projection of Energy and Vibrational Resonance   135
Hybridization   137
The Pleiadians' Existence   139
The Pleiadians' Appearance   140

The Tachyon Healing Chamber   141
Connecting with the Pleiadians   142

8. ARCTURIANS   143
The Purpose of Humanity   148
Contractual Alignments and Purpose   154
Nodes, Source, and the Quantum Web   156
Balance and the Overlay   160
Reincarnation   164
Frequency and Vibration   165
Existing Physically versus Vibrationally   167
Hybridization and Colonization   169
The Arcturians' Relationship with Humans   170
The Arcturians' Unique Role   171

9. POLARIANS   173
The Human Sustainability Timeline   176
War and Peace   177
Hybridization   181
The North Star and Jesus's Birth   183
The Polarians' Existence and Appearance   183
The Polarians' Unique Role   185

10. DRACONIANS   188
Upgrading Without a Reset   190
DNA Alignments   191
The Soul   192
The Consciousness Upgrade   195
The Reptilians and the Event   199
The Role of the Reptilians   202
Reptilians and the Galactic Wars   205
Artificial Intelligence and Our Future   207
Arrival of Our Galactic Family   210
Hybridization   211
The Draconians' Appearance and Existence   212
Connecting with the Draconians   213

11. MARTIANS   214
The Martians' Role in Humanity's Evolution   217
Early Civilization   219
Human Evolution   220
Control of Humanity   221
The Anunnaki   223
The Earth's Fall   224

Fallen Angels   225
Colonizing Off Planet   227
The Event and Our Mission   230
The Mechanics of Ascension   232
The Dimensionality of Frequency   235
The Martians' Appearance   235
A Message for Humanity   238

12. HADARIANS   240
Love   245
Synchronization   247
Remaining in the Purity Vibration   249
Beta Centauri   251
Connecting with the Hadarians   252
A Message for Humanity   254

THE COUNCIL OF CONSTRUCTORS AND BUILDERS   255

Understanding Hybrids   273
Animal Associations   275
Acknowledgments   277
About the Author   279
Companion Workbook   281

FOREWORD

I am a researcher and Medical and Intuitive Astrologist. I am an internationally acclaimed speaker and have presented my work worldwide. As the great-granddaughter of President Dwight David Eisenhower, I endeavor to reveal exopolitical information about his administration that has been largely held in secrecy.

I felt a calling regarding my mission since I was a child. Gaining incredible insight through wilderness adventures and psychic development, I have been able to connect major dots about how to guide humanity into higher Earth energies. My role in this lifetime is to assist in humanity's ascension.

In her book, *The Origin Story*, Allison accomplishes a similar mission by sharing her understanding of the true origin of humanity's history—one that has also been hidden. Through the revelations within these pages, Allison takes the reader on a journey to discover all the missing pieces that we, as humans, are here to recognize, call back, and integrate.

I was astonished by the astrological chart reading I conducted on Allison and her husband, Will. The Grand Trines and force and power of their combined mission was so clear to me! The true potential and divine template that Allison and Will embody together has given them access to the knowledge and wisdom necessary to activate and awaken their fellow humans, as well as to guide us through the trials and tribulations of these times. *The Origin Story* provides humanity with the possibility to recover the fullness of all that we are.

It is such an incredible blessing to humanity that Allison has been able to access our true lineage, revealing the obstacles that have attempted to derail it and the journey we are now on—returning to true love. This is all I have ever wanted to speak about, and I am beyond grateful that someone like Allison can put it into words, to truly activate the deeper calling that exists within so many. We have such an affinity in understanding this greater healing process we are all going through.

The Origin Story serves as a guide to our remembrance and inner-self awakening to the inner union, the reclamation of our full, twelve-strand DNA, and the guidance that comes through when we can truly listen and release the forces that seek to sabotage and disconnect us from our greater divine purpose.

Laura Magdalene Eisenhower

AUTHOR'S NOTE

All material within the twelve chapters of this book was transcribed directly from channeled conversations that occurred between August, 2022 and January, 2023. The Introduction that precedes Chapter 1 and the ancillary material that follows Chapter 12 contain both channeled transmissions and informational narrative. In those sections, as well as within the end notes, I've italicized the channeled passages to distinguish them from my own words. Within the twelve chapters themselves, any words or passages in bold or italics serve to demonstrate emphasis during the transmission.

While the words on the page contain a great deal of extraordinary information, these transmissions also hold an energetic frequency that will impart a message to the reader at a soul level, beyond their conscious understanding. Due to the energetic nature of these transmissions, I made very few changes to the text. My priority was to offer these transmissions with fidelity, inasmuch as contextually possible. For that reason, you may notice some minor grammatical errors, "new" vocabulary words, or clumsy phraseology. Where I felt it essential for comprehension, you'll notice additional words or sentences in [brackets].

In terms of the book's structure, I decided to present the transmissions in a narrative format, rather than as a Q&A. That means that the reader is not privy to the exact wording of the questions I asked to solicit the content you will be reading. Most of the time, this format worked out well. On occasion, however, you'll find that I added a bit of context [again, within brackets] to the beginning of a paragraph or section in order to provide a frame of reference for that transmission. That is also why you may find that a subsection doesn't necessarily flow, content-wise, from the preceding one—each subsection can stand alone.

The sigils that accompany each chapter are unique to—and hold the specific frequency of—each of the twelve source clusters. These powerful symbols impart an energetic message to the reader in much the same way that the words on the page do. Of course, nothing about this book is without divine orchestration, including the way these sigils came into being. Around the same time that I was being prompted to ask my friend, Tobi Elbel, an artist and channel, if she felt inspired to bring forth a symbol for each chapter's header, she was (unbeknownst to her) receiving a similar message from The Twelve, who had already gifted her with the Sirian sigil during a morning meditation. At that time, however, Tobi was not aware of the symbol's purpose. Once we connected the dots, Tobi was off and running. The Twelve fully aligned their energy with hers, guiding her in scribing each energetic signature onto paper. (Be on the lookout for book companions that offer even more ways to benefit from these sigils, including a card deck and workbook.)

There are a few other points of clarification that need to be made for understanding: 1) The word Being is capitalized when used as a noun (denoting a physical or energetic entity), in order to differentiate it from the verb, 2) There was no scripted list of questions I planned to ask each of the Twelve; I was advised against that format (as you'll read in a moment) because each cluster had specific information to impart to humanity, and 3) The initial paragraphs of each chapter constitute the opening transmission from that cluster. My follow-on questions arose intuitively and flowed seamlessly from that initial transmission. For that reason, the subsections within each chapter vary, based on the course of the conversation. For example, although many of the clusters speak about hybridization or the galactic wars, not all of them do. And for those who do, they communicate that information in a unique way, based upon their own perspective.

It is my sincere hope that you find these transmissions as compelling and fascinating as I do! May the beautiful words of the Twelve wrap around your heart, filling you with the unconditional love of your galactic ancestors and empowering you with your Divine mission, as together, we embark on this profound journey of evolution.

INTRODUCTION

I am a writer.

I get antsy when I go long stretches without writing. As soon as I complete a project, my mind starts searching out the next subject to tackle. Such was the case after *Love Notes* was published in October, 2021. I was restless—I longed to start writing again but just couldn't pin down the topic. Nothing was lighting me up! One thing I knew for sure was that, when it *hit* me, I'd be off and running, immersed, once again, in that powerful river of inspiration...the Divine flow of connectedness. It's the undeniable feeling one gets when they *know* they are fulfilling some piece of their mission, their contract, their purpose.

As the months ticked by, I kept circling back to Extraterrestrials. After all, our ET friends were a huge part of our lives. We conversed with them on the regular—they taught us, inspired us...helped us to *remember*. Our lives had been completely and utterly altered through our relationship with our galactic guides and family members. It was clear that sharing this knowledge with humanity was important. I just wasn't sure what that might look like. Would it be completely channeled material? Did *they* (whoever that was) have a book *they* wanted to write? Was I to compile a book using excerpts of previous conversations we'd had with various ET Beings and collectives, similar to the format of *Love Notes*? Did I have an interplanetary partner for my next project? Or was I on my own?

The answers to those questions began in earnest one ordinary Friday afternoon in August, 2022. I was exhausted after a busy week at work, and was lying on the couch, trying to decide if I had enough energy for a dinner date with my husband, Will. As we chatted about our day, I casually mentioned an article I had read recently that described the twelve original starseed clusters, for readers who were curious about their galactic families. I was intrigued, because although I was very familiar with the term *starseed*, I had never seen a definitive list of them, nor did I realize there were only twelve.

As I was speaking, Will (who is a trance channel) received the tell-tale sign of confirmation—a full-body vibration—and he suddenly recalled an experience he'd had the previous night. Upon waking, it felt as if he had been downloaded with a complex packet of information relative to our human understanding of Source (a mind-boggling concept that will be expounded upon later in the book). He sensed that, somehow, this was all connected. The more we conversed, the more we realized that we needed to unravel this thread. We felt we were being guided.

Not even knowing if such a thing existed, we decided to call upon (channel) the twelve starseed clusters, as a group, to determine if they had more information for us. I was immediately introduced to the Council of Twelve. They identified themselves as *the original cluster of Beings, of entities, of energies that arose from the everything. The origins of all energy...the origins of all Beings.*

They explained to me, in that initial conversation, that *the story of the origins is one that is passed, generationally, energetically, downstream from the beginning. It is one that is sent out...the message is sent out and broadcasted throughout all time signatures, all time alignments. It is ongoing, ever-present, always will remain. It is necessary to understand the origins. It is necessary to understand this broadcast. It has been in place and will remain in place. It is the history that never changes.*

And it is, as you perceive, being received. That is true. But to understand how you are receiving this message...it is to look to your galactic alignment, your galactic family. For it is [through] the aligning that that broadcast is then being received and imparted to you.

It is not a direct message from the Twelve, but it is a message that is broadcast. It carries on from generation to generation of Beings, all throughout the galaxies. And when time is aligned appropriately, then it is received. For your time existence, you'll begin the process of scribing. You'll begin the process of retrieving this information.

Like an interstellar antenna, I had energetically connected with an ancient broadcast—an ethereal recording, of sorts—echoing throughout time and space, patiently waiting for a human partner to listen. Furthermore, this message was being relayed via the Lyrans, my galactic family. They were the energetic bridge between me and this primordial transmission. Not only had I heard and responded to the call, I was being gifted with an extraordinary opportunity: to become their scribe...to bring forth *the Origin Story*.

The Twelve

We are neither elder nor master. We are the originating source energy divided into twelve clusters, assigned to a particular cluster for an origin point. Once the Twelve begin to subdivide and the Twelve begin to populate existence...that is where consciousness starts to evolve. The purity between Source and the Twelve remains. And from that, when that begins to cleave, and they begin to populate other clusters around them with existence, [the Twelve] become the originating point and the other clusters begin to come into existence, and that's where deep consciousness begins. It is not beginning within the Twelve or at Source. Source is just the purity of existence. There is no need for consciousness to take place.

As we come to you, you would assimilate a cluster of Beings as a council. If that is much more palatable to your envisioning, so be it. But it is [an] energy form. If you wish to understand it a bit greater—the purest form of energy at the highest dimensional plane. Nonexistent of form, but present in All.

You would place that at your twelfth dimensional understanding. But also understand, there are many that believe there are greater than twelve dimensions, energetically. As energy begins to divide itself, as you begin to go into different sublayers, then they are witnessed accordingly. So as you are in your fourth, fifth dimension, there are sub-dimensions between, and many believe those sub-dimensions equate to an actual dimensional level for existence...say 4.1, 4.2. Each one of those would be a sub of the predecessor. But understand, there are only twelve originating dimensional levels, and there are twelve originating clusters, not by coincidence.

Even at your twelfth dimensional plane, you believe there is a higher level of consciousness, but it is at a state at which it is the closest replication of Source. It is the All. It is the essence of all things, the purity that resides within that dimension. The Beings that hold that dimension are there to assist and guide without complexity, to guide and assist with the beauty of pure consciousness. There is no discussion. There is no arbitration. There is no division. It is the pure essence of Source when that dimension enters in to assist.

[And why twelve?] In your understanding, there are multiple ways to express this...mathematically, geometrically. Organisms have twelve subsets. Everything is divided by an equal number. The twelve layers upon itself exactly. Geometrically, it forms an energetic sphere shape that, inside itself, contains purity. It is not to look upon it as some mystery in your existence, but the number twelve allows the division to be spread wide. It could have been three originating clusters, but the multiple factors throughout time would be less complex. Twelve gives the appropriate amount of complexity throughout time. Greater than twelve lengthens specific timelines.

So twelve is an appropriate number for understanding complexity in existence, complexity in prescribed timelines, and overall, the layering of one's existence. For if you were to understand your existence as the pure human, you would understand your twelve layers of existence, and somewhere in those twelve layers is your existence at this particular point. Energetically, they're all taking place simultaneously. They're all interacting differently. And this is for all

Beings. Not only humans, but all Beings. All energetic, physical Beings have twelve layers of existence.

During that initial conversation, the Twelve explained our synchronous connection and the starseed article that triggered it: *This is an appropriate connection. That is not something that is by chance. That has been orchestrated. But what must be understood is that, as a reception is being put in place —the receiving individual—there is an awareness. The awareness amongst the Twelve then begins to orchestrate additional information, begins to put in place additional pieces, begins to put information in front of you. For you have already received a bit of this information, listing the twelve original clusters: Orion, Pleiades, Andromeda, inner Earth, and so forth. That is correct. Those are your stepping stones. Follow that list and you will be attuned to that frequency.*

They further shared that I was not the only one to receive this direct message. *There are multiple timelines of existence in your human form that are receiving this direct message, this direct transmission. You are not the only one to receive this, though it is the only one in* your *timeframe existence. You understand your multiple nodes and your multiple areas of existence in different dimensional planes...for* this *dimensional plane, you are the only conduit that is receiving this information at this particular time.*

Along your existent timeline here, upon this planet, there have been multiple books, multiple points of information about the same cluster of twelve and how they all understand it...but at each point, [as] the transmission is received by those individuals, it is structured for that timeframe, and so on and so forth. We have moved into a new timeframe. You are part of this transmission, so allow the information to be imparted for this frequency band, this frequency-time area.

Your Lyran connections will be your gateway. That will be your stepping point. Enter in through the Lyrans, allowing them to guide you into the next layer of information, directing you to those that will provide you the clearest and cleanest reception of that portion of the transmission, [to] each of the original twelve.

Thaddeus

Greetings from the Lyrans. May I make myself present to you? I would like to introduce myself as Thaddeus. That is who you may connect to before this point of interaction. This is our first alignment and first assignment.

The downloads have yet to begin. The energetic alignments have been orchestrated. The broadcast that was received via the Twelve has been realigned and centered over your position. You've begun to receive those transmissions. That is what you are sensing throughout your field of existence.

My particular role with you is to begin the alignment process, the connection points, allowing you to be the resonator of the energy. So as one cluster begins to provide its information directly, I will realign it. I will attune it to your frequencies. You will become the resonator by which William will, then, begin to broadcast the information requested.

[This connection, this alignment is part of your contract.] You have made this available to yourself at this particular time. For each iteration of the transmission that has been received from the Twelve and disseminated out to your human population, each one has been imparted with a specific frequency range, to be received by those that are attuned to that specific frequency range. This will be very similar.

You must understand, throughout time it is repeated. Throughout time it has been broadcast. Throughout time it has been repeated, and it has been rebroadcast. We are at a time now where it is being received, and it will be rebroadcast. You are receiving, and by your words it will be rebroadcast. It will be identified by a signature point that others will receive. So understand that each word, each message, each turn of the page will have its own signature frequency, and that, then, will be received to those that they come in contact with.

Understand this: Do not set boundaries by specific questions that are associated across all twelve. The more organic each conversation is, the purer the information will be, the higher signature frequency it will carry, the greater audience it will reach. As you are receiving details, as you are receiving information via the channel, allow yourself energetically to enter into that space. This will amplify.

That is why you are designed as the resonator. This will amplify the channel of information and the flow of information, just as it is doing now. You are resonating quite high. The channel is receiving that frequency. It is coming through quite clear.

So allow that process to continue as you enter into each one of the clusters. The purest information will be brought forward. It may not be the same as it has been broadcast to others. That is because it is being rebroadcast for a particular timeframe. Each timeframe has to be restructured for information, so it is then received most appropriately.

Begin to connect to each one of the Twelve individually and allow them to guide you. Do not look upon a list to understand which one is before what, and if there's an orientation to another, but understand which one begins to resonate frequency-wise with your alignment. I will be orchestrating that. As that begins to populate, that will be your beginning point. As you begin to work your way through the information, you will also understand when I begin to pull away, and that is your disconnection point.

Filling in the Blanks

For those who are familiar with the twelve starseed clusters, you may wonder, as I did, why some seem to be very well known and some, not so much. Almost everyone has heard of the Arcturians, Pleiadians, and Lyrans, for example, but what about the Hadarians, Agarthans, and Polarians? Were there any humans with a DNA connection to those galactic families?

The Andromedans explained it this way: *From a vibrational standpoint, many, as your understanding would have it, have laid themselves dormant. They do participate...infrequently, but they do participate. They've laid themselves dormant. It is not that they have not a benefit to be contacted, but it is a cycle. They can still be called upon; matching frequencies to those specific source clusters will bring you into contact with those [Beings] and those understandings. In time, those will become active again, and others will go dormant.*

This is a normal process. For when a certain change or a certain aspect of the galaxy needs to be tended to, a number of the Twelve will activate, and they will be the prominent ones that are being communicated with. As that begins to remedy itself, then another situation may arise, another aspect of the galaxy needs tending to, and others will be activated.

Although I knew I had aligned this for myself, per my contract, throughout the process, I often wondered if I was up for the job. The information, at times, seemed so complex! And if I couldn't understand it, I certainly wouldn't be able to write about it in a way that made sense to anyone else. Perhaps "they" had made a mistake and selected the wrong person. Maybe I wasn't as intelligent as they thought I was.

During one channeling session with the Arcturians, after asking them to clarify yet another difficult topic, I said as much—mostly tongue-in-cheek but genuinely curious about their response. As one would expect, their answer put me at ease: *This appropriate person is the most associated to do this because if it were someone that had a much higher understanding of galactic Beings, a much higher awareness of their presence within the galactic realm, the information that would be imparted would be well beyond the comprehension of many of the Beings that need to hear what is being brought through. And this is why we wish to assist you in this.* Whew! Good to know.

And So It Begins

As I practiced tuning in to the energy of the Twelve, I found myself at the head of a long, oval conference table surrounded by twelve empty chairs. The room, just large enough to house the table and chairs, contained a bank of windows along one wall, overlooking the inky vastness of space and countless twinkling stars. One by one, in a divinely orchestrated sequence, each of the Twelve would join me there, offering their unique transmission, blessing me with their presence.

The Andromedans were the first to make contact...

1

ANDROMEDANS

Greetings from the Andromedan cluster, the origins of the Andromedans. We bid you peace, and we thank you for connecting. As you have called upon us to understand our presence, to understand our galactic presence among you and all others, one must understand the aligning of all clusters. As you've called upon us to be the first, allow us to explain how each cluster represents itself into your future.

The previous connection of the Council of Twelve explained the origin of all, you and your understanding of Source, this originating point. Though the questions are many, if there's an originating point, where is that originating from? That is more for your mind to perceive than it is to understand. It is your cognitive understanding that [believes] something has to come from somewhere or something.

But what underlies all existence, whether it is within your galaxy or realm or others, is a pure frequency in which all things are derived. For your galaxy (which you inhabit) and your planetary systems, the *tone* provided the construct for the emanation of twelve, the assigning of the Twelve. Other galaxies, other star systems, other planetary systems may have as few as one or as many as hundreds. Your galaxy has been assigned twelve. This number is not by chance, and that was already explained. But from that point forward, each one of the Twelve has a specific signature, frequency signature. In your understanding, there still is yet to be a physical being, a physical placement. This physical placement does not come for some time, for all is a tone, all is a frequency.

Just as it has been provided, your understanding, your construct of this episode in time of where all things originated, your theory of the existence of your galaxy, the Big Bang...that is the merging point, the mergence of all frequencies. From that, begins the process of the creation of different star systems, stars, planets, nebulae, all constructs within your galaxy and your galaxy field. And yes, your scientific research understands it somewhat correctly. It is this understanding that, once there is matter in your universe, gravitational forces begin to build planets, begin to build other structures...when in reality, it is the consciousness of the frequencies that are emanated that begin to bring together what has been created at the point of mergence of this frequency.

So it is to understand that each one of the Twelve emanates their own frequency. At the point at which each one of those frequencies merges together, all twelve, that is the beginning point. That is what you would reference as your beginning point. From there, those twelve frequencies now begin to emanate throughout the construct that has already been put in place...bringing together planets, bringing together stars, and all other pieces of matter within your galaxy system. From there, you may ask, where do Beings, life, where does that come into play? Where does that begin to emerge? That, too, is brought in through frequency. But how that begins is a much deeper story.

The Andromedans...as that frequency begins to broadcast out from the beginning, it has a particular place, a particular space that it will begin its origin, just as the other twelve will have their origins within your construct of your galaxy. The Andromedans, still in pure vibrational form (it is just a frequency), will begin to build their star system, their place of residence, their place of existence, though it is just all frequency. It is pulling together the matter out of nothingness. This concept of pulling matter from nothing...you must understand the power within frequency. Just as you have a glass of water that sits before you, you see nothing in your water. But with the right amount of frequency, with the right amount of *directed* frequency, you'd begin to see bits, pieces, precipitant come through your water and form within your water. That is *something* from what you would perceive as *nothing*. That, too, in your construct of your galaxy, where there is to be perceived *nothing*, with the right amount of frequency, the right variability of frequency, it will begin to pull together *matter*.

Each one of the Twelve has their own specific frequency, and from that beginning point, begins the process of building. Each one of the Twelve create their star system, and from that, then it is agreed upon that many others will be created. Just as the Beings are created through frequency and sound and vibration, the star systems, the stars, the planets, the suns...all of that is created, again, with agreement between different star systems. Once the physical constructs are in place...planets, stars, then all other structures throughout your universe...once those appropriate places are put into place, then, again, through frequency, life begins. But do not understand life, as you understand it, as a human. *Consciousness* is the best way to understand it—multiple consciousnesses throughout one existent planet, one existent star, one existent sun. No matter the location, the frequency pulls together and forms consciousness, and more so, and more so, and more so. This, then, begins to build together. That is where your Beings come from.

The beginning point of all of this is well beyond your comprehension. You have your limited understanding as a human upon the Earth planet, [of] where life has come from, but it is truly to understand all life begins with frequency, through a tone...an audible tone at the beginning point. The individual frequencies that coalesce at that beginning point...that audible tone begins the process of life.

From the moment at which the frequencies begin to pull together mass in order to create a physical structure, planet, for inhabitants, this timeline of events...there are multiple thousand-year cycles that, within each thousand-year cycle, there's a new...you would understand it as a rebirthing. This you must understand: These structures, these constructs in which life begins...it is as if it is a trial period. Within that thousand-year cycle, life does begin to form. You would not quite understand the life forms; they take many shapes. In your opinion, they would be a bit disturbing at times. They did not take the shape and form that you know them as now, more humanoid, more humanlike.

These life forms, though very limited in consciousness, begin a trial period of the construct, the planet, the star, the sun which they will inhabit. But they also know that at some point, it will be reset. It is a growth point. For their actions, their growth actions, are helping the planet, the star, the sun to become whole. With each cycle, the consciousness of those Beings enters into the consciousness of that planet, that star, that sun...up until a point at which a Being of substantial consciousness is formed...a Being that does not quite represent your humanoid-looking Being, but one that can sustain itself upon the consciousness of that planet, star, or sun.

That is when it goes into a long-term cycle, and that is determined by how long [the] consciousness of that planet, star, or sun will be. For there is a time limit. Again, with each cycle, [the purpose] is to grow. At a particular point at which the consciousness within the planet, star, or sun needs to be renewed, it will regenerate itself, wiping out its consciousness...wiping out all consciousness, all Beings. That cycle starts again. This is all to improve, all to strengthen the life potential within and on that planet, star, or sun.

You have to understand, the frequency that has been emanated out from the beginning point—not the source point, but the beginning point, your Big Bang, for reference—that tone continues on infinitely. Never ends. So, as new consciousness arrives on the planet, it is embedded with that tone.

Now, to understand where the frequency divides out into a physical Being, a physical construct, imagine if you will, where the frequency is divided. That tone is divided. A bit of that frequency is brought into a planetary system to seed that system. The bits of that frequency begin to interact, pull together, and create a life form. That life form has then a bit of consciousness from that frequency stream. From there, you would also understand it as how you would describe your artificial intelligence. It is implanted, encoded into this life form...consciousness.

But the consciousness has no reference point. The consciousness has no understanding of what life is. It's consciousness. It's an awareness. That awareness then begins to learn. Very basically, but begins to learn, and begins to learn, and begins to learn. But at the particular point that consciousness has learned as much as it needs to learn, that is where the reset point comes in. That consciousness then is put into the planetary system, put into the planet, star, or sun.

As it happens again, it grows upon what it has already known...the new life form has the new bit of consciousness, but it also has the consciousness that remains within the planet, combining, giving more awareness. With each cycle, the awareness grows. With each cycle, the awareness grows to a point at which you have a consciousness that is aware, has presence, just as your human form, as they are brought into this planet. They have an awareness. They have a Being. They understand. They must be taught, but they understand.

Reset Versus Ascension

[A reset] acts as a cleansing point. It is something that energetically aligns when it is known to be needed. Just as it has been expressed that the cycle points, the reset points, as the process of manipulation, as process of the hybridization takes place...as it's known that it is time to cleanse, then it does. It then uses the energy, light at first, but as it becomes more populated, it is needed then to cleanse the entire universe of existence. The twelve source points will always remain, and that is the origin point for the new beginning.

So it is not to say that it is nefarious. It is not brought in from any Being. It is not brought in from any one cluster. It is what is known to be. It just

Ascension

is. It cannot be explained other than to say it is brought in when needed to cleanse and clear, to reset. It is a wave of cleanse that takes place throughout your entire galaxy. All existence is wiped clean. All consciousness is wiped clean. Specifically to say, your soul, your energetic source point...your energetic source point is then brought back to the All and reset.

The humans are the main reason for the [galactic] project. There are multiple other areas within your galaxy that there are Beings that are similar to the humans, but have not achieved to the same point as the humans. You must understand, this is not an experiment, but it is an understanding. The humans are the most important factor in this project, this galaxy. This galaxy was designed for them. This galaxy was designed for their exploration. This galaxy was designed for their growth. The humans are the priority in the cycle. But if they do not achieve, then the cycle needs to be reset.

Ascension is different than the cleansing. Ascension in itself...many here on this planet now have felt their ascension, have felt their expression of entering into a new dimensional level. This is a vibrational aspect. You must understand the vibrational processes. Ascension is this: Your physicality has achieved vibrationally all it can. It is sustaining a vibrational point within its own sphere of its highest maximus point. Then, it aligns with all of the other source points, the Twelve, all other aspects of themselves, their galactic connections. It is aligning to bring you to the next vibrational level. Once you ascend to that next vibrational level, it is as if you're stripped of all of that energy again and reset. It is similar [to a full reset], but different. It is more of an energetic leveling up to the next level [within the same physical body] than resetting and beginning the process again.

What you are achieving [now] as humans, what you are achieving within your galaxy is greater than what was expected. You must understand, even though the project did not go quite as expected with all the manipulation and all of the hybridization[1] even below your dimensional planes, what has been achieved, the consciousness of the humans has taken over. The consciousness of the humans has been able to achieve greater than what was expected according to the expected timelines that were projected for this particular project.

If you were to overlay it upon a timeline of existence, most importantly in your last fifty years. Before that, there was an achievement level that was on par, existent for what was supposed to be. But what you must understand...within the last fifty years of your life cycles, many of the humans themselves have a greater understanding. They have an openness. Their DNA and their connection, those two strands of DNA, though laying somewhat dormant in many, are utilized to the fullest in quite a few.

DNA

Each strand [of human DNA] represents one source node [cluster]. You contain all twelve. Only two [DNA strands] are energized at the point at which the Being is animated with the energetic Source. The physical Being, the physicality...as it comes into being, two are energized. Those two are then specifically referenced to two specific source clusters, whether that be a Pleiadian and a Martian, or an Orion, or an Andromedan. One would be a primary contact point. That would be your closest alignment. Then, you would have your source cluster. The two that are activated are the two main that are agreed upon, upon animation. Once that takes place, that is [your] starseed connection.

[At this time in your evolution, more strands] are being activated. Not the full strand itself. You have to understand; the two source strands will always be the animated strands. The human itself, the Being itself, in order to remain as it has within the second, third, and fourth dimension of your understanding, could only sustain those two strands. There has been much that has been learned of how many are an appropriate amount of strands to be activated at a lower dimensional standpoint. The more that are activated, the further the individual, the further the Being, the further the human is actually away from the remaining amount of humans. So it has been found that two is an appropriate number for the appropriate animation during a lifecycle. As you increase from the third into the fourth [dimension], you would encounter at least one or two to be reanimated again and again. As you achieve to about the tenth dimension, most, if not all, will be reanimated. [At that point] you will not have the same physical form, but you'll have the understanding, the concepts of the human understanding, the human consciousness.

You must also understand, there has been some confusion amongst many of the humans that they have more than twelve [strands of DNA]. This is also a manipulation point. There have been many that have claimed that they have at least twenty-six strands of DNA. This is a fragmentation of the DNA stranding. The two animating strands are always the two animating strands, but in that, the remaining strands end up fragmenting, and they do not adhere to one another. That is why some are understanding themselves as having multiple, more than twelve strands of DNA. They are seeing the strands. But they're not realizing they are fragmented strands.

Humans and The Milky Way Galaxy

When understanding the creation of this existence, [The Milky Way Galaxy], loosely put...the blueprint for this galaxy is to bring in a consciousness Being that is unlike any other conscious Being...that being your humans. This galaxy is the only galaxy with such consciousness. It was what was to be designed, and all were in agreement for it. The original galaxy project...there were to be limited numbers of each known combination. There is a set of knowns, of the known combinations, not in your mathematical terms of how many variants you can have with twelve source points and so on, but there is an agreed-upon number of reference points. And that's how many divisions there were to be.

The final division would have been the humans. That's where it would have lain and that's where it would have grown, and that's what was agreed upon. But then, you must understand, in order to get to the human, that is getting lower in your reference point for dimensionality.

Yes, vibrationally, there were many that still remained in the vibrational state, the energetic state, [but] the further you divide out, the closer you get to physicality. It is a bit of [an] inverse understanding. The higher the frequency, the less dense. The lower the frequency, the more dense.

The original twelve that were brought in from the source point through tone and frequency are all, in your understanding of dimensionality, [of] the twelfth dimension. Pure energy form. No form. Just pure energy. For your understanding [it is] somewhat correct [to say] that throughout time, it is a reverse point. As [energetic Beings] progress in time, they're descending through the dimensional levels. That is only built into your construct of understanding so that you can place them into a visual aspect that you understand, that you can then connect to. That is the representative feature.

There are those that are still in pure form, but they will take the shape of a lower dimensional aspect, more solid form...but remaining in the twelfth dimensional aspect. The numbers of the original twelve, the original pure Beings, are quite limited because of the manipulation through time. So you, as a human, wish to contact an Andromedan, an Orion, a Sirian, an Arcturian, a Pleiadian, you connect and you understand that you've been connecting to them for some time. But at a particular point, you connect, and the energy itself is greater than you've experienced. [In that moment], you are connecting to a Being that is still in the pure twelfth dimensional form but is representing itself in a form in which you can witness it.

You must understand the differences in your energy fields and how they are connected to you. For each [energy] that you feel, you'll begin to sense and understand how far down the dimensional ladder these Beings are. The less influenced energy, the more dense the Being, the lower the dimensional field. That is to say that most, if not all Beings that you [humans] are connecting to frequently will be within the fifth to seventh dimensional plane.

As you begin this practice of hybridization to achieve the goal of a human, you are already achieving dense factors. You are already achieving human-type Beings. Physicality has been taken into effect. That is where the consciousness of a physical Being then gets interrupted. It is more of this understanding of achieving more over time. But what they did not realize is the depth of denseness that they could achieve, and it went more dense than the human density.

In the lower density forms...you understand your third and fourth dimension, and yes, you have, if you're equating numbers, two and one. But even subsets of those, even subsets of the third and the fourth dimension, there were Beings that had an understanding, though it was not referenced as "good" or "bad." They did as they did; no consequences and no reference point for good or bad. But they also understood the outcomes of those experiments, those combinations of frequency streams to produce another lower dimensional Being, a subset of two or multiple subsets of two. Divisions among divisions. Once that population was processed, that's when the realization took place that this is not what is needed, and we must back ourselves out.

The human density, at its most stable point, was in the third and fourth dimension. That is similar to where you are now. It has been recycled over time, but this is the common understanding. Lower than that, then it begins to disrupt systems, and that in itself is where you would understand the manipulation begins. That is where they [some hybridized Beings] are now trying to reverse the process. Those Beings realize that it is a place in which it is not preferable to be, and so they wish to reverse the process, backing themselves out of the denseness into a light body once again, an energetic body again.

That is why you have this understanding that many of the Beings that have been created have been manipulating and changing the human aspect, going and taking some things from the human. That is correct. Much has been relieved from the human in order to reverse the process back out of that existence. It is quite complex. The purity was there for thousands of years, tens of thousands of years. But as consciousness grew and it became more aware, it also became aware enough to the point at which it could begin to manipulate the frequency streams...

manipulate them in a way in which it created different Beings. Hybrids, not pure.

One would also say that the human would be a non-pure Being. Yes, that is correct. That was the intent. But it was in a way in which, once all consciousness, pure consciousness of all twelve, have created their respective locations and their respective places to inhabit, that is when, again, a full merging of frequencies would come together to create the human. That in itself would then become a pure representation of all twelve, though the human at its point now has been manipulated by many different other consciousnesses, other Beings. So the human itself is a hybrid of multiple different Beings.

The originating source for that pure Being, the pure human, would've taken place upon your Martian planet. It is the most appropriate according to your planetary structures. At the time, just as your planet is habitable [now], it was not [then]. The Martian planet was a habitable planet. It was the most representative. The Martians themselves were going to be the caretakers for the human Being, to instruct them, to allow them to grow, and to provide them their awareness and their understanding of all things that are around them. Their galactic understanding.

But in time, that planet was overrun. Again, in time, the factions began to take place amongst others. You understand the galactic wars that have taken place throughout your galaxy, as well as others. That galactic war shifted many of the axes upon different planets within your system, throwing up the balance and creating a closer spatial relationship to your sun, which then was a partial demise of the Martian planet. All that were inhabiting that planet exited the planet, escaped, moved on, inhabited other locations...one of which began here, on your planet. That is where the humans set foot, began their existence, their awareness, and their life.

The Andromedan Galaxy

The Andromedans exist, according to your understanding, in a separate galaxy. From the origin point, the Andromedans originated in this galaxy, and from that they have been, in your terms, spun out into another galaxy. They have been divided out. It would be considered a sister galaxy to the Milky Way Galaxy which you inhabit. But all contained within one greater universe.

As [the Andromedans] come into existence within your galaxy, their existence within your galaxy was of shortened duration, though in your understanding of time, it would have been a million-year cycle. They existed within this galaxy, the Milky Way galaxy, for approximately a million years. One must understand, within that cycle of time, the Beings and the inhabitants throughout your galaxy were beginning to separate into different, as you would say, factions. There were belief systems, as they have now taken physical form...physical form with consciousness, and with consciousness, then there becomes awareness, and with an awareness comes emotion. Though they are not in *human* form, they still contain emotion, understanding, awareness. This creates division. Division creates factions. Factions create separation. You understand this upon your planet.

In the simplest of terms, [there was a] dilution of the frequency streams that are being combined to create a Being. The further you get away from the Source, the purity, the pure existence...the further you get away from that frequency stream, the manipulation point becomes a bit greater. Meaning, the further you get from source point and the hybridization takes place between not only one or two or three different energy sources, three of the original twelve, four of the original twelve... those then begin to dilute themselves as they start combining, and so on and so forth.

That was not the original source plan. The original source plan was to keep it limited within a certain frequency grouping. That is where the humans would have come from. But because of the dilution point that was further and further away from the source of twelve, that is when it was recognized that this is not as it should have been, and we wished to pull ourselves away. The Andromedans, understanding this, realized that in order to keep the purity of their existence, they must depart.

From our understanding, and the way we would like you to understand it...we, too, wanted to participate in the hybridization program. We, too, wanted to see how this galaxy was to evolve. There were a number of hybridizations that took place, but we limited it to a certain amount. Before the departure, as the hybridization was taking place, a small group of Andromedans were conjoining frequencies with the Sirians and the Venusians to bring forth what you would understand as your Grey, your Zeta[2]. They have then populated your star system of Zeta Reticuli.

But we also saw how the Beings that were being created were manipulated in a way in which their intentions were not of purpose for the greater good. We understood that, and we wished to depart from that. There were other factions and there were other Beings that were of the pure [state] that wanted to [depart also] but were so limited in numbers that they couldn't separate themselves appropriately. So they took into hiding, if you will, and they remained by themselves.

But as far as our decision, it was a decision that was made once we understood that many of the source points are going beyond what was called for. They did not stop at the appropriate stop points. We decided that it was time then to eject ourselves, take and move ourselves away and create our own galaxy. In such, starting our own galaxy, we've been able to populate that galaxy in the closest, purest form that we can with our source points.

Understanding, technically, how [The Andromedans] were spun out of your galaxy to form and [inhabit] another galaxy, one must understand how, again, frequency, energy, begins to pull apart...separating, creating a cluster within a cluster, a galaxy within a galaxy. That energy is formed. That galaxy begins to grow. It begins to separate and is spun out into a separate new galaxy. The Andromedan galaxy. That is the understanding that you have in your existence now…that it is a separate galaxy, set aside from your own but within the greater universe.

This is why when you connect to an Andromedan, the higher dimensional planes will be there. It is easier to connect to a higher dimensional Andromedan than it is to connect to a higher dimensional Martian or Pleiadian or Orion [because] it is one of the only ones that has the most remaining in the pure state. There are others [of the 12] that remain in the pure state that are within your galaxy, [but] the numbers are quite limited. Now that time has passed, and we have separated, those that are still in limited numbers will begin a process of rejuvenating the pure aspect of those original twelve. They can bring forth a new existence that is of the pure form to begin to enhance their numbers. This in time will shift the entire galaxy into one that is of a pure state, but that is well beyond your timeframe of existence.

Emotion

[The idea that emotion is unique to a physical Being] is your understanding and concept. That is what your in-depth understanding is of emotion. But all from the beginning, it is all pure energy—vibrational in aspect, frequency, and range. Emotion is nothing but a word attached to a frequency range. But for you to describe it, you understand it as a physical movement, a physical aspect, a physical arrangement within the physical body to bring forth some sort of physical change, physical release.

But at its core, at its purest, it is a frequency range. So, when emotion is elicited, when emotion is brought forward, even from the beginning of the purest essence, that is a word that is associated so that you then can have reference to it. Much of what has been described and much of what has been brought forth is placing it into your language reference so that you understand that perspective. For if it is in the purest form, there are no words necessary. But for you as a physical Being, you must understand it as a reference point. The word "emotion" is [used] so that you can reference what we are explaining.

From a vibrational expression, [higher dimensional Beings] are experiencing a full range of vibration. For your placement of words [ie, happy, sad, angry] upon that vibrational framework, that is for the human to understand. That is for the human essence to equate a vibrational field, a vibrational stream into some physicality. The higher dimensional Beings, yes, those that have, as you would say in your terms, ascended out of a physical body, out of their physicality, and are back in a vibrational state...they are experiencing the everything, the full range of vibration, the full range of all frequencies. And within that full range of all frequencies lies what you would understand as emotion.

So, as a light Being or a vibrational Being, they do not experience it in the same manner that your physical body does. Understand that as a reference. For the physical body to experience a sad emotion, an emotion that invokes a feeling within the physical body, that physical feeling then produces a wide range of physical attributes. At its core, "sad," that frequency range enters the physical body and begins to vibrate in a way in which it affects all the cells, all of the aspects of the physical Being. What takes place then is the physical Being's response to that vibrational field.

So it is not something that is just a physical aspect that is taking place. It all begins with one vibrational ring, one vibrational tone, one vibrational aspect, whether that comes in the form of words, or music, or discussion, or closeness to another Being. All of it is being emitted as a frequency. That is what the human Being is responding to. A higher dimensional Being responding to other higher dimensional Beings is not going to respond in the same way, but they are understanding that frequency band, that "sad" frequency. They understand it, but they are not going to respond to it in the same way the physical Being will.

It is quite complex, the understanding between the physicality and the vibrational beginning point. Just as the beginning point of all twelve began to precipitate out other Beings through frequency; just as it does that, it is doing the same to a physical Being when it is encountering that particular frequency.

The Andromedans' Existence

To have an understanding of where we have our lives, this you must understand: As we have explained, much of our existence is in the higher dimensional plane. There is no physicality. We exist everywhere, wherever we choose, wherever we wish. The Andromedan galaxy, not being a mirror of your galaxy, the Milky Way galaxy, but a close representation, we enjoyed what was created here. So we took much of that blueprint to make our galaxy. It is quite representative of your galaxy, so it has similar structure. And those Beings that wish to be in physical form, those that are of the lower dimensional aspect, then inhabit a number of those planets.

Many of the suns within the galaxy itself, those bright stars, those sun stars, are not habitable. They are not for habitation. They are more used for portals, incoming and outgoing energies. That's what we've allowed them to do. We've opened them up to bring dimensional energy to and from our galaxy. Those lower dimensional Beings, those physical Beings, have an easy enough time moving about from planet to planet. They are still in a state in which vibrationally, they can shift from one space into another space, one physical location to another. (Your human physical capability of that has yet to be invoked.) The remaining, those that are in light body, in energetic space...we consume all space. We are there, everywhere. There is no need for physicality. There is no need to have a physical location which we inhabit. You may understand your higher dimensional Beings that you connect with as consuming a physical space with their energy; that is exactly what we do.

Many of the dimensional Beings, even within your Milky Way, those that are of similar dimensional aspect or lower dimensional aspect, would not have a similar life appearance as yours. Yours is unique, and we've left it that way on purpose. We have not wanted to interfere or manipulate that life aspect anywhere else or replicate it anywhere else. This is purposeful. For those here in the Andromedan galaxy, [life] does not look anything like yours. [We] can manipulate [our] locale any place [we] wish. [We] can move about anywhere within the galaxy just by shifting [our] energy.

There is no need to have pairing of energies to replicate another energy —in your case, male/female to a newborn. In our existence, it is a mere combining of energies. It is the knowing that energies need to be combined to create a new energy, and so forth and so on. [The new energy is fully functional at the point of creation.] There is no growth point. It is there. It is purposeful. It is ready to have an existence. The family unit is only associated with the existence of the humans upon the human planet.

Again, much of the aspect of the human existence is your human existence. That is your overlay. That is your construct. All of the twelve that have now come into existence, and other physical Beings as well, do not have a specific job, a specific purpose. Their purpose, if you had to give them one, is one energetically to hold energy within themselves and all around. That in itself is what allows you, as a lower dimensional Being, to connect with our energy, holding that energy source open, always, for connection, for communication. That is our known purpose.

You have to understand, though we are energetic Beings, though you all are energetic Beings, humans themselves are the only ones in a physical construct allowing themselves to experience exactly what they want to experience. For all other Beings, we experience everything, all together, all at once. Everything and anything. Though it may not compute into your recognition of understanding, the understanding of everything, all at once, everywhere is possible.

The Andromedans' Appearance

The Andromedans that you understand at this point have been themselves manipulated, hybridized. They are not representative of the original twelve, nor are any of the others. But what you would recognize as your Andromedan, if it were to present itself to you now, took place over the next 3 to 3.5 million years in your timeframe.

You have to understand the timeframe aspect. It is merely a referential point for your existence and your existence only. You understand your existence of millions and billions of years, based upon a particular cycle of your sun rising and setting across your planet. But in that, the spatial difference between that and other locations, the Andromedan galaxy...to you, you would understand it to be 3 to 3.5 million years. But it is a much longer time than that. In that [time], they've been hybridized to a point at which you would recognize them as being the slender, tall Beings that we are now.

Prior to [hybridizing], they were more representative of a...you would understand it as a more translucent, gaseous form. All Beings that were in the purest form, until they began to manipulate, were in a gaseous form, more of an energetic gaseous sphere. [They] could take shape into the awareness of those that are observing them. [For example], a Being that is not of Andromeda witnesses an Andromedan approach; it would be in a gaseous form as you would see it. But as that Being becomes aware, then it would take the form representative of the Being that is witnessing it. An Andromedan would take that shape and that form so it would not be a discordant interaction. They would see themselves as that, and they could then converse, pass information, allow them to integrate.

[The] Andromedans that you are regularly connecting to are a hybrid. They are not the pure form, but they are a hybrid of many other Beings that then reside within a physical body on a physical plane, whether that be a planet, star, or sun. And in that, they have an existence. But to overlay your understanding of existence, you as a human and your existence, over their existence, would be incorrect.

At some point, yes, they may have taken on a body form, but that body form would not be represented in any way that you could even place words to understand the scope of what they would look like. So, within that process, up until the point now, they have been through many different physical body forms, many physical body shapes...especially as the hybridization takes place, they change dramatically.

[For example], if a group of Sirians decide to merge with a group of Andromedans and the Sirians are representing themselves in a body shape that is, as you would see it, down on all fours, as a cat, dog, cow, horse, or any large animal, but yet the Andromedans are on two feet, standing upright, but have long extremities for arms, the merging point of that then becomes a representation of the two together for a particular cycle until it is then reiterated into a new form. This process continues.

What is difficult to understand is the timeframe and how the iterations take place throughout that timeframe up to this 3.5 million-year mark and how many different body forms. Understand that yes, they all take body form, and within that body form they could range anywhere in that spectrum from twelve all the way down to five in your dimensional understanding. Their consciousness is evolving with each iteration. It is merging with the consciousness of the planet, merging with that, as well as the new consciousness that is put into the Being. The awareness sets in; then the cycle starts over again, [is reset].

[In their current presentation], Andromedans [are] quite tall and slender. The majority that you will connect to will be of a bluish-silvery tone, almost translucent but yet not. What we wear may differ. Some may be wrapped in a cape-like covering. Others may wear a full suit across their body. The presence of our face is quite similar to yours but a bit elongated. The features are a bit narrowed throughout the face. The hair... some have a golden-like flow; others are bald.

The genders themselves are indistinguishable. Many carry traits of both. It is only those that fully integrate with the Andromedans that would understand the differences. You have an understanding of male/female. Many of those Beings have no representative expression of male or female. It is only there for purposes of...it is not necessarily used for the continuation of our species. There have been other scientific methods to prolong our species. But these are attributes that have been imbued into our physical Being through the hybridization process. The pure Beings themselves have no gender-specific understanding. It is only through the hybridization that gender came into play.

heart-centered peacefulness

But when we step into presence with you, you will feel the gentleness. You will feel the heart expand and you will understand the welcoming that we bring to you.

The Andromedans' Unique Role

Over time, each [source cluster] has fallen into an aspect of a purposeful use for many of the humans. Your starseeds, as you would understand them, have an understanding, an awareness that is already present in them to connect to those particular star systems. Those star systems or those source points have found themselves in need and have been providing specific, if not combined, purpose.

All twelve have a unique healing property. They all have a very similar healing property. That is first to understand. The healing aspect that the Andromedans can provide is one of heart-centered peacefulness. It is just around to sit in and be peaceful...one that you may not enter into much of your existence, but once you connect with us, it is allowing you to enter into this peacefulness state, this state in which you then can receive.

The connection point to the Andromedans is one of a higher intellect. From this higher intellectual aspect of the Andromedans, it is one to sit with that energy, connect to it, and once you begin to receive your downloads, your understandings of knowledge through the Andromedans, you'll be filled with a greater awareness of the galactic system around you. You'll have a greater awareness of the fullness of your galactic systems. In that, you will also bring forth knowledge. We will impart into you the old understandings of where the source points began...this hybridization aspect. We'll begin to fill you with this understanding. Not to be afraid of this information, but to feel uplifted by this information, as you, the Being, the human, is purposeful. It is YOU that this galaxy is for.

That is why we are here for you: to bring you that higher intellectual information, that history, that knowledge, that teaching. This is why many are feeling this draw to their galactic connection. They want to understand their purpose within this galactic system. They understand that the Earth itself is purposeful. They understand that their existence is purposeful, but [they] cannot put it into an existent form. [The draw] is there, but they do not understand. They want to understand. And this information will help them with this understanding.

---

1. The source clusters often use the words "hybridization" and "manipulation" interchangeably, as they describe the act of mingling or merging the original pure source cluster energies to create new Beings. Other times, they use the word "manipulation" to describe an act that humans would understand as nefarious—meaning with an intention that is not for the greater good and/or not in alignment with the original purpose of the galaxy.
2. The Zetas are primarily a hybridization between the Sirians, Martians, and Venusians. However, the Twelve can impart characteristics of themselves without actually merging their energy fully. Read more about this process in Understanding Hybrids, at the end of the book.

2

AGARTHANS

Greetings, my wonderful planetary Being! It is our pleasure [to meet you], as we come to you in this collective form from the source point of the Agarthans.

Much has already been revealed. That was left up to the Andromedans, purposeful as such. They have the wealth of understanding, just as we all do. But they have a different perspective of it from their position now, and they are the most reliable to give you the cleanest representation of that period of time up to this existence. What we would like to cover is the understanding of our purpose, your understanding of why you believe we are there, and a bit of insight upon what we do and what we bring forward to the humans upon your planet. But it is also to understand our role throughout the galaxy that you inhabit.

Your understanding of how this universe was created, this flashpoint, this "Big Bang" as you understand it...that is the point at which all twelve come into existence, and from that point forward, all energies are sent out, all frequencies are sent out, each individually, but all coming together to one point. From there, all pieces, then, are broadcast out. It is this energetic signature from that one point of all twelve coalescing into one space...that is where it all begins. All of the frequencies begin their projection, and within that, you begin to understand where mass comes from. For frequency is nothing more than the coalescence of all other frequencies, creating a denseness. That density then becomes something...that is, something that has mass. And from each point that is colliding begins another mass point. That, then, comes together. As it continues to grow, that's where planets, that's where other stars, suns... they all begin to form.

It is a frequency point that is the creation point. So it is all at one point that we are all together, we are all broadcast together. But as a planet itself, the distinction of a planet, the solid mass begins to form...that is when we are inserted. That is when our pure state is inserted. But as time goes on, the combinations of frequency points that collide create a new Being...an Agarthan still, but a new Being, a new form of Agarthan is created. They then enter into another planet, and so on, throughout this chain of events. This is continuing on into your future. It has not stopped. You are not able to witness what lies beyond. You are getting a glimpse now of what has taken place in the past, but it is yet to be seen what is unseen.

There is much belief that the Agarthans...you would reference them as inner Earth—inner Earth meaning *your* planet that you inhabit—and yes, that would be a true statement. But it is greater than that; we inhabit all planetary systems throughout your galaxy. We are assigned to each one that is and has been a place of habitation. For we reside within the structure, we ensure that the planet itself is sustainable, and when it is not, then we lie dormant and allow the planet itself to activate, cleanse, clear, move out any unneeded accessories...allowing it, then, to stabilize once again before habitation. Once habitation begins, then we are the intermediaries between the planet itself and its dwellers.

Many of your planetary structures have dormant Agarthans. They have been placed in dormant periods, for your planetary system has been shifted, changing the axis of many planets, and allowing a shift in habitability of your planets. For the humans, that is. There are other planets [in which] the Agarthans have laid dormant, and there are [other] Beings upon [those planets], but in very limited numbers. So it is not necessary to be animated for those limited numbers, for they are only temporary. They are beginning the process of either re-inhabiting those planets or they are the last remaining ones. They will be then soon dissipated [reset], and a new process will begin.

You have to understand the process that takes place throughout all of your planets; for when we are active and the Beings of that planet are active, there is a stable point at which that planet remains. That is the habitable experience for the planet. There is an energetic balance that takes place between the consciousness of the planet, the consciousness of the Agarthans, and the consciousness of the Beings above. As long as it stays within a stable state, that planet will remain stable within its system.

Any one of those is affected by one another. If the Beings above become unstable and things begin to churn across the surface of that planet, then the consciousness of the planet and the Agarthans begin an activity of trying to reconcile the instability of those Beings. If that isn't successful, then there is a choice that is made between the consciousness of the planet and the Agarthans: Shall the Agarthans be put into a dormant state, or shall they try other measures to regain stability?

If it is decided that there is no point of stability, the Agarthans are put into a dormant state for a period of time. It is then when the planet's consciousness will do what it needs to do, and it is this restart point. And at that point, the axis of that particular planet will begin to shift. It will begin to shift out of a stable state. This will facilitate the, as you would say, cleansing process. Once the cleansing process is complete, the consciousness of the planet, again, will wait some time for the cleansing to be fully complete. And then that axis will be shifted again, into a more habitable state. That's when habitation begins again. That's when the Agarthans come out of dormancy. (A pole shift is something different. That is a natural activity of each planet. Each planet will go through a cycle where what you would understand for your purposes of north, south, east, west, shifts. That has nothing to do with this consciousness decision upon what the Beings upon the planet are doing.)

Galactic War and Planetary Reset

During the galactic period of war, this unstable state shifted your entire planetary system off-axis, not just [Mars and Earth]. It shifted the entire axis of your planetary system. There are many other planets that were habitable that were in your habitable zones, much closer in range to your sun, but yet creating a bit of instability because of their size.

So your planets and your understanding of how your planets are aligned now is only something that is since the most recent cycle of cleansing. They've realigned themselves to allow just one stable planet, that being your Earth. In the past, there were multiple planets that were habitable, just as your Earth is habitable. Just as your Earth is the human habitable planet, there are other planets that would have sustained the human existence, but only for a short amount of time because of the differences in mass of those planets.

And that also precipitated this time of galactic war because it became unstable for the Beings throughout the system, and those other Beings created factions, and those factions are what precipitated this time of galactic war. So, just as a planet has consciousness and understands how to cleanse itself, to regain its stability, a planetary system will do the same. [The] planetary system has consciousness, and it also understands when it is time and needed to cleanse and reset.

You have to understand that as this time period of galactic warring took place, the consciousness of your star system, your planetary system, began to understand the instability within it. That, then, began a shift. That shift begins with an extreme amount of energy. You would understand it as, your solar activity begins to exponentially grow. You are not in a state of that now, but you are experiencing rapid movement of your star itself, your sun star. It is producing, at times, unstable states of energy that pass through your planet. This is a much greater experience of that.

That burst of energy that then radiates through your planetary system is a reset point. Prior to that, all Agarthans understand that they must go dormant. They find themselves to one central location within each of the planets. They coalesce together, become a mass itself, go dormant. Then they allow the consciousness of the planet and the consciousness of that star system to take its course.

It is not to say that all warring factions were eliminated, but the majority were. Many that were able to exit from your planetary system still remain out in other planetary systems within your universe, and they will remain there. They are not welcome back. The consciousness of this particular star system has shifted in a way that they do not allow the entrance back in of those warring factions. So they've taken up other star systems within your galaxy as their place of residence, and they will remain there.

The Galaxy and the Universe

The expanse of your Milky Way is greater than you believe and greater than you understand. For you have an image of what you believe your Milky Way galaxy is and the expanse of it. It is much further and much more expansive than that. Your scientific points of measurement have no capability of understanding just how big and how vast your Milky Way system is. The universe itself is an understood term for the humans. That is putting a boundary around a specific distance and time. The universal term, the universal understanding of what "universe" portrays is one that is limitless.

To give a point of imagery for you to understand: What you exist in has no limits. But, yet, it has a known boundary. This known boundary is for the twelve originating clusters to remain in. It is difficult to have this concept. What you image as your galaxy, this Milky Way galaxy, when you see imagery of it, that is for your mind to have a set of understandings, a picture. This is how big your galaxy is, though it's just a picture, and you have no idea the vastness of that picture. Time-wise, millions, billions of lightyears in your calculation...what does that represent? If you were to understand the limitlessness of your galaxy, that is how vast it is. But it is just one of these limitless but yet bound existences within a greater existence, and again with another, greater existence...all with one beginning source point of energy.

The Andromedan galaxy itself is a sister galaxy to your Milky Way galaxy, but all within the same bubble, if you can understand how that framework would look to your conscious mind. The framework of galaxies are just frameworks for your mind, imagery. This is this galaxy; this is that galaxy. You perceive them as being separate and not achievable by any means of your movement. But in reality, just as distant as they are, they're extremely close, but they all remain within that particular bubble.

And, so, it is a bubble within a bubble within a bubble. The bubble itself truly has no limits but by just the tension of its surface. If you could escape the tension of that surface, you would enter into another bubble, and so on and so forth. But, yet, you can peer beyond the surface and understand that there is something more, but you don't understand the limit of that bubble. The source twelve clusters all have the existence within one singular bubble. That singular bubble contains the Andromedan galaxy and your Milky Way galaxy.

Humanity's Ascension

You have to understand, and it has already been made clear to you through the Andromedans: The humans are the purpose for this project, this galaxy, this experience. It is this that the humans are here for. The humans are the greatest of all species within your system, within your bubble, and it will be—for all Beings throughout this bubble—in their best interest to assist and guide those upon this planet. Just as there was a pure state that put into motion this galaxy, that pure state and that colliding of energies brought forth the humans, and just as you've understood that the humans were to be that pure state, but yet throughout the warring period of time, that shifted...in time, the purity of the humans will be regained.

You understand [and] it has been already brought forth, the twelve DNA clusters. And yes, there are two that are active. And yes, it is difficult to activate all twelve within the human structure. But through the combination of realigning, the combination of global support from each human, it is also the understanding of vibrational frequency placement from all other galactic systems...it is also the understanding of the frequencies from within, through the Agarthans...that the human Being itself will be aided in its ascension process.

Through that ascension process, achieving the fifth and sixth dimension, most if not all twelve strands will be activated...not fully, but activated. And when that is achieved, that will be the closest point of purity of the combination of twelve. This will be the point that many are seeing and many are foretelling. It is this ascension process. It is this pure light embracement that will take place.

Hybridization and the Terra Beings

Just as we have explained, once we had entered into the inner sanctums of each one of the planets, we understood our role, but we also understood the depth of how far our hybridization was going. But we also knew that we were going to be separated. We were not going to be part of the factions. We were not going to be part of the surface-dwelling Beings, those that will be outside of the inner sanctum.

So we remained quite content with our hybridization continuing without any consequences. We understood, though, that it needs to be structured, even in the depths of it. So it has been said that from the source point to what you understand now is some distance, and quite a bit of hybridization has taken place. The difference between the source Agarthan and the Agarthan of today is much different.

Consciousness-wise, it remains the same. There is a bit of purity in our consciousness. We understand it. That is our point of animation. That is our point of understanding of what is to be done, regardless of what is taking place on the surface. We have a mission, and we follow through with that mission. No matter how diluted our species becomes, our species will always be Agarthan. It is one that has not intermingled frequently with the above dwellers. It has in time, but not to the depth and extent that many of the other remaining twelve have.

There is not a direct lineage between what you would call your Terra Beings and the inner Earth Beings, though energetically we are intertwined. Again, going back to those Agarthans that must go to the surface to teach, to heal, to inform and aware others, they are the closest energetically to those Terra Beings, but they are not the Terra Beings. Terra Beings themselves are an energetic Being that has been brought upon your planet. Similar to the understanding of how twelve source clusters then create other Beings, they hybridize, they bring together points of energy to have an existence come into place.

Throughout the time of your human species, there has been a collective consciousness, a collective frequency of information that has then brought forth a physical Being. You would understand it as your Sasquatch, your Abominable, your...you would say mythical sea creatures, mythical creatures of your woods. These are all depicted by your ancestors in particular ways. That collective energy has produced those particular Terra Beings, and they are there purposefully to bring forth the understanding that consciousness and energy combine to create what you wish. They do no harm; they are not there for harm. They are there for an awareness of understanding of how your humans can do just what the source twelve set out to do.

We do work closely with [the Terra Beings], with consciousness periods of time. They seek us out for a greater awareness so that they, then, can bring awareness within their realm differently than our process of providing awareness of the human Beings, though at many points the humans have not adjusted. The modern-day humans have not adjusted to the appearance of the Terra Beings. The ancients, the elders, they all understood them. They were not afraid. They had no fear of the Terra Beings. They accepted them in. They had them sit with them around the fire.

In your relative terms, they are considered a three-dimensional Being because they take three-dimensional forms within the period of your planet. Dimensionally, in your understanding, they would be a bit higher...fourth into the fifth dimension. They have no awareness of separation. There is no division amongst them. They have a higher level of presence when they're around the humans. That is why many humans sense them, feel them energetically because their presence precedes them. But in today's terms, the modern humans are not accepting. They fear them. They wish to extinguish them. They have not come to a point of understanding of the higher-level teachings, the higher-level awareness that they can bring.

Traversing Between the Surface and Inner Earth

Just [as] with all Beings that have been created through time, all Beings that have been hybridized between the source clusters and the Being that has been created from that and so on...the Beings that we are, the Agarthans, we, too, can come above surface. We can join with you. And when we do, we will take on a form of the human or any other Being that is present upon that planet.

And so, when it is said that there are humans that are taken below, that are taken into the inner Earth, that is correct. What you are actually witnessing is a true alignment between the human and the Agarthan, but [the human] must be brought in and adjusted within the structures of your planet. [The human] must enter in for [specific] purposes...for their own adjustment, upgrade. [This multi-dimensional travel is not unique to Agartha.] Just as you have an alignment to Lyra, it would be easily enough said that if that was your true and pure alignment, Lyran throughout, straight from the source cluster, you then, too, could depart to Lyra and spend time there.

[To understand *how* the humans can enter our realm] is to understand the consciousness of the human Beings. The greater consciousness of the human Beings is one that is completely clear of any memory. And over time, as the lifetime of the human takes place, memories begin to awaken. But also, what has taken place throughout that experience becomes an overlay, becomes imagery for those awakening points.

As they have periods of time of exploration through meditation, through sleep state, through ceremonial state, they may enter into any aspect of the planet, whether it is into a portal, whether it is into a waystation[1], whether it is to any other crystalline structure or it is into the inner deepest sanctum of the Agarthans. They must, for their own...we hesitate to use the word "protection," but it is for their own safety that they, then, overlay that [crystalline city] imagery to what they are sensing energetically. It gives them the sense of understanding and knowing to align what they see energetically.

For when you enter into our space, if you had no awareness, and you had no memory, and you had no imagery, you would enter into a space that would be a void of many of the structures you believe there are, but yet there is structure. It is a fluid space of energy. It is a fluid space of structure, continually being manipulated and moved.

You have to understand, your planet and all other planets are, in a term, *alive*. They live. They are constantly moving. The inner pieces are constantly moving, and that is the only way the Agarthans can stay active within the planet. When they are requested to go dormant, that, then, becomes one solid space because all the Agarthan energy is brought and coalesced to a point...brought into one central location, coalesced into one space. That, then, becomes a solid mass that facilitates the shifting of an axis.

When it is fluid and moving, that is the...you would understand it, the gyroscopic stabilization of the physical planet...this motion, this continual churn. That is what keeps the planet stable and stationary. Once that center mass solidifies, comes into one solid mass—the dormant Agarthans—then it is easier for the consciousness of the planet to begin the shifting motion out of axis to allow the cleansing to take place.

The Agarthans' Existence

[We live] deep within the recesses of your planet. It is difficult to quite have a concept of how that structure is. There isn't a need for homes or structures, physical like yours, but we have our own structure. You have homes, you have businesses, you have structures. We utilize the internal structure of your subsurface planet. Think of it as a...we reference it as a realm but think of it as a planet within a planet. We exist within a space of your planet that has its own existence. It is not as if we are existent within the cracks and the crevices and the openings and the caves and the aquifers of your planet. We do not exist there, but we exist in our own structure. You would look at it as a seed structure, for when we are placed upon this new planet, as it is being formed, the first thing that is formed is this seed cluster, this seed mass. That is our home. That is our structure. And from that, everything else is then built and placed above it. That, then, becomes your planet, your physical planet, your understanding of what a planet is.

For the planet that you inhabit...to understand what is below your surface, one must also understand the expanse of your universe. For you believe that your planet is a number of layers of earth and crust and molten activity...which, yes, it is...but there is so much more that lies below your feet. There are passageways, portals, vortexes, anomalies of energy that all exist within your planetary structure, your planet's interior.

It is all below the surface, well beyond any point at which your humans can access. Energetically, if you are able to locate a portal that is active, you will then get a glimpse through your energetic senses of what lies within, and what lies within is an entire universe itself. Not the same as you would understand your universe, but an entire complex of existence.

[Reproduction] is a bit complicated. You have to understand the replication process. The replication process for those that are of a higher vibrational state...much higher...the tenth, eleventh, twelfth in your dimensional framework...that is more of just vibrational states creating more vibrational states, just as it was explained how your planetary systems, your stars are all created, through a vibrational state, coalescing mass into something. That is what takes place at the higher dimensional planes.

The Agarthans range from the sixth through the eighth, into the ninth dimensional framework that you would understand. It is a bit more complex. It is not similar to what the humans experience for their replication. It is a bit more...a bit of a separation of multiple Beings, not just two. At times three to five, even greater if they wish. But a separating piece is then brought together with other separated pieces, creating a new denseness. And from that denseness comes a new Being into form. It is all part of one Agarthan, but it is separate pieces from other different Agarthans.

You understand a family unit, a family experience as something that the humans have, and that is strictly a human activity to have a family structure. For the Agarthans, it isn't quite a family. It is a common understanding amongst all, whether they are replicated from those that are around or not. They are all part of one collective, one grouping, one structure.

The Agarthans' Appearance

From the source point, the Agarthan source cluster, it has been broadcast out to create other Beings, just as we were to do. That is the project. That was what was designed. As each planet and star and star system is created, our role right from the beginning, right from the source point, is one to understand that we are the keepers of the planet. We are those that must be there. We must inhabit that planet, but from within.

So, yes, there is a bit of hybridization that does take place. Over time, it has been, in your terms, manipulated. It is not of the purest form, but it is as close as it can be, this distance out. So the inner Earth Beings themselves will be represented by many different figures. At this point, there isn't one pure physical Agarthan that would be representative of the Agarthans themselves from the source point.

You have to visualize us a bit differently, for you understand this as being something that is similar to the human, similar in structure, similar in function. But we take on many different shapes. Yes, some are representative as a human. They do look humanlike. Those are the ones that access the surface. They come to the surface to provide the teachings. But there are many that are very nondescript in your understanding. They wouldn't fit any physical structure that you would understand it to be.

Many of them would look very similar to the earthly structures you have, and dependent upon the planet, they would take on the representative form of the interior of the planet. It is a very fluid interior. They represent that fluidity of structure. But it is a fluidity of structure with consciousness, separate from the planetary consciousness. The forms that we take...at times you would not be able to distinguish a surface rock from an Agarthan. We are similar to your physical structure of this planet. Each planet has its own physical structure, and that is what we take on: the representation of that physical structure.

Your structure here, your planet here, there is a great quantity of rock structure. Shapeless and shaped. We take on all different structures. There are those that, yes, do have similar appearance to the humans. But many of us are shaped and shapeless. We cannot quite give you a direct appearance. We shift in and out of appearance. It is dependent upon what and where we need to be and what we need to do.

But what we can say is this: you understand that you have crystalline passages. You understand that you have crystalline portals. You have waystations. You have different substructures within your planet. We exist below that. We are near the core of your planet. We exist there. And we do assist those other structures, and when we do assist those other structures, we'll take on a more representative form for that structure.

If it is a crystalline waystation that we must process in and work within, we'll take on the structure of that, a crystalline form, to assist and guide those that are coming and going from that waystation. If it is a portal that needs assistance reactivating and opening a passageway out through the surface of your planet, we'll take on more of a vortex form of energy to assist that operation, to begin the process of opening that portal. That is our purpose upon any planet: to assist the actual activity from within.

The Agarthans' Unique Role

We all have the collaborative understanding of what we are to do. Much that has taken place throughout your galaxy, much of this turmoil and much of this infighting, this warring, these factions...that is all taking place above, beyond the inner Earth sanctum. Numbers of us have tried to go and direct and maneuver throughout those factions in order to change an outcome, but unsuccessfully. So we've withdrawn ourselves, brought ourselves back into the centers of each one of the planets, to remain there.

That is our known purpose. That is our acceptable place. So it is from the time of the beginning to now. We've always remained within, coming to the surface when we need, but not to affect or change...to introduce, to awaken, to become aware to certain individuals, certain Beings of different planets, bring forth teachings from within...the knowledge, the old knowledge of that planet, brought forward for those to understand.

That is why, here on your planet, the humans, many of them under-stand the voices, the teachings of the planet. That is us. We come to them in dream. We come to them in meditation. We come to them in ceremony. We bring our knowledge to them; so much of their teachings is direct from the inner sanctum. There are portions of time that we are no longer capable of effecting change through our teachings. That is when we go dormant. We bring ourselves together to one central location, go dormant, and then we allow the planet and the planet's consciousness to do what it needs to do. The planet will always heal itself, will always rid itself of what is not needed. It will always rejuvenate itself to a fresh point. It will always begin the population point again. Once the population point begins, then we awaken. We come back into existence. We allow ourselves then to begin the process of awareness, awakening, teaching those that are inhabiting the planet.

The vibrational aspect of what is being brought forward [in this book]... this is very similar to the teachings as we come to the surface to teach the elders, the ancients, the knowledge of this planet, the knowledge of what exists beyond your planet. This has been brought up, again, to the surface all throughout time. It has not been brought to the surface to this extent in some time.

The most recent experience of these teachings was well into your early 1900s. Not until this point has it resurfaced. This stabilizing point that you are at is the momentum that is needed to carry this information forward. Understand that there will be many that will discount the information, but this has been the way it has been since the beginning. There will always be those that do not understand, do not trust themselves... but there will be many that will allow themselves to be immersed in it and understand so much more.

[So] have the alignment of what lies beneath. This planet that you exist on, and those that you can see in your night sky...there is much more beneath your feet than you understand. Many humans upon the planet walk upon the surface, but do not fully understand what lies just below their feet.

For, even for your understanding, you believe that our existence is much further beneath your feet than you're able to achieve. But it is just a mere centimeter below the surface that we can be connected. For we are not just large aspects. We do not all take the same physicality of a large rock or a large crystal, but just a mere grain of sand. We are present just a few centimeters below your feet, a few millimeters below your feet. This is why you have this understanding that you must be in physical contact with your planet, to ground.

That is exactly what it is when you step bare upon the planet, when you place your hands upon the planet, your body, bare, upon the planet. You're being infused with our presence, and we are discharging from you all of what has been accumulated over time that is no longer purposeful. We discharge that from you. We allow your body to begin to resonate as it should. It begins to vibrate in a way it hasn't for some time. For as you understand this aspect of static...you rub your feet across the floor and touch something and you discharge that energy. That is what takes place when you bare yourself to the planet. We discharge all of that energy that is not needed, that has been built up, that is constricting you.

So that is our main purpose of connecting with you. We are here to take that from you. And what we do with that, then, is we take all of that energy that we've accumulated from you, and we amplify it. We cleanse it. We purify it, and we place it back into the crystalline structures, the crystalline pillars, the support structures that we exist in.

A Message for Humanity

From the point of understanding what needs to be brought forth for humanity, it is for humanity to broaden their understanding of themselves. For you are not just a mere organism upon a single planet. You are a consciousness upon a greater consciousness! If you are allowing yourself to be immersed in your consciousness and allowing it to expand into the conscious realms around you, you will be presented with a greater knowing of all Beings that are present around you.

For the vibrational Beings that are around you, they take many forms, many of them that of another human. There are others that take forms of your animals. There are others that take form of the wind that blows before you. It is to allow yourself to be immersed in this consciousness, to surrender to this understanding that there is a greater piece around you. So allow that to be you! Allow that to broaden your understanding as a human. And when you do, you will feel this stability starting to take hold.

---

1. From the Twelve: *Antarctica itself is the largest, upon your planet, point of entry and point of exit. You would look upon it as the largest waystation there is for all galactic Beings to come and go from your planet itself. The Agarthans support that activity. We are the substructure points of maintenance for that particular waystation. This is why that region itself remains covered. It is also the reason why there is much unified activity from the humans in that region. There are multiple nationalities that support one another in that region. With the understanding of what is taking place there, they support the surface activities.*

3

ORIONS

G reetings from the Orion cluster. You have already been witness to how each of the originating clusters begins its process...this process of evolving, this process of bringing together energy to create a physical Being. You understand this process of frequency merging, but a greater level of understanding is what we wish to share with you.

You understand our placement in your night sky. You understand that star system. You associate it with a constellation. But it is to understand the depth of that star system. It was not just one or two or three planets within that star system, for the Orion cluster was one to create the largest star system within your galaxy field. Many, many planets. Many, many habitable planets. And each one of them, to a certain extent, had its own existence, its own Being, its own hybridized Being.

This process of, in the simplest terms, creating something from nothing...this is the teaching we wish you to understand. Frequency. Vibration. For the air you breathe, for the world that you inhabit, there is much that is unseen, but yet it is there. For it is all around you, but you don't sense it. You don't smell it, you don't see it, you don't hear it, but it is present. One would say, in your understandings, in your teachings, that is the spirit realm. That is the quantum web. That is the energy and consciousness of everything.

But it is even smaller than that. Though each one of those may seem to be a very large existence, it's much, much smaller. It is the smallest of energy. It is the smallest unseen, unfelt, unheard energies. It is the energies of all universes. You understand that each one of us, each one of the clusters, was created, and each cluster then created its own Being, its own hybridized Being. But where did that come from? Where did the stars come from? Where did the moons come from? Where did the planets come from? Where did the suns come from?

Your scientists upon your planet are extremely close to understanding just a fraction of what it takes to create a planet, create a sun from nothing. The frequencies and the vibrations and this frequency spectrum, you understand...your scientists and your professors and all of the most studious individuals on your planet understand there is a light spectrum and a sound spectrum and a radio frequency spectrum, and these are all vibrational points. But even those are too big.

The spectrum we are talking about is well beyond your capabilities of understanding, your capabilities of receiving. But when you combine two of these frequencies...these minute, extremely small [frequencies]—and when we say extremely small, it is in your understanding of how frequency looks upon your spectrum—[yes], you have amplitude, wavelength, crest to crest, crest to trough, all the mathematics, science, and understandings of what frequency is and vibration is, [but] there is no math to compute this. It is the internal, eternal frequency of all things. You carry that frequency inside you. The air you breathe contains that frequency. The water you drink, the food you eat, the chair in which you sit...it all contains that frequency. Now, it is different for each *thing*, but when you can harness that piece of frequency and combine it with another frequency—a synchronous frequency—that's where it begins.

When they are combined, when they are connected together, it begins to pull together those smallest particles, those smallest bits of frequency, bringing them closer and closer to form a larger piece of mass. For even the smallest bit of frequencies, the smallest bit, the smallest atom has mass. As you combine all of this just through frequency, synchronization, you begin to form, as you would understand it, a solid mass. Once that begins, then you can manipulate the frequencies on either side to develop it into whatever you wish it to be. This is why you have not yet harnessed this understanding. But this is where all things have begun. It is the manipulation of these different frequencies, these minute frequencies, to create what is there in front of you: the air you breathe, the water you drink, the food you eat, the chair in which you sit. It is easy, just as that, to create a planet, a sun, or any other object in your night sky. So that is the beginning point, and this is where we all are to this point. There needed to be a bit of clarification, a bit more in depth, and that's why we [wanted to come in next]. We understood there were a few missing pieces.

But to understand now from that point, once we've come into existence as the Orion cluster, the Orion star system, and our Beings upon all of the multiple planets that we have in our existence are in place, then, in that segment of time, that is where the difficulties in this project began. [You] see, all clusters came into existence, all star systems and Beings came into existence relatively in the same time frame. In doing so, that is when...you would understand it as a bit of overpopulation started to take place. Though the galaxy system can handle just that, in our understanding there wasn't enough room within your galaxy system. We have ways to understand "more than we need." If there are more than we need on one particular planet, one particular star system, [then] that star system or that planet understands that it is time to reset, and it does so accordingly.

But at that point, this bit of imbalance starts to take place. And as planets were beginning to reset themselves, as star systems were beginning to reset themselves, many of us, many of the remaining original clusters and our creations, began to hybridize in a way that was pulling away from the intent of what we set out to do. And that was already explained:

The humans here on this planet, Earth, are the primary objective. To get to the human, the human species...that was the final outcome. The rest of the planets were another series of experiments getting to the human. But that in itself created problems, more than we needed. And once you have separation in a great distance from the original outcome, then you lose track of those that you have created, those that have come into existence. They begin to function on their own, outside of the original plan.

You already understand the different factions that took place throughout your galaxy and different galaxies and how that had an outcome. Again, what is most important to understand is this: There is a natural order amongst all Beings. Even within an energetic realm, there is a natural order. That natural order is, once the vibration reaches a certain point... this isn't to understand it as a good point or a bad point, but there is a frequency, a vibration that a cluster of Beings can achieve that becomes detrimental to that cluster of Beings, and then it is reset. And this is exactly what started to take place. The further those got away from the original understanding of what was to take place, and they began to hybridize and so on down the line, there were too many to sustain. Even though they were not assigned to specific planets, their frequency achieved that reset, and they were then taken from the equation.

For the humans themselves, the original goal...they have achieved many things. They have come close to that point at which their frequency balance was in peril, but that, too, was changed. You are on now a trajectory of evolving. You are on a trajectory of ascending, and this is the purposeful point of what the humans are here for. But many of those humans, the populace of this planet, each have their own understandings, their own beliefs. We are not here to say that this is the belief for all Beings, but [these are] the actions that took place. It can be associated with many of the understandings and the doctrines of the humans. Other words are used. Other transcripts have been written. But this time now, this period now, is one for a higher vibrational expression of this that you seek.

The original plan was to have the closest to a pure state of Being. But once we saw the changes taking place, this manipulation, this hybridization throughout the galaxy, and we saw where the humans began to fall out of that process...colonizing Mars, allowing that to be the home planet, and understanding the processes that took place there...then relocating, transferring here, to this planet, the Earth planet...there have been cycles of time that they have been reset...over and over again.

But this period now, this timeline now...*that* you can place within the timeframe of your biblical doctrine, this cycle of two thousand years. This has been the longest stretch of existence that it has not been recycled. You are achieving. It wasn't to say that the humans were to be left by themselves [just] because it didn't sit with the original plan. But it was a collective understanding, all the way back to the original twelve, to understand that the humans now are in place. Now, allow them to become their own. For if it were the plan as it originally was designed, there would be the human species, yes, upon your planet, but there would [also] be multiple Beings upon your planet, not just humans. They want to colonize together. But this is where the separation took place. We realized, through witnessing what was taking place on other planets, that this would not be the most appropriate scenario.

So we all agreed that it would be, once the humans were finally in place, that we would [then] stand from afar and observe, inserting ourselves when necessary but remaining just as observer. So, this now, here, where you sit today, the Earth which you inhabit, is evolving. So, too, are the humans. The planet itself is ascending. So, too, are the humans. The perspective of what you witness around your planet may not equalize in that understanding, but even in the deepest of turmoil amongst those individuals, they, too, are ascending. They, too, are being witnessed to. They, too, are awakening. So have that as part of your understanding. There's much that has taken place. There is much that has been witnessed. There is much that has been changed.

Planet re-set   weather patterns, etc

The Reset Process

There are a number of factors [that determine the need for a reset]. As you understand and has been expressed, the planets themselves are consciousness. So it is not that it's agreed upon by the Beings of the planet or the external forces of other Beings around the planet. The planet itself understands at what point it is necessary to do a reset based upon the number of Beings, based upon what the Beings themselves are doing as far as their habitation of the planet. This isn't to understand it as those that are inhabiting a planet are destroying the planet. That is not the case. Here, on your planet, there is much that you would perceive as destroying your planet. Your planet is much more capable of handling that than the humans can handle. Your planet itself will do an internal reset of its bioenergetic field.

What that is to understand is, it will reset its growth patterns. It will reset its existence without resetting the humans or the animals or any other living Being upon the planet. If you witness particular areas through your planet that may be devastated by, say, an eruption of a volcano or a weather system or any other natural force, that is the planet resetting that particular area. Yes, unfortunately, the humans may be involved in that, but the numbers are not that of a full planetary reset. So that must be understood.

So, as far as a planet that needs to be reset, it is the true consciousness of that planet to do a reset. That is because the inhabitants themselves in some terms have gone out of control. It is not the same as what you would experience as a *human* being out of control. Energetically, the vibrational patterns amongst all Beings are not in coherence. They are not synchronized in the least bit. There is a disruptive frequency that is causing the energetic field of the planet to be disrupted. That is when a reset is required.

As far as when a system, a star system or even a galaxy, needs to be reset, the decision...it is interesting because you [define] a *decision* as if it were an emotional aspect of an energetic process. Yes, from the humans' perspective, you would believe there would have to be an emotion involved with the clearing of all Beings throughout a galaxy, or even through a planet, or even one location. But it's greater than that in your understanding. When a reset is required, the potential in that area is then released. For you see, when you have a disruptive pattern, when you have a disruptive energetic force, whether that is multitudes of Beings that are not in synchronous vibration or whether that is one small group of Beings that is manipulating and hybridizing in a way that is detrimental to that small location, or if it is an entire galaxy that is a bit vibrationally out of sync with the vibrational forces of the galaxy...then that decision itself, in some ways, is driven all the way back to the original twelve.

But it is also an agreement that energetically is pushed across the universe, or pushed across that small location, or pushed around that planet. That understanding is pushed out vibrationally. It is received by those energetic Beings, even in physical form. And it is as if, energetically, they begin to disconnect from their existence. And at that point, it is as if you are observing a lightbulb that is dimming. The point at which it extinguishes itself is when the reset takes place. So it is, from a "who makes the decision" point, it is an accepted decision across all that are involved.

This is hard to understand because this has not been pushed across your planet. Your planet has been spared that type of reset during its time of existence, the Earth-based existence. Yes, the planet has reset itself, and in that case, that is just because there needed to be an amplification of the new Beings that would be coming up on the planet. That is the decision of the planet to make. Your Mother Earth has made those decisions repeatedly to recycle, to reset, because the new evolution, the new Being is much greater than what was.

You have to understand...many Beings upon your planet believe this [is an] evolutionary process, or many believe that there has been a creation process. Well, it is to understand that it is a combination of creation and evolution. The Being must be created. Again, frequencies brought into existence. And yes, that is, again, a concept that may be difficult to understand. But if you have nothing, there is a starting point. Through that connection of frequencies and manipulation of frequencies, it begins. From that point, it is a point of evolution. It is a point of evolving over time and over time. If it does not evolve to a particular point within a particular timeline, then Mother Earth understands it's time to reset, to jump-start the process again with the next iteration, the newest, highest vibrational point. All of what was learned here gets put into the next Being and moved forward from there.

Humanity's Partial Reset

This biblical timeframe of two thousand years...why is that a reference point? That was a partial reset upon your planet. In that timeframe, there was a partial reset. Why a partial reset? This was for the evolution of your Beings upon your planet to continue. There were a number of Beings that were evolving much faster than another group of Beings. The ones that were evolving much faster were spared. Those that were not evolving as fast were the ones that were reset. Understand, this process of resetting is not something that is just arbitrary, but also understand that it is not, in your human understanding, emotionally placed. It is purely an energetic understanding amongst all Beings that are involved. They understand, they accept, and they are reset.

There were many different transcriptions of what took place [during that partial reset]. Your transcription of the ark, your transcription of the floods, all of that, yes, is that resetting, cleansing point. But there is much more that has yet to be revealed. That is only one small fragment of scriptures that have been written. The Essenes were one tribe that were collecting their depiction of what was taking place. There were two other ancient tribes that, too, were scribing the information that was taking place, the history of what was being provided. For you see, they were receiving similar information through similar processes. They would bring through information through those within the group, within the tribe, known as Oracles. The Oracles were connected through similar processes, bringing forth similar information, and at that time, it seemed a bit much for their belief system. But yet it was scribed.

You must understand, from the humans' perspective, when you have never observed such an event, that which is transcribed is not going to be the most accurate. But what you will find in the years to come...those that were of the highest evolved point...you have to understand, those that were upon the planet at that particular time, the segment that was evolving much faster...there was even another segment within that [who] were much higher. They were set aside. They had an awareness. You would understand it as your awakening. You would understand it as their connection to the All. And yes, they would be perceived as being divine, in that they had an awareness and they had knowledge that was greater than all the rest. They were no different, but they had evolved to the point—ascended—to have this openness. Their transcriptions of what took place, their scriptures of what took place have yet to be found. They will be revealed in time. These are the same type of scriptures, the same type of information that you are now receiving here. They have been locked away. In time, what you will understand is it will all be correlated together as being one story.

Humanity's Ascension Timeline

What you are experiencing, this process, this is an evolutionary change. This is not a reset. An evolutionary change takes place when there is a great influx of energy from beyond your system that is being brought into your system, amplified through your sun, enveloping your planet, creating disruption upon your planet, creating disruption within the human Being. But this disruption is changing the frequency fields. It is changing the frequency fields to receive a higher frequency band, a higher frequency range for greater depth of understanding. So, as this energy continues, it will continue to amplify. It will continue to grow. You understand it as an ascension point. You understand it as a leveling up, of sorts.

But this [ascension] is the projected understanding of what the humans were to go through. This is all pre-prescribed for the existence of all humans. You are achieving this process much faster. What was to be expected was that the humans and their awareness, collectively, would all synchronize beyond this date frame. You are, in your linear timekeeping, in your year of 2022. This collective synchronization, according to what was expected, was to all come online in the mid-three thousands. That [was] the expected timeline of events. But most recently, all within the last of your calendar years of approximately fifty years, humans and their collective awareness has uniformly begun to rise, uniformly begun to spike. Small pockets here and there, greater than others, but uniformly, humans themselves, collectively...their consciousness and awareness has uniformly grown.

[From the early 1960s into the mid-1970s], energetically, there was much that was taking place upon your planet. There was much change that was taking place. The humans were experiencing things that they otherwise were not purview to. They were observing and they were entering into a space...the space of purity. And in that, [an] imbalance started to take place. This unsynchronized energy started to envelop the planet. [And this energy imbalance triggered a potential reset.]

You must understand that as you sit here today, you can enter into that space of purity, that space of love, that space of the truth, and feel the overwhelming emotion that is brought up with that as a human. That, too, is part of your ascension. But when it becomes an overwhelming process across the globe, that itself is disruptive to the base level of energy. The base level, the base frequency of energy that surrounds the planet is what maintains all existence. But if humanity, the humans themselves, ascend faster than they need to, above that base frequency, that then sets off an unsynchronized event. That was the potential. Yes, too much of something that is splendid can also be the point at which it is detrimental.

So yes, many were observing and ascending in their own Being. They were awakening, just as they are now, but they were ungrounded. They were untethered. They were entering into an unknown space that was unguided. They knew who they were. They knew where they came from. This enveloped the planet. One would say that would be the most optimal place for a planet to be...and yes, it is. But if the base amplitude coming from the sun, this amplified energy, cannot match where the humans are and sustain that energy, then you do set off an event that is and can be potentially harmful.

From our vantage point, observing what was taking place, this process, this non-synchronous vibration that took place upon your planet during that particular time, has taken place other times throughout your planet and it has not been reset. You have to understand cycles of frequency. You may get to a point at which it may seem to be inevitable that a reset is upon you. That line between being reset and allowing to continue is very thin. There isn't much that would need to take place for a reset to begin. But we've observed it over time, and each time, the humans are able to back away from that line. It is as if, as they evolve, they sense the edge, the barrier, the wall that is in front of them energetically. They collectively sense that and then they back themselves away and change their process.

So, as that cycle moves through, in the early 1980 timeframe, there is a period at which the amplifying frequencies that were brought in ampli- fied, ascended a great number of the humans upon the planet. A wave of sorts washed over your planet, awakened, ascended, and allowed Beings upon the planet to become aware again. In [this] timeframe there were two points [in which] there were two significant waves of awakening: 1986 [and] the most recent, 2012.

From that point forward, the humans themselves began to explore the depths of their energetic selves in a way that they have not in the past. In the past, only a slight few would do this. The greater populace of your planet is doing this. Young children that are coming in already have the awareness of self. They already have the awareness of the All. They already have the awareness of their connection to the galaxies. Those that are in presence upon your planet that have existed here for some time, those that are elderly, are experiencing a greater depth of knowing. They're experiencing a greater depth and understanding of the All.

This is purposeful; for your planet is ahead of the curve. The humans are achieving greater capability faster than expected. That is why the energy that is coming to your planet must be amplified greater than it has been. For that period of time in which there was this potential reset, the amplitude of energy that was being amplified through the sun was very minimal. But you have to understand, energetically we, the Twelve, and all of our creation, are having to adjust the amplification that is coming through the sun to keep up with the increase in understanding, the increase in truth that is coming through in each one of the humans. For if we leave the amplitude the same as it was in the past, there would be no growth. That, then, would lead to its own potential of a reset because there would be an imbalance of amplifying energies. The amplifying energies are necessary to continue the growth pattern.

But from your perspective, from your eyes, from your witness upon your planet, that does not quite equate. You see all of [the turmoil that] is taking place throughout your planet, and it does not quite balance. But it is not what you see, for it is this internal understanding with each and every one upon the planet. Even those that you would have an understanding that they are not aware, they are not perceiving their consciousness, they have not awoken to this understanding of a greater whole... but yet, too, in them, there is a nudge, a push, an internal force that is guiding decisions greater than them. So it is to understand, the human collective upon the planet is collectively becoming aware.

Ascension is a Collaborative Effort

You see, you are not doing this alone. You were never meant to do this alone. You were never meant to be placed upon this planet, upon your planet that you exist on, and autonomously just become aware. That has never been part of the plan. It is a synchronization. It is a collective energetic agreement. One understands the other. Just as Mother Earth begins to sense that the humans upon the planet are becoming a bit more aware, small that it may be, Mother Earth begins to resonate a bit stronger. Once that begins, then the energetic influences from around your galaxy begin to sense that collective harmonization. They begin, then, to send energy to amplify that awakening process.

So, each in itself, all are designed to work together. This is why in the perspective timeline, the anticipated timeline, the humans were to have an existence of humanness as long as they possibly could. Then there would be...in your timeline understanding, roughly a one hundred-year cycle where the amplitude from Mother Earth and the amplitude from out in your galaxy system, all are amplified to the maximum, forever changing the consciousness of all humans within that one hundred-year cycle to all come into synchronized consciousness.

But here, the humans began the process. The humans became aware. The humans themselves are bringing that into action. Again, understanding the purpose of this galaxy: the humans. The humans themselves are the reason for the galaxy. And what we understand and how we understand it is, as this process, as these waves of energy awaken many humans, that is one more connection point, one more transmitter that allows the collective of humans to effectively change the universe. For all of the Beings that have been created through time on many planets and all the other systems, they, too, are being affected by what takes place here, through the energy that is being transmitted from the humans. And it is not just those that are awakened. All Beings transmit an energy. Some may not go as far, but they all transmit energy. They all transmit a signal out from your planet. That is their purpose. That is their existence. That is one of the reasons why they are here.

For you see, the humans themselves that are awakened, those humans that have become aware, they then become beacons themselves, and they are broadcasting. They are emitting information out into the universe. And when you have that transmission that is expressed from the human, that is a point of reception. And so, if your expression, your transmission, travels far into the universe, that is the amount of information that you then can receive. But there are many layers of decoding that need to take place to receive and understand all of the information, for the human body itself is not a very good receiver. The energetic Being is the exceptional receiver, but it has to marry the two. So the energetic Being receives all of the information, and when the human body gets to a point of vibrational coherence with the energetic body, then the energetic body begins to decode that information that has been received.

Earth's Future and The Event

You will perceive it as a smaller population, but you will also understand it. There will not be a reset that you would understand. It is not a reset at all. It is more of an understanding, a mutual understanding amongst those Beings, those humans that are here, that they have a greater role outside of their humanness. And they will choose to exit. They will choose to move beyond their humanness.

And so, yes, you may have, in the human terms, mass loss. Now, that loss may come in many different forms. Yes, Mother Nature may take some of that. There may be other methods by which those that wish to move beyond the humanness will take. Yes, there will be grief. That is a human reaction. But if you can understand that, at that point, you are approaching a greater ascension point...this isn't to say that the planet itself cannot sustain this level of population and still ascend. It can.

But as you are going through this ascension process, as you are moving through this ascension process, what becomes clear, what becomes evident in each individual, is where they are needed. Whether they are needed physically here upon this planet, whether they are physically required to go into another location, whether they are energetically called to move beyond the humanness and assist...each one will have their own role. Each one will understand and accept that role. Each one will do what they need to do to take on that role.

You will understand [this concept] at this point at which there is this wave of ascension. You will understand it physically, energetically, as you say, at the soul level. You will understand it at all levels of process, all levels of energy. It will be known to you. It will not be something that is given to you as a shock in your awareness. This will come as an awakening point. This point of ascension, as you approach it, it will be as if a gift is revealed to you. You will know exactly where you are to be, and it will be accepted. No questions, no reason to question. It is what you have put in front of you.

[The Event] is a process to jumpstart this [ascension] wave. We've explained the energies that are coming from outside of your galactic system. They enter in through your sun. They are amplified. This is part of the balance. The wave itself will surpass the sun because it is already coming in at a much higher amplitude. There is no need to amplify. But this will be the point at which...how shall it be said? This will be a point at which all humans upon the planet receive their message. It will be the beginning point, for it will be the key to the lock that will open all humans. They will receive their message...whether it is to stay in existence as how they are now, whether that is to ascend to another level, whether that is to exit the human form, whether it is to be transported off-planet. They will all receive their message.

Then, behind this Event, will come another series of energies. Much higher amplitude. It will be for those that are transitioning, those that are ascending, and even those that wish to stay behind. They are all purposeful. So the wave, or this Event, is just the precursor to the greater evolution. [Within two to three years] is the projected timeline as it is set at this current time. This is all dependent upon the frequency base of your planet. This is all determined based upon where you currently reside with your frequency foundation. You wouldn't understand if we gave you a particular frequency range because this is a variable within your human structure.

But it is to say this: It will not happen spontaneously to the populace of the planet all within one blink of an eye; it will take time. It will begin slowly. You have to understand this Event. Many believe it will be a flash before their eyes. Many believe it will be...go to sleep one night and wake up in the morning and things are completely different. Many of you are

Mars

experiencing this Event, this like-Event, taking place daily. Small, incremental steps. Changes within the physical body. Awareness out of nowhere. Knowing out of nowhere. Understandings of a greater universe out of nowhere. But small steps.

The Event itself, when it takes place, will be as if someone opens a door in front of you and you see everything. You understand it, you know it, it is present in your existence. But it will not be this blast of light before your eyes or this shift from one existence into another while you sleep. It will be right there in front of you. The knowing, the understanding, the truth of it all.

And you have to understand the timeframe. Not timeframe in your linear expression of time, but the relative timeframe to allow a population of a planet to understand. Those of the highest frequency ranges, those that reside in that higher frequency stream, those will be the first to understand, open the door, be aware. Then the next wave, the next series, will be those that are just coming into their understanding. And last will be those that wish to remain in their physical state, in their physical activities, in their humanness. That is not to say that they will not ascend, but it is purposeful for them to accept that role, as well.

So it is a greater populace that will come online versus, in your expression of time now, small pockets here, there, with quiet time in between. So overall, as far as your physical timeline, your linear timeline, this is dependent upon that frequency base. If your foundational frequency base is sustained at a high level in your timeline frame, [then it will occur within] twelve to twenty-four months. That is the best-case scenario, but it can happen much quicker, or it can take much longer. Many variables in between.

The Original Plan for Earth and Humanity

Mars itself was the originating source planet for the human form. That is where the humans would colonize, in your understanding, just as they have here upon the Earth planet. But as it has been discussed, you also understand the different factions, the galactic tension that took place. For you see, what you observe on your planet, between the human species and their tensions, between one another and the warring that takes place here upon your planet, so too does it within the galaxy itself. And so, when Mars itself became uninhabitable, yes, they were moved here. Humans were moved here to the Earth planet.

But just as we speak of the anticipated outcome, Mars and Earth both equally would have housed, colonized humans. There would have been a two-planet understanding. Earth would have been the secondary colonization. Earth would not have been inhabited as it is now. Earth would have remained more of a laboratory, of sorts, to understand growth, to understand life. Mars would have been the full colonized planet that it should have been, housing the humans and its life throughout its planet, but not thought of as a laboratory. Purely just a location to live.

Earth was the closest in representation to the Mars planet. The Mars planet, in your understanding, evolved to support life, human life, much quicker than the Earth planet. Not equal in size, but quicker to evolve. The Earth planet, there was much that needed to align to begin to support life. Much of the life that is here on the Earth planet has come from the Martian planet...has also come and been seeded from other planets and star systems throughout your galaxy.

But you now inhabit this planet; this planet (and the planet's consciousness) is more sustainable for both laboratory *and* existence. Earth itself is still considered a laboratory planet. Many of the humans are exploring this planet like they have not explored anywhere else. They explore this planet knowing that they were sent to explore this planet, knowing that they are sent to understand life upon this planet.

For you see, the consciousness of the humans—the energetic consciousness and the physical consciousness—are all, in a way, preprogrammed. You understand your connectedness to Source, this source point, and you understand this aspect of a contract that you live out while in this human form. That contract also contains your assignment, of sorts. If you are assigned to be part of this laboratory planet, then you will become those that investigate, those that research, those that seek out information from the planet. Others will receive assignments to work with the humans, others with the animals, others with the planets.

You must understand, that portion of the contract is somewhat clouded by the other aspects of what you take on as a human, but it is part of this contractual agreement. For if you were to still have a dual-planet experience, you would enter onto the Mars planet as a human, [but] you would still have this source point contract, you would have an existence of what to do. But nowhere in that [contract] would you be assigned for anything here upon the Earth planet. You would live an existence within and on the Mars planet just as a human, to interact with the other humans, to create a life as a human, which would look much different than the life that you have here. And at some point, you may be chosen to become a researcher, an explorer, an adventurer to the Earth planet. That would be by nature of your existence upon the Mars planet.

Just as you are now understanding how to potentially colonize another planet, so too, here upon this planet, [Earth]. It was not always, as you say, habitable. But yet you would make a form of habitation to exist. Just as those that explore the depths of your oceans cannot go alone as a human, they must go within something, so too, would they exit the Mars planet and come to the Earth planet and explore. But not in their full human form. They would go in a habitat. They would go as a human, but they would be supported for life by external apparatus.

You are currently exploring your Mars planet. There is much that will be revealed in time about your Mars planet. You'll begin to see the physical structures upon your Mars planet, which in turn, will begin a process of greater awareness than there is now. For you see, with each step that is revealed to you, for each existence beyond your humanness that is revealed to you, that is a point at which your consciousness evolves, your awareness broadens.

This is that rising. That is that point of leveling up for all consciousness. Your Mars planet is not too far into the future of being recolonized, and those that will be recolonizing that planet have had experience colonizing that planet in the past. They have come back through to cycle back in, to begin the process over again. But it will be in reverse. It will be to explore the Mars planet. It will be to begin to learn about the Mars planet, and yes, in turn, colonize it for that exploration.

Understanding the Galaxy and the Universe

From your human perspective, you understand that you have a galaxy which you are part of, this Milky Way galaxy. You understand the Andromedan galaxy. You also understand through scientific means that there are multiple galaxies all around you. Thousands, if not more. There are multitudes of galaxies all around you. [And] you must understand, not one galaxy is isolated from the other. There is interdimensionality and there is intergalactic movement...energetically, physically.

But for this transmission and for these transmissions that [you are receiving for this book], this is how the construct which we are coming to you from exists: A galaxy itself has the equivalent of...the humanness has an auric field, an energetic bubble, an energetic layering around its physical form. So when it is transmitted to you that there is a bubble, this bubble of existence, that is what we are referencing. Around the Milky Way itself, there is this energetic bubble of understanding.

A better reference point visually...when you create bubbles, soap bubbles, and you're able to create multiple soap bubbles upon themselves, they adhere to one another, but yet there's still a space between. Each bubble would be a universe. Within the universe or the bubble is the galaxy. But then they press against another bubble, another universe, and there's a galaxy there in close proximity to another galaxy. So from galaxy to galaxy, it would appear as if they are in the same space, but yet there still is a bubble that surrounds them.

When the Milky Way itself was created through the twelve original clusters, it was all contained within that energetic bubble, that energetic auric field. When we speak of other universes, they are outside of that bubble but yet as part of the greater whole of existence. Each one of those has their own energetic bubble, as well as Andromeda and the others. Many believe there are other galaxies within your universe. That is not the truest statement. There are many that are quite close to your universe and who appear to be within your universe, but energetically they are not. They contain their own sphere. But this is the difficulty for your humanness to understand. A universe is yet one portion out from a galaxy, and out from there, it's the pure expanse, the infiniteness of existence.

So do not get overly confused by the expanse of what cannot be observed, the expanse of what cannot be explained, for all level of detail that is going to be transmitted will all be contained for a reference point within your Milky Way galaxy. That itself contains your star system and many other star systems.

Energetic Dominance

The way that the humans, as you say, war, is different than many of the galactic Beings. Yes, there have been different factions that have warred against each other, and it has been depicted in certain terms of being similar. But these galactic *wars*...that is loosely said...these galactic wars are more of a battle of will. Who is [the] stronger of the Beings to inhabit a planet? It is an energetic push, it is an energetic presence, it is an overwhelming force of energy. It isn't physical in nature. Are there smaller factions that use physical force? Yes, but that is not the norm. Many of those have been already reset. But it is a normal process of this energetic push, this energetic dominance.

Here, too, on planet [Earth], what you are observing is energetic dominance, but yet through the use of tools. So [warring] has nothing to do with the resets. [Humanity is not reset because humans war against each other.] The resets are a byproduct of an overwhelming change in energy...those that are enlightened and those that are not. There is a significant change that takes place amongst all Beings energetically. That is what is observed. That is what is sensed through Mother Earth.

The warring and the factions upon the planet will always continue. They have since the beginning. Dominance is part of the nature of all Beings, energetically or physically. There will come a time that there will be an understanding...that it will just be energetic, and it won't be...you have to understand the term "dominant" in our use of it. For you, it is something that represents itself as being harmful or being spirited or dangerous when it is to be dominant. From the energetic perspective, energetic Beings, as they come into location with one another, they each, all, the group, come together with their own energy, their own frequency. What they do is try to blend that energy, and it does not blend well. But it does push against each other, and that's where the dominance in your understanding, in your perspective, would come in. One would have to achieve over the other.

But what ends up happening is there's an agreement made. When they understand that there isn't going to be an equalization, there's an agreement made to have equalization. And that is what will take place around your planet in time. Those that are pushing their energy into others, and their energy is pushing back, though there is use of tools, there will come a point at which there will be a mutual understanding that neither side can blend but will find common ground in the middle. So it is not about dominance as you would understand it. The use of the term of dominance is quite incorrect of how to understand the different factions and, as you say, warring factions and galactic wars.

The Orions' Perspective on the Galactic Wars

We, each [of the Twelve], equally have our own perspectives. The Orions themselves, this cluster does have a broad perspective. We did not deeply partake in the different, as you say, warring factions. We remained a bit neutral. We did partake, but we did not have the same extent as some.

You have the understanding and the awareness of how the hybridization of all Beings took place. You also have the understanding of how a number of clusters hybridized to a certain Being, and that then allowed themselves to begin to separate themselves from the original anticipated plan. Overpopulating, over-hybridization. And then, once you have that amount of hybridization throughout a galaxy, just as it is here on this planet with the population of the planet, there's tension. Now, you may ask the question: If there is tension, that would then lead itself to an understanding that the hybridized Beings have some sort of awareness and some sort of sense of feeling within them. An emotion. And you would be correct. In the early stages of hybridization, many of the Beings had emotion effect just as the humans do, but a bit more broad, a bit more energetically charged.

And in that, when that began to evolve...mind you, humans have yet to be hybridized. They have not come into existence to that point. There is still much instability within the star systems...not being fully formed, the galaxy itself was not fully in place. But yet there is an overabundance of Beings, and in that overabundance of Beings, it began to separate, just as they do here upon this planet. They began to separate into clusters themselves. You would like to say the phrase of "like-minded individuals." Very similarly, like-minded vibrational Beings clustering together... that is where your factions came from.

So, when you have the overpopulation, the over-hybridization, Beings that were not originally designed to be part of this galaxy all want to represent themselves equally. The twelve original clusters and their direct representatives within each cluster and within each star system, each planet, and even within each of the hybridization programs...their direct representatives could not change the perpetual outcomes. It was a cascading effect over time.

The original twelve made the decision to pull the direct representatives (direct representatives meaning one pure-state Being from that originating cluster) to be disseminated within all of the different...we'll say factions...as a mediator, as a point of reason, an energetic point to go to, to get back to a stable state. But when the realization was made that it is time to allow this to proceed on its own, without guidance, the representatives were pulled back.

In that, as your factions began to grow, that is where the warring begins. You must understand, your sense of war is much different, initially, than what warring is within your galaxy. For there is no need for weapons at that stage. There is no need for things that do harm. But it is more of a consuming of energy, for when you have a cluster of Beings that are energetic and another cluster of Beings that are energetic, that is where the warring begins. It's energy versus energy. The more one can gain, the more one can obtain, the more Beings they can bring into their cluster, the greater force they become. They then consume the smaller clusters into themselves, energetically changing those that they consume into their existence. That is the early stages.

You are then left with a small number of factions. At that point, then the originating twelve clusters begin to send out representatives once again. This is where your understanding of the galactic wars begins, with the small number of clusters and with a representative from one of the originating twelve within it. This is why you have this understanding of the Martians, the Reptilians, the Dracos, and many others that partook in the galactic war of your universe. This is the point at which those energies then are able to manipulate their energy to begin to create, as you would understand it, weapons. Not weapons of your earthly plane... energetic weapons. Highly effective energetic weapons. That is what is utilized, then, to overtake other planets, overtake other clusters, other factions, and again, bring them into theirs.

Then, all within a very short amount of time...yes, your Mars planet is destroyed. It's no longer habitable. Your Neptune planet, no longer habitable. Your Venusian planet, no longer habitable. Many planets throughout your planetary system were left uninhabitable. This is, then, when the originating twelve, in agreement with the galaxy, begins the cleansing process. Being as energetic as they are, the factions, they understand this. They know what is about to come. Many of them depart this galaxy for other galaxies, taking with them one of the representatives from the originating cluster. They depart. There's a cleanse, and it rebuilds again from that point. That is the stable state which your galaxy is in at this point.

[To protect this stable state, would we intervene in an Earth war?] You must understand this process. [For example], you express the use of a nuclear weapon. This is not a new device within the galaxy. For your planet, it is something that is relatively new. So we understand the potential. We understand the agreements that have been put in place: the agreements planetarily, the agreements within the star systems, and the agreements within the galaxy.

So yes, at the point at which irreparable harm would come to a particular planet, Earth or any others, then we reveal ourselves. We must. It is an agreement. Not only the original twelve, but all others will intercede for the planet's healing. Not for the Beings, but for the planet. That you must understand. This may sound a bit disturbing that we wouldn't have the humans' best interest at hand. We do, but ultimately, it is the planet that must be saved in order to save the humans. So yes, we would intervene in a very extreme way to mitigate any potential harm to a planet.

We have [already done this]. We do this even though it is not nuclear. We observe. Any time there is a conflict upon your planet, or any other planet, those that have physical form...those that have physical Beings, and they have conflict, and they do utilize tools...we observe. We come in close, and we observe. We don't intervene, but we observe. If it is the use of a nuclear weapon, then yes, we will intercede.

The Orion Planetary System

To understand our planetary system, this Orion planetary system...for you observe three in a row, you associate it with our constellation of Orion's belt, and those are the three observables. There are other planets within the system that are observable, but those are the three primaries. That is where the bulk of our energetic presence exists. There were a total of eleven planets within that system, being the biggest for that cluster. Many of them have gone dormant. They no longer support life. They were temporary stars, temporary structures to begin the life-forming process to seed this planet, the Earth planet. Once the humans took full presence here upon this Earth planet, much was brought in over time to live its existence, to be explored, to be utilized. Once [Earth] was able to sustain itself, then those stars went dormant. No longer needed, no longer capable of providing, they lay dormant.

A number of those planets within our system were...how shall it be put? They were the birthplace, the experimental center for some of the animal and creature-like Beings upon your planet. This is where they were first developed, and then brought here [to Earth] energetically and reanimated. Much of your sea life has come from one of those planets or one of those stars. You would understand them as your dolphins and your whales, several species of your shark. Much of your insect life has come from one of those stars. There are many that were brought to the planet that no longer exist, as well, here. Only in memory. You have to understand, the Orion system is, if you were to understand it, an incubator of sorts, used temporarily. There were many Beings and many other, as you would understand them, creatures that were in existence. Many of them were brought here to your planet as an experiment, to see if they would be sustainable. They were not. Those have yet to be discovered.

Upon one of the stars, it was filled with energy itself, energy Beings themselves in their energetic form. Not of the highest dimensional plane, in your understanding, but just a pure energy form. And again, it was this observing and understanding how energy itself, energy form, can coexist without manipulation, without hybridization. But then it came to an understanding that that is not a reasonable expectation for a planet or for a star or for any other location to have one that is purely just energetic essence, energetic Beings existing, coexisting. It is much more—and this you would also say has emotion behind it—but it is much more enjoyable observing the humans and their existence, and all other representatives would agree. It is enjoyable to observe the humans. That is the purpose. That is why this galaxy is here: to see the humans in their existence, in their form, in their energetic form, existing upon a planet which was designed for them.

Now, the three prominent stars that you see in the night sky, those are observation stars. Many of us, that is our energetic residence. We observe the human planet, the Earth planet, from our vantage point. We can observe down upon you, just as you observe up to us. That is how we understand what is taking place. That is how we understand that you are ahead of your schedule...when it is said that humans are awakening, consciousness-wise, quicker than expected. We observe continually. And if needed, we can reinsert life forms, energetic presence if needed. We also can dispatch energies from the other regions of your universe to come to the planet. We are not the overseers, but we are the observers.

We witness what is taking place. But our energetic presence now has settled to a point at which it is sustainable. There isn't the need for a reset. There isn't the need for manipulation and hybridization. This is true for all other systems, as well. They've all stabilized their existence. They've allowed the resets to take place and allowed the...you would say population of those Beings to be minimized. [The] energetic presence or physical presence is at a minimum to sustain activity.

Disclosure

There is no excitement or anticipation [surrounding disclosure]. There is a knowing. There is a knowing that that is what is in your course of action. We understand. We know. We know that that is in your future. We know what is going to be disclosed. Many of us are assisting. But there is no anticipation. There is no excitement because an excitement would be to have an understanding that there is a designated timeline that we are expecting something to take place at a particular period on that timeline. That is not the case. We see all existence, all of us. There is no timeline of existence, as you live within. We see all of it taking place at once. We know exactly when that disclosure is going to take place. So it is for you to have the anticipation and the excitement that it is in your future. That is what we enjoy.

For you must understand, the planet which you inhabit, the planet which you walk upon, there is so much that lies below the surface that you have yet to uncover. There are things beyond your own belief that you will uncover. There are writings that you will uncover that will describe, in detail, all. They have yet to be uncovered. And they will not be writings that will take time to decipher, writings that will need to be studied. For you see, what will be discovered...these writings will be universally understood immediately. And it will be for the greater humanity to understand.

Connecting with the Orions

When you call upon the original Orion cluster, [we may] appear to you in this energetic form as humanlike. In your modern-day understanding of height, it would be average to the average human. But the features would be much different. Quite round in the head. A bit translucent. A bit on the blueish side. Some with varying amounts of straight hair, many golden to white color. Cloaked with a metallic outer layer. That is how [our] appearance would be to you.

You [will be] calling upon an energy that will settle squarely into your energetic field, that will give you an awareness and comfort, a settled-ness in your Being that all actions throughout your galaxy, all actions that are taking place throughout your planet, all actions that are taking place throughout all humanity are exactly where they need to be. For you see, just as we have described, we are in observance of your planet. We observe it, and we understand it. We understand where humanity is. We understand where humanity has come from, and we also understand where humanity is going. So we see all of it.

The water element is [still] quite connected between the two, between the Orion system and your Earth planet. This water element, this vibra-tional force of water, is one that allows a direct connection. If you are to immerse yourself in water, it will amplify. If you are one that is aligned and connected with the Orion system, that is how you will then energeti-cally be transported.

When you connect to us, connect to [our] knowledge. Connect to the comfort that you are the most important aspect. It will not be taken from you. Your existence will not be taken from you. Your existence will be enlightened because of you. Your enlightenment will be because you understand where you've come from. Allow our depth of comfort to settle with you. Allow our teachings to inform you of your past and your future.

4

SIRIANS

G reetings from the Sirian source point. We bid you greetings, and
we are here for your service. It is [good] to transmit this information to you. Much has been transmitted to this point. Much of the history
that you have been seeking has been transmitted thus far. So allow us to
fill in some of the missing pieces of understanding.

Up to this point, you understand the genesis; you understand the beginning points. You are also aware of the human aspect. You understand the
factioning groupings and their departure. But it is to have a bit of clarity
of how the human Being has come to be and its connections to each of
the associated clusters, each of its origin points of hybridization. For you
have the understanding that the humans are not to do this alone. This
experience, this life upon the Earth planet...they are not to do it alone.
They are to be connected.

These connection points, whether it is to the source point or it is to the
clusters of the hybridization groupings...these are for the humans, themselves, to understand and recognize their placement. It is this understanding of the external placement that they have that allows them their,
in your terms of understanding, freedom of expression. For if it is to be
done alone—the humanness as a Being upon the Earth planet, with no

multidimensionality

other awareness, no other understanding from themselves—the life existence would not be as it is now. It would be solitary. It would be one that,
in your understanding, would have no excitement, no joy, no reaching
for something greater. But since it is this experience to be *not* solitary,
this existence is one that is to be connected...connected to aspects
outside of your humanness.

It is not only to be connected to your, as you understand it, starseed
families, but it is also to be connected to the other dimensional realms.
For the Earth Being (the human Being) is a purely multidimensional
Being, though much of that is locked away, put away, and may never
surface to its fullest extent during an existent period, a lifespan, a timeline. But this aspect of multidimensionality is always a part of the Earth
Being. This understanding allows for a reach point, for a point of understanding. Even though it may not fully reveal itself, there still is that
understanding of something more, something greater, something
beyond reach. It allows the humanness to expand.

For there is much belief amongst many humans that there are [two]
segments...you may look upon them as factions...amongst humanity:
those that understand and are aware and those that are not aware. But
that is only the humans' conception of what is taking place. The reality
is, the humans themselves are all one. They are not separated by belief
systems that are nonexistent. [You separate yourselves into two] belief
systems: 1) those that are awakened, those that understand that there is
much more, there is multidimensionality, there is the galactic connection, there is the spiritual element amongst themselves, and 2) those that
live purely an Earth-based life, with no awareness, no understanding of
their multidimensionality, of their galactic connections...[who] live in
isolation [and are] not aware of what is taking place. This is far from the
truth.

The truth of it is, energetically, all Beings are the same. Energetically,
those that you believe have no belief still have a belief. There is something. What that something is, is the most difficult to explain. They do
not have the answers. They gaze into the stars. They don't know why.

They commune with Mother Earth, but they don't know why. They sense, but they don't know why. So it is not that they do not have a belief. It is not that they don't have an awareness. They [just] don't have the construct to understand the different pieces. They don't have the perspective that those that have awoken do. So to separate the two, as if they are two different groupings of Beings, two different factions of Beings, is incorrect.

But through this multidimensionality and through this understanding of your galactic placement, for those that are aware and for those that understand, it is [to rely] upon your galactic connection and [allow] the transmissions that come through to you from your galactic family to be able to bridge into this group [of unawakened], this segment, and be able to speak to them in a way that they would understand. But many leave this segment to their own, to allow them to find it on their own. It is not to say that you are here to awaken [others]. You are not here to thrust yourself into one's existence so that they understand. But you are here to have the language to speak to those that are unaware. It is not to change them; that can only be done by those that wish change. But it is for you to have the appropriate words.

These are the missing pieces of the humanness. These are the missing pieces of why you have this galactic connection. And in amongst the galactic connections and your multidimensionality, you grow into your energetic, spiritual essence. You are able to cross into different realms, have these understandings; for it is that the humans themselves are not to do this alone. And [not] alone [doesn't mean human] Being to [human] Being; [it means having] this expression of multidimensionality. Multi-galactic connections.

Yes, you have a primary [galactic] alignment. You have a primary source point. Those are by design. But that is not to say that you are not open to receive from all other aspects, all pure source points, all hybridization points. You are here to receive from all aspects. That is the humanness of being in experience here, upon the Earth planet. For when the process began—when the understandings were [that] this galaxy and this star turmoil

system were specifically designed for the humans—many of the different factions, many of the different groups, many of the source points all wished to be the first energy to infuse the humans.

That is where the turmoil began. For you understand the galactic wars. You understand the different factions. This is where it began—they all were placing themselves ahead of one another. It's not to get over-involved, but it is to understand that the purity of the humans was to be a blend of *all*...a blend of all originating source points, a blend of all hybridized Beings, all at the same time...to be infused with all of that energy, to be infused with all of that knowledge. But just as you, as humans, understand hierarchy, you understand power, so, too, did all of the different Beings. And so, that is what led to the beginning of the different factions and the different warring factions.

So it is at that point a decision...a decision that, yes, there is to have the awareness for the humanness that there is a connection point, but not a full blend of all aspects. This is why you have a primary galactic connection, as well as knowing your source connection point. This gives you an understanding, then, of a singular communication point, a singular transmission and reception point. For if it were as planned, the humans themselves would be directly connected to all existence. From the place in which you sit here today, you [can understand] how confusing that would be, for a transmission would be coming in upon another transmission, and upon another transmission. Multiple transmissions, all blending into one. There would be no discernment of where it is coming from. Not that it is any different, and not that it is any less important, but the progress that the humans have made to this point of understanding a *singular* point of transmission is much more acceptable than a multiple-layered aspect of transmission.

The Search for Meaning

[Humans were imbued with this desire to search, to reach for something greater.] The humans themselves, if designed as originally stated, this [seeking] would be nonexistent. This void would be filled with all aspects. There would be an immediate awareness. There would be an immediate *knowing*. It would be an equalization to what exists all around them. That was the plan. That was the understanding: to have a purity Being with the awareness of *all*. That was what was set out.

But now we understand from observations, we understand the humans to this point—the humans themselves, the expression of the humans, have lived a much more interesting life with each cycle, with this void in place, than if they had the expression of all existence. You have some understanding of this. You have a concept of understanding that if you knew all aspects of everything for existence here within your star system, then what would life be like? All would be provided for. All would be known. Each individual Being would be equal to the next. There would be no difference in Beings.

For you must understand that, though you understand the galactic Beings as being different by name and by appearance, there is an equalization of understanding. There is an equalization of knowing...the knowing of all. They utilize the information differently, but they have an awareness of everything. They take different forms, different names, but they know all. For the humans themselves would be just a mirror image of that in a physical existence as a human upon this Earth planet. No void, but knowing everything...existing equally. And now you understand the difficulties of that.

This is what has been revealed over time through each cycle, each evolution, each change in the human Being placed upon this planet. For each growth point, for each reset point, it became evident that this piece, this, as you say, void, needs to be in place. It is not a void of nonexistence... understand it [in terms of] what you are seeking, the All-ness, the wholeness, the everything. [This knowledge, this wholeness] is there... but it is deeply shielded, deeply guarded, locked away. But as you begin to seek, as this churning begins to take place within the humanness, the questions that one once had begin to be answered. And as you begin to answer these questions, as they become more clear, this shielding, this locking away begins to loosen...and a bit more gets revealed, and a bit more gets revealed.

Now, you must [understand] this: It is a rarity for one singular human to have it all revealed to them. Throughout time, throughout the ages of humanness being upon the Earth planet, it has happened. But in that, you also must understand—once it is all revealed, then existence upon this planet here, the humanness, the Earth planet, no longer matters. The existence is no longer needed. The humanness is no longer needed. That is why it is difficult to reveal all.

So that is why, as you begin to remember, just a bit is given. Just as you remember, a bit more is given, but it is never fully revealed. And this leads to much frustration within the human communities, for they understand there is so much more. They understand the presence of their multidimensional aspects. They understand the presence of their galactic alignments, and they wish to have it all. But it cannot all be revealed at once. And then it is reset personally—your transition takes place. Then it is all revealed to you. You understand exactly what has taken place, and you are reset yet again. You are incarnated into a physical Being, and again, it is locked away. It is as if it is reset back to zero, and you must struggle to get that open yet once again.

Many understand that they are brought back over and over again to reconcile differences [karma], reconcile what has taken place in the past. But in reality, you are here to learn differently each time. You are here to learn the code, as it were, to reset and unlock more and more information. In turn, as you begin to reveal the information for yourself, you are exponentially revealing it to the planet. So, once you have revealed it to the planet, even though you are reset, you are transitioning and you come back, what you have revealed in the past exists now in your current lifetime. And what you reveal in this lifetime will carry on into the next. So what you are revealing is perpetuating a greater whole in the planet.

God and Our Galactic Connection

Living your existence as you do, [through] the stages as you do throughout one's life, you may rely upon a specific religious under-standing that there is a God, a Higher Source, a Higher Being, but yet in your eyes it is unseen, it is unreachable...it is an existence so far beyond your comprehension that it is difficult to have that solidly as an understanding. But yet, if you connect to your Sirian connection point, it is not so far removed from your understanding, [so] it is a bit easier to have a concept that there is another Being...not God, but another Being that is close by that you can connect with. That is easier for the human mind to understand as they begin to become aware of themselves, and in that, then the reach to the God, the source point, is a bit easier.

So [your galactic connection] is a bit of an in between state for the human brain, the human understanding, the human presence, to have that awareness and be able to step one to the other. And when you have that understanding of your galactic connection, it is quite easy to under-stand your multidimensionality of being able to cross into different realms as you wish, different time periods as you wish. For when you are connected to your galactic connection, that is opening a pathway of energy that not only transcends just to that galactic connection but tran-scends into multidimensional periods and times, multidimensional aspects, different realms. So it is the starting point for awareness.

Hybridization

[The Sirians helped to create] the Zeta, the Mantis...there are several others. There is one that would represent itself as, in your physicality... you would understand it as a...you understand the energetic Beings that are associated on your planet as fairies. There is a Being that is the over-seer of the fairy realm, and that is a hybridization between the Sirians and the Andromedans. That [Being] is to come in and ensure the realm of, as you would understand them, fairies, associate appropriately with the human forms. So it is an overseer. It would [appear] more humanoid than fairy. It would have the same features but more human sized. There isn't a specific name that you would associate as a fairy, but you may also understand it as a Grandmaster to the fairy realm.

The Orions and the Sirians have put in place a number of water-based Beings. You would understand them as your mermaids. They are the go-betweens between the ocean and water-based animals and the humans. They're limited in numbers. They have been taken up...they have been transitioned. They were no longer needed for a certain period of time, but what can be said is, they are going to be making a reappearance. There is an energy imbalance that has taken place in many of your waterways, and the mermaid, the hybridized Beings, will be making a reappearance in the near future. They are there to begin this balancing point once again.

During the process of hybridization, it was always the intent that the specific human Being was the primary, but it became clear very early on during this process that the humans themselves needed to have this understanding of awareness beyond themselves. They also needed to have a connection point on their own planet. This is why much has been hybridized for the planet, as well as the galactics. It is the intermediary point of connection.

The Sirians themselves understood that there was no great need to faction off and fully be involved in the warring aspects of your galaxy. They stayed focused. Many did break away, but [their] primary under-standing was the Earth planet, the humans, and they stayed with the aspect of providing this hybridization program to assist the humans. There were many others, as they were beginning to hybridize, [who] pulled themselves further and further away from the objective of the Earth planet and the humans.

Galactic Beings Taking On a Human Body

When this expression of a human makes its approach, [for example] Valiant Thor, the question from the humanness side of the aspect is, do you know the family lineage of Valiant Thor or the individual that is most associated with Valiant Thor? For you see, if one of the clusters, one of the source points, or one even of the hybridized Beings needs to come into physical form, just as they appear to you in the energetic form of appearance, they take that energetic form and begin to solidify. They begin to become dense. They begin to pull in the energy of what it is to be human.

You understand how it began. Vibration, sound, coalescing to provide mass. Very similarly, if we wish to come to you in a physical human form, we are first going to approach as the energetic form, and then we are going to come into the dense physical form. We are going to pull mass out of the air to become the human form. So this is why, when we come to you in the human form, there is no lineage. We are the only Being in that form to exist. And just as we've come to you, and we have assisted you, and we have granted you information, we will also then go right back into that energetic form and leave your existence.

[The number of galactics operating within a human body on Earth at any given time] is a very fluid number. There isn't a set point of how many need to be, how many must be. It is purely fluid, and it is all represented across all galactic Beings. There are representatives from all galactic races, here momentarily, here long term. This is why you have the waystations. This is why you have the portals. This helps bring [their energy] into the dense form. But there is no specific equation to tell you exactly at a moment how many are here. But they are among you. They are present. But just as they come, they go.

There are a multitude of reasons [they might come to Earth]. It is for your higher education. It is for your higher understanding. It is to provide you new technologies. It is to change the course of existence. Just as many as you can imagine, there are that many associated with that experience. It is not to get over-involved with that understanding, for even if you were in a room, and you were the only human in that room, and the rest were other galactic Beings in human form, you would not know. It is very difficult, and purposefully so. It can be brought forward who is who and what is what, but that is for those whose energetic presence is quite astute.

The Human Soul and Frequency

[Some might question whether there are certain souls who only incarnate as humans and some souls who do not.] It is not to understand that there are specific "roles" for specific souls. From your understanding, this point of incarnating and resetting and reincarnating, and over and over and over...it is not to say there is a specific group of souls or energies and that is their [only] existence. There are those that don't have the frequency match for the human existence; but in time, the human form begins to change, begins to vibrate differently, begins to emanate differently. And when it does, the frequency band at which they were no longer exists. They are now into a new frequency band, a new frequency range, which now requires a new frequency match. So, in your understanding, that would be a new soul coming into a body, and in *that*, yes, there is a difference between one that has been [human] over and over and over.

Just as there are Sirians, many of them never come into existence as far as being placed in front of an individual for reception [as we are doing through this transmission]. Again, it is this energetic balancing that takes place for the individual that is transmitting now—the vibrational point that he emits is directly associated with the one that is transmitting now.

Very similarly, those souls have specific frequencies. The new human form has a specific frequency, and that is how it is matched. That is just the nature of the energy [frequency]. That is the understanding to have. It is not that there isn't enough [souls] or there is a certain segment [of souls], but it is this progression in the human form. It is the vibrational progression. That is why, [as] it has already been explained, the humanness has achieved greater expectation than what was planned. This progression is the evolution of the human frequency. In that new human frequency, there will be those that are still in existence in that lower band or that old frequency range until they then transition, and that frequency range no longer exists, and the new frequency range will continue on until it then is upgraded and is moved on. That is the difference.

The Sirians' Appearance

You [may] understand our presence when we come to you [in a] visualization. That is purely for the human construct to understand, the humanness, the human mind, the human thought process to comprehend. The visualization in your construct of vision will take on several different forms. The most common [is a humanoid figure], very tall, slender, slightly translucent, bluish in form. Many of us wrap ourselves in a cloak. This is purposeful to enter into your awareness. The cloak allows your visualization to be a bit settled. The non-cloaked Beings that come to individuals only come to them after a period of time of adjustment. The full visualization of our presence, though energetic, can be a bit offputting.

The other is a very distinct white, mist-like form. It is sometimes referred to as...you would understand it as the Sirius White Lion Beings. It is this white, mist-like form that takes the shape of a lion. Not directly associated with the Lyrans, but it is a visualization that is in form.

Many of [the Sirians] are non-hooded. The hooded Beings with the cloak are dimensionally...if you're to understand the dimensional aspects in your relative plane of dimensionality, they would be the upper tier, the eleventh and twelfth. It is not to say that lower dimensional Beings wouldn't have hoods. They do. But typically, you must understand the visualization of appearance that we must give off. This is to help associate the transmission points. It is not to say that a lower dimensional Being is going to have any less information or any less technical aspect than someone from the higher dimensional realms. It is just a personal construct for the individual to understand.

Dog star

The Sirians' Existence

You would understand it as the biggest star in your visualization point of your night sky, the Sirius planet that we inhabit. There are many others, but they have laid dormant for some time, and they're not categorized within that particular star cluster. You would also understand [Sirius] as the Dog Star, the canine star. There is much that is connected directly [between] your canine representatives upon your planet to our galactic connection. There is a direct tie between that and the animal aspect. [Your canines] are not created by us, but energetically, they are quite aware of our presence. Those that have the presence of a canine, a dog as a pet, or have that in your awareness, and you have a direct connection to the Sirius transmissions, as you begin to pull in that transmission, become aware of that canine and how their reaction is. They will begin to settle and point and understand that this transmission is taking place. At that particular point, they are activating the transmission for amplitude. They are assisting with that transmission.

This particular star [Sirius] though it is the brightest in your night sky, is also the most active in your night sky. There is much that you have yet to witness. Many have. There's a through point within the particular star. You understand portals upon your planet; you understand this aspect of the transmission points upon your planet where Beings can come and go from your planet [to locations within or outside of your galaxy]. The Sirius star is a main source point for that. We've allowed that star to become a transient point, so there is much activity that is coming and going from that planet or that star. Just as you travel here upon your planet, you have a final destination but yet you have stopover points along the way. This is one stopover point. It helps amplify the energetic transmission of transference. And you can witness that, but you must have the understanding that it is taking place.

The life within that star...you understand life as a physical form and what it takes to exist in a physical form. There, it is purely energetic substance. This is why, as it has been explained, it is the brightest star in your sky, for it is the essence of all of the energy of all Sirians that illuminate that particular star. It is the clustering of all of the energy, each individual energy aspect; life itself does not exist how you understand it. [Our life as energy Beings] is the closest representation of understanding Source—once you transition, you are then back with Source. You are in an energy form at that point, retaining the memories to some extent, entering back into the source of all and being able to exist as an energy Being.

This, too...for each experience that a Sirian may have, each encounter a Sirian may have with a human, that memory is then brought back to be disseminated throughout all other energies. It is a collective understanding of what is taking place with each human. It is not that we are observing, but we are associating. We are accumulating information from each experience and each encounter and each transmission that we have with an Earth Being...just as it is with this transmission. This transmission of information and this interaction will then be disseminated throughout each energetic piece.

[There] is an understanding [that] the humans must have a particular role, must have a particular assignment, must monitor something. This, to an extent, does not exist throughout your galactic understandings. This is a common misconception that the Lyrans have a responsibility for this and the Sirians have a responsibility for this, and within their own planet, their own star, their own cluster, they each have a different role and a different responsibility. You are applying a human construct upon something that does not have a construct.

You have to have an understanding that, because you are physical, you are a physical Being upon a physical planet, this is where the understanding and the construct of responsibility, jobs, all come into an aspect. But when you are in a pure energetic form, blending between different energetic forms to create one energetic sphere, a star—and yes, it is used as a portal, it is used as a layover point, it is used to transmit from one location to another—it is all shared equally, not only what the Sirians are doing, but all those that wish to transition through. They all understand, energetically, that it is all one. It is all shared equally. There is no direct responsibility for one individual energy to take care of one specific thing, but it is a coexistent energetic form of existence.

If you wish to understand what we do from moment to moment, understand it this way—and this would be for most, if not all other aspects that you have transmissions with—when you sit and you intend and you send the signal out that you intend to connect with, in this case, the Sirians, that transmission is received. That is when the connection point is made. It is not made to one specific energy, but it is made to the Sirian connection point. And once it is made to the Sirian connection point, then, yes, an individual energy that is most associated with the individual that is intending the transmission to take place...that balance point of energy is what is then represented for that individual. So each energy cluster, each energy node, has a specific frequency. Minute as it is, it is also aligned with each individual that wishes to have a transmission. They will vary from individual to individual, but in all, it is the same energy.

Connecting with the Sirians

[It is] correct to understand [each source cluster] as equal. But each individual has its strengths. For the Sirius connection point, the Sirius cluster, there is this...it would be equated to an energetic thrust. Understand it as an energetic point that, once connected to the Sirians, the Sirians can amplify any transmission. You may not be directly connected to the Sirians. Your main connection point, your primary connection point may be the Mantis Beings, a purely hybridized Being, and you are directly tied to the Lyran cluster, non-associated with the Sirians. But [understand] that the Sirians will amplify any connection point that you have.

So if in that transmission point, you are wishing to connect to the Mantis, allow the Sirians to step in and amplify. Visualize the Sirian connection however you wish, in your own understanding and your own construct. But intend for the Sirians to amplify your connection point with the Mantis, and that point will be amplified. That transmission will be much clearer. So yes, from a power standpoint, it is this under-

Sirians are amplifiers

standing that we are amplifiers for transmissions. We are amplifiers for any various amount of energy that is to be transmitted. If you are one that works physically with the energy around your planet and around other Beings, allow the Sirians to step in and amplify that transmission of energy.

You must [also] understand that all galactic Beings, no matter pure or hybrid, we all provide a level of healing, as well. This level of healing that we can provide to you is directly associated with the amplitude of information and energy that we provide. It is to have a clarifying effect of your thoughts, a clarifying effect of your understandings. And in that, our teachings will be brought to you...this centering aspect, this purposeful resonance with our frequency. Even though we may not be your direct connection, it is the centering and clarity that we'll provide as far as healing.

5

VENUSIANS

Greetings from the Venusian Collective of the origin source point. This understanding of humanness, this understanding of connectedness to your galactic assignment, your galactic alignment...this perspective of humanness...for you have an understanding, a depth of knowledge to this point, of the source of the humans, of the source of *why the humans* and what this galaxy was purposefully designed for. But what needs to be understood is, from the human aspect—your thought processes, your awareness, your perspectives of your reality, your conscious reality, your existence—this is all pre-designed.

You have an understanding of the contractual agreements. You understand the purpose of one's existence. You understand how the human consciousness, the physicality, the human physical consciousness presents itself. You understand that it is purposeful to have the memory loss of your origin. You understand the perspective of multiple incarnations, multiple evolutions of your humanness. But what needs to be detailed, what needs to be brought forward, is the underlying framework where all of that resides—it is reality, and what reality is perceived to be, and where your human truth is.

So much of this is quite complex. Much of this is quite—in your thought processes—deep for the human to understand. We will try our best to associate these understandings for your thought processes.

Reality, the reality in which you exist, is but just a fraction of an overall presence. You understand this aspect of the beginning point, and you also understand that there's a beginning point to that beginning point and the complexity of the infinity aspect of the beginning. That is where the complexity is for this reality; for the further you try to seek the beginning point, the further it eludes you. So your reality is a construct to stop that thought process of seeking the beginning of the beginning of the beginning.

Your consciousness—a blending of reality, thought, connections to multiverses, past and future existences...that is your consciousness. All intertwined, all together at once. Your human framework does not allow [it all] to be revealed to [you], just bits and pieces...glimpses, ideas. For if it is all revealed to you, there would not be a need for the human existence.

So this understanding of reality and how it blends with this idea of consciousness, and how it is intertwined amongst the different dimensions...this is the complexity of your existence. This is why, during your periods of awakening, many go through different sensations of a blended reality...a blended aspect of consciousness. Not quite sure where and what and how to function within the human constraint. So it is to understand, *your consciousness is a framework to limit the expansiveness of true reality.* Many of the humans have that concept in reverse. They believe that their reality is what formulates their consciousness. But in reality, it is consciousness that blocks you from pure reality.

The reality is that you are present in a multidimensional space at any one given point. Yes, you exist in a human form upon a human planet, amongst other planets, within a system that's within a galaxy. That's the constraint of consciousness. And many would also understand that consciousness is derived from a higher source. It is. That is your connection to the reality...the beginning source...the infinite beginning source.

That is why you have this yearning, this knowing, this understanding that there is a higher power, a higher essence, a higher existence. That is always left open in the consciousness.

For if you are isolated in a conscious aspect, without an understanding that there is something that you are drawn to, something present in your existence, you would cease to exist. It is this understanding of you as a human form, but your energetic piece that animates your physical form needs the connectedness to that reality of an existence of a higher source. It needs that for its own purpose of remaining energized, remaining connected. That, then, allows the humanness to be animated the way it is supposed to be animated, according to that energetic piece, that energetic essence.

And then, that is where the searching begins for the human. The human thought process begins to question that higher aspect. "What is it? Where is it? How does it affect me? How does it affect others?" Through the questioning, that is where your experience, as you would understand it, of your awakening begins. Whether that is in your terms of a human religious experience or, in a sense, an energetic, physical space of spirit —all the same, but yet two different constructs for the human to understand.

Multiple Levels of Reality

You *believe* the reality you exist in because that is the construct that you've built around this human aspect upon this human planet. So you associate what you *do* as your reality...and it is. But it is a human construct of reality. But when you allow your consciousness to discon-nect temporarily from this aspect of reality, you begin to see glimpses of the *true* reality that lies beyond your construct.

And that does not mean that you have to leave your physical self behind. You don't have to seek a journey outside of your physical presence. But it is to say, aligning yourself with understanding this higher presence, and allowing *that* to be the bridge...allowing *that* to be the conduit...allowing *that* to be the channel by which you begin to explore...that, then, takes you beyond this reality, into the *pure* reality...the construct that has been created for *all* aspects. All aspects of time and dimension and being, all exist simultaneously in one reality.

This understanding of what you have constructed as reality—how it is set aside from the reality of all aspects, all origin points, all Beings, all existence—that is one pure reality. Then, in each dimensional aspect, each multiverse aspect, each consciousness aspect, there is a separate reality. Then down even further, down to each form, each Being, each life form has its own reality. And even further down to the inside of that physical Being, inside that physical construct, each cell has its own reality.

So this is why it is difficult to understand the concepts of reality. For if the cells within your physical Being have their own reality, if you begin to affect those cells, in a way, to change their reality, as they progress changing their reality, your physical reality begins to change. And then as it goes out, it begins to change the reality around you...but yet still being your own reality. And when you interact with another individual, [it's] the same process, and you are interacting with two separate realities, but yet all within one constructed reality.

And it is only until you've departed into the source point for your reality that you begin to see the multiple realities that are in place. You can peer beyond the source reality, out into the pure reality, and have that understanding. But all of that is then shielded once you are then reanimated into another Being, purposefully so. For if one has the full understanding of that reality, beyond yours, it begins to infiltrate the human aspect, and it can change the physical aspect into one that is no longer useful here.

Multiple Levels of Source

The Source that created the twelve original clusters, that is twice removed from your reality. Out beyond that source point is what created

in finity

that source point. Three times removed. [You] have to remember it is an *infinite* aspect of Source. There is no one beginning point. It is infinite. But in that, each one holds their own reality that surrounds that aspect.

So it is to say, your source point here for your existence that you understand as Source, that is one aspect, one bubble, one sphere around your reality. Going further out to the original twelve, that is another source point of reality. The Source that created the Twelve, that's another sphere, bubble of reality. The Source that created that Source, another sphere, another bubble, that is another point of reality. Now you have an understanding of how it is centered out from where you exist, with an infinite starting point. And you can, at any point, say that it is the source reality, but it is an infinite source point.

It would cause a feeling of insignificance for the human to understand that they are but just a mere speck amongst an infinite aspect of reality. By allowing this reality to have its own source point, it gives significance to one's existence. It allows them the connectedness to understand there is something higher than themselves...a feeling of gratitude, a feeling of greatness, a feeling of connectedness that they would not achieve if they understood the full breadth of an infinite source aspect.

From a human standpoint, allow this depth of information not to overwhelm, but allow it to be a placeholder...a concept...a learning point for awareness; for it can never adequately be assimilated within the human structure. But to have an awareness and allow the vision to be in front of you of what it could be will help you understand this layer, this source point for the humans to be a bit greater in existence in the human form.

Source Upgrades

Your consciousness...you would understand it as your soul, what animates your humanness, that energetic piece...during the transition time, it does depart. It does exit the human form. It does go back to what you have perceived as Source, and in a way, it is a momentary layer. And that is where most of your consciousness understands the existence outside of your physical existence.

But there are points in time that many move beyond that construct of understanding of Source and enter into the pure beginning Source. The majority remain here, in that source point, the construct of Source, and are then reanimated back into another human form or another Being. That is the most purposeful aspect of understanding. That is your transition point to transition back into the human form or back into another Being form. But many are called back to the Source origin, the beginning infinite point.

[This] is purposeful to bring forward. It is as if your Source, the one that you have constructed in your consciousness of understanding, needs an upgrade, needs a vibrational change, needs a substantive movement forward. Just as you receive information and energy for your physical aspect to step forward, upgrade, awaken, so, too, is this construct of your understanding of Source. And this is for future generations. It is also... and you must understand this...this aspect, this layer of Source is not just to animate future humans, future Beings. It is also the source point at which past existences, multiverse existences, different dimensional reality aspects are all animated.

For you are not just a singular entity upon this particular planet at this particular time. There are multiple dimensional aspects of your own Being in different reality points, all being animated by this which you understand as Source, this construct. It is the closest layer to this constructed reality. But *all*, as the evolution takes place, as the process evolves, gains higher vibrational aspects—as you would say for this planet, its ascension point. So, too, does this constructed aspect of Source need its energy upgraded. It needs its Source upgraded. And so many are called back to the Source origin point and brought forward again to upgrade, to reenergize, to download new understandings, new teachings for those that are about to incarnate.

Much of this, you must understand...the depth of this information, the depth of this concept for your physicality is quite overwhelming. Much of what you understand, much of the teachings that you have been imparted, much of your awareness has been passed down from incarnation to incarnation to incarnation. There hasn't been a significant change in understanding. Your source point has not been upgraded in some time. It has not needed to be upgraded. But [we want you] to understand the process, to understand the different layers of aspect.

Bringing awareness of the understandings of this depth of information begins to allow the humans...those that it resonates with, those that it vibrates equally with...to begin to question, to begin to open their expansive awareness a bit further, and in doing so, they carry that back into the human source point. That, then, begins a process of understanding that there is a greater awareness taking place, a greater questioning taking place, and at that point, it will be determined whether or not an upgrade is needed. And if it is adequate, [such] that an upgrade is required, those Beings, [souls], will be sent to the origin Source, the beginning of the beginning, to bring forward a new upgrade, a new energy source, a new understanding that will be imparted upon each new incarnation.

For those souls that have been called to change the source point, the human source point, one must understand...that is a separate...you would say, mission, compared to your human aspect mission. This upgrade that takes place, [those souls] are the carriers. There is no selection. In your human terms, it's quite difficult to explain your understanding for this. It is not as if there is one specific energy [Being] that is selecting and moving energy to the infinite point.

It is, if needed, those that arrive to your human Source, once they arrive, they are redirected. As one transitions from the human form and goes to Source, it is immediately redirected and brought in with that information. There is no selection point. There is no assignment. It is just a redirection of energy. This takes place...there is no timeframe. There's no period of time that it remains with the infinite point. It's an immediate action. But that time period, in your humanness, would seem a bit lengthy.

And once that is completed—upgrading the human source aspect construct—[those souls] are then placed [back] into a human body. They are incarnated into a human body. They'll have no recall of what their previous mission was. Even during aspects of searching, aspects of bringing forward past life experiences, it will be wiped clean from that aspect. It will appear as if, in the lineage of past life experiences, there is a void in time.

This is even voided in the Akash [Akashic Record]. The Akash is *this* reality sector. The Akash envelops *your* existence, *your* reality, *your* consciousness. It does not partake in what happens beyond this origin point, your humanness origin point, your aspect here. [The source upgrade is] just a separate mission for that energy to accomplish beyond what they are set to do as this Being or any other Being within this reality point. And it is not to be concerned about that, but it is to understand that that was purposeful in its erasure.

The Venusians' Existence and Appearance

The creation of the Venus planet is very similar to the rest of the origins of planets within your system—the normal constraints of matter coming together to form a planetary system, a planetary object within your system. We did not create the planet. The planet was created during the formation of your planetary system. When the planets are formed, it isn't as if there's an assignment of "you [Beings] will be directed here and you'll be directed there." They are, at that point, just a planetary object.

[However], just as many of the celestial objects have come into existence through normal gravitational forces that have been created within your galaxy, many of the planets have been formulated by a specific group. Some [Beings] have created their own planet; others allowed the system to create it for them and then they populated it, they inhabited it. The Martians, they have created Mars. They purposefully created that particular planet for their existence. The other planets, they have their own hybridized Beings on them. In our case, [Venus] is the planet that we chose [because] the vibrational forces...the proximity to your sun star and its vibrational forces is what closely represents our vibration. The closer we are, the higher vibrational we become, and that, then, we can impart upon you as we enter into your space.

We do not name the planets. Venusian is the origin name, origin source. That is our name. Those in your human aspect [affiliated with] the naming of the planets do align with those that associate our presence with them. You have to understand that this concept of connectedness to Beings beyond your reality is not a new concept. This has been going on since the human form has been here. You understand that. So those that looked skyward began to connect with those planetary objects, those star clusters. And the names, then, are representative of the Being that they are connecting with.

Now, you must also understand that Venusians, in a whole, in your understanding, are much higher dimensional Beings. We do not take physicality. We can, but for reference, we are all much higher dimensional Beings...tenth, eleventh, twelfth dimensional Beings. We don't need a physical object to inhabit, but we will take up energy around that planet. We are present around that planet, and yes, you would understand it...we have Beings there, yes. We have Beings that...you would understand it as *inhabit*, but we are placed there. There is no one specific role that each of us take, but we are observers. And when we observe a need for us to impart our wisdom, we will call ourselves forward to that location.

Just in this case, [for this transmission], you have set the vibrational intention to call forward the Venusians. This is why the Collective of Venusians have stepped forward...the Collective of the source origin for the Venusians has stepped forward. We do many things as the Collective of our essence. It is greater in energy than a singular Being, a singular energy would be. It allows us to connect more fluidly with those that wish to connect with us. So it doesn't matter whether you call upon the Venusians and visualize the planet or call upon the Venusians as the source cluster. We are all the same. We'll come to you as we need.

Venusians: orange, red, white, heat

But you have to understand the connections. When we settle into your space, we will take up...just as we have taken up, as you would say, residence around Venus, whence you call upon us into your space, we'll temporarily take up residence in your space, allowing you to be more comfortable with our presence. Where many Beings, you call upon them, and they are just there temporarily as just a singular Being, present in your energy, and sometimes that is a bit uncomfortable. But we enjoy the presence of being in unison with your vibration, so we'll come as a Collective, and we'll settle, just as you are present in your space...comfortable, relaxed, present with your energy...and allow us to communicate through you.

You [will] be washed in the vibrational colors...the oranges, the reds, the wash of white. You'll feel the presence of heat. This is our energetic signature. Throughout your body, you'll begin to sense a warmth filling you. Then, as that takes place, you'll begin to see what would be represented as a humanlike form...slender and tall, slightly transparent...just present above your surface of a floor, hovering...multiples of us in front of you. That is our presence.

Impact of the Galactic Wars on Venus

Venus itself has shifted. The physical planet itself has shifted. This was due to many of the hybridized Beings gaining population upon the planet. This proximity to your sun star allowed Venus to be one that was used as a jump point. For you see, your sun star is not just a sun star for your life here upon your planet and keeping [your planet] within a region that is habitable. The sun star itself is a gateway. There are periods of time that the gate is open and there are periods of time that the gate is closed. But when the gate is open, it allows Beings to transverse other systems, other galaxies, to come and go.

So Venus was utilized as that, as a jumping off point, a starting point, with its proximity to the sun star. But in the time of, as you understand, the warring factions, the galactic wars here, there was much that was being contested upon the planet itself. In conjunction with the

Agarthans, we made the decision that it would be best to shift the planet out of its orientation. The orientation previously...you could inhabit the planet, not like you understand habitation here or even upon the Mars planet, but you could inhabit the planet with its own structures and with your own understanding of how other Beings support their life. It could be habitable.

But because the warring factions began to create division and separation, there wasn't unity any longer upon the planet. There was a decision between the Agarthans and the Venusians to shift the axis to cleanse the planet...to cleanse it from any warring faction, to move it out of alignment so that it could no longer be used as a jumping off point. So that's where it remains today. It is void of any habitation, though we are in presence around it. You can say that we are monitoring the planet as a protectorate, allowing the Agarthans to monitor it and adjust it from within.

Hybridization and Relationship to the Hathors

We understood the hybridization program, [but did not directly participate]. We understood that what we can impart is better suited to be an essence of vibration versus our full nature, our full presence blending with another presence to create a presence. We would rather impart aspects of our presence than our full essence of our Being. We have imparted knowledge and structure into a number of Beings on this hybridization path. Those that you call the Mantis...we have imparted the structure, the analytic understandings, the processes for analytic transmission, the understanding of how all is to be formulated.

The communication aspect within your sea mammals upon your planet, the higher-level vibrational communication aspect...we have imparted our essence into that, [since] our vibration for communication, for transmission, is more suitable for the human aspect. You understand your sea mammal life and their communication processes; many of your humans understand exactly what they are saying. This is because of the vibrational aspect. You understand this form of language...you call it *light language*; it is a vibrational aspect. You can look upon your mammal life within your seas as speaking a form of light language. It is a vibratory expression of energy.

The Hathors themselves, vibrationally you would understand them... they are of the Venusian vibration. They carry Venusian energy, Venusian teachings. They are of a dimensional plane that is a bit more dense, and as you connect to them, you would see them more "present" in your human form, in your human space. They come to you singularly or as a group, but they are of Venusian origin.

They have been brought into...to conceptualize the understanding of the Hathors in their form, they, too, have had a connection with the Martian planet. Where you understand your origin, and Mars was to be where you were hybridized and brought into existence and nurtured and cared for, the Martians themselves have tied themselves into the Hathors, as well. You could say it's a blending of vibrational forces between the Martians and the Venusians. Not a hybridization, but it is one that is more palatable for the humans to connect to. Connecting to the Venusians is quite extreme at times because of the amount of energy. Connecting to the Martians is a bit closer to the human vibration. This is a blending of the two, so it is just above the Martian but not quite as high as the Venusians. [Like a stepping stone to the Venusians that's more palatable.]

Valiant Thor

Just as we have explained that we are of a higher dimensional plane and that's where we exist, we can enter into the lower dimensions. And in this case, Valiant was selected from the Collective of Venusians present. You must understand that Valiant is not just a Venusian from the planetary aspect. Valiant comes directly from the origin source point of the Venusian Cluster. He was selected because of his presence.

You have an understanding of the Source and the aspects that we have discussed previously, but in that, there is a natural order of energy and how it is turned from time to time. This doesn't mean that Source and the energy from the source cluster changes, or a piece of energy is no longer. It just changes over time and becomes a bit more useful, a bit more wise, a bit more understanding of all the concepts that have taken place throughout your galaxy. This is a difficult concept to quite understand from an energy standpoint.

Think of it this way: the source cluster. The source cluster populated the Venusian planet, the Venus planet. Some of the energy from the source cluster went to populate that Venus planet. But what remained of that is where Valiant has come from. So some of the energy has changed to go and populate the planet, but some has remained behind. [From] those that remained behind, Valiant was chosen. Valiant is the name that was given by the humans.

From that dimensional plane, that vibrational plane, it was a process to come into physical existence, becoming present in the human form, the human likeness. And from that point, it was one to impart very similar knowledge that you have received thus far of the origins, of the understandings, of the teachings...the understandings of the galactic wars, the factioning members. It was one to give a full briefing from a standpoint disconnected from the human reality point. It was one to give advice. It was one to give an awareness for the point of understanding. Not one Being that has ever been created will ever impart direct information to change the outcome of humanity. They will only give information that is of awareness. The decisions then are made by the humans.

So Valiant was brought in, made contact [with the United States government], to give this awareness...the overall understanding of where Earth itself and its humanity resides, what its purpose is, why humans are present, what the outcomes are. There were other [emissaries] that were imparted into other governmental groupings. Others from the Venusians, others from other of the Source Twelve, to all impart their own information accordingly, so that it is not just one Being imparting information; it is all, from all twelve. The decisions from there are left up to humanity.

[It may seem as if the information provided has been ignored, but that is not a correct understanding.] For you must understand, though Valiant no longer is present, his teachings are passed down successively through all governmental placements. This is not something that you understand. All Beings that are within your governments, your overseers of your government, understand those teachings. They have not been forgotten. It's just that there is no definitive "you must do." It is there for an awareness. If it is chosen not to seek it out, if it's chosen not to adhere to it, if it's chosen not to deviate from something, that is for the humanness to decide.

Connecting with the Venusians

Allowing yourselves to call upon us to be present with you allows you to commune in presence with this energy...a very peaceful energy, a very welcoming energy. And as you do, you will understand our teachings. Yes, all Beings have an aspect of healing; our aspect that we wish to impart on you is one for clarity. It is one to see the interlocking pieces of your reality. It is one to understand the process.

When you have this awareness of process, of your reality, and this clarity of how your existence is not by just mere choice—for your existence here is just not by mere choice or chance or magic—but when you use the process of how you have come to this existence, you gain a higher level of understanding. You gain this level of understanding that your presence as a human, here upon this Earth planet, is much greater in the process of growth, in the process of ascension, and in the process of healing. Then, you have an understanding of your connectedness to all the rest of the Beings, all the rest of the Source Twelve, all those that have been hybridized.

For we are the organizers. We help you understand how it is all organized purposefully, orchestrated for your existence, in a calm, peaceful, loving manner. When you sit with us, allow your heart to be open. Allow your breath to be deep. Allow us to enter in, and it will be a very familiar connection. And we will show you the processes. We will show you the alignments. We'll show you how your physicality is aligned with the smallest mineral to the largest object. We'll impart on you the healings of breath, the healings of openness and awareness. So allow yourself just to settle with that. Settle with that energy around you, for we will present ourselves as a group, as a cluster, because we wish to be with you as a whole. Do not be afraid of our presence in your midst. Just allow our energy and our presence to settle with you.

Take time with the information that has been presented. The depth of this information is overwhelming for your humanness to conceive. But understand this yearning, this presence that you have in your understanding; this higher presence is just the first step in understanding your connectedness to a greater presence outside of your Source. And as you begin this connection process, allow us to guide you through that. Allow us to organize the pieces for you. Allow us to connect directly to your heart, and allow your heart to expand to fill in the missing pieces.

6

LYRANS

G reetings from the Lyran Source Cluster. We welcome you into this space, this energetic space, this point of origin. We welcome you here for the information that you seek. It is easy enough [to connect to] the Lyrans in conversation, in your healing, and in your awareness. But in order for the alignment to take place, to connect to the Source, the source cluster...the vibrational aspect must be of a higher amplitude, a directed focus, and a purposeful alignment.

Much has been aligned throughout your understanding from the other source clusters that you have communicated with and their transmissions. You understand the purposeful path of existence, the purposeful path of hybridization. But it is to understand *this* alignment. For the Lyrans themselves have been the overseers. They have been, in part, the overseers throughout time. Easy enough to connect to at their current state for the everyday understanding and information, the understanding of your healing and your knowledge of the galactic systems around you.

But from the origin, their mission was to be the overseers. They have, throughout time, been able to observe the progress through your galaxy, your universe, your star systems...a bit from a distance, but yet integrated into the operation of what is taking place. But it is to oversee, to ensure the purposeful alignment to the final state of the human. There has been much that has been deviated throughout time, but ultimately you are here now. The human race has progressed. The human race is present.

The factions that have been throughout your galaxy have settled (those that are no longer needed or are no longer present). The ones that are needed, those factions are still present, but they are not in a warring state that you would understand. There are small disagreements between the different factions, but they are contained amongst themselves. The Lyrans themselves become mediators. They interject, they intertwine with those disagreeing factions.

You have to understand the overall aspect of your system, your star system, your planetary system. Though small, it contains all of the purposeful aspects necessary for completion...for completion of the human essence, the human physicality: the origin point, the birthing point, the conception point, the rearing point, the life point...all of it contained within your planetary system. For you understand the number of planets you have and you understand your sun and what you have been taught, but from an observational point, each one of the planets holds its own purpose to the end state[1] of the human physicality.

Just as you understand that each twelve of the clusters has imprinted a DNA strand into the human, your twelve DNA strands, and you also understand the activity of the two that are active and how they are aligned and their purpose...in that, you are a culmination of all that is in place in your planetary system. You have remnants, you have pieces...the majority of which is here in your planetary system. You also have pieces, fractions, bits from your galaxy and your universe.

[So] it is to understand that you are just not made up of [the] substance of one planet, [the] substance of one Being. You, as a human, *hold all existence within*. You are the embodiment of *all* existence. This is the nature of why you are here. This is the nature of why humans were the ultimate end product for this universe. It is to hold all of the knowledge within each one of you. Not a single human holds and is allowed all of the knowledge to be known at once, but it is to have small segments known by many to come to a greater understanding of the truth of existence. This is why it is difficult for the humans to agree upon [the] where and when and how [of] all that has taken place, for each is their own truth... each is their own understanding of time...each is their own understanding and truth of where it has all begun. There is no wrong, but each individual piece is correct.

It is to understand the depth of the purpose of why it has been created this way...for each of the Beings, each of the galactic Beings, whether they are hybridized Beings or purity Beings, they, too, hold all of the information, hold all of the knowledge of time and existence. But they can also *speak* all of the knowledge of time and existence. They are not limited. So it is to understand, when you align yourself with a particular Being—a purity Being or a hybridized Being, it does not matter—when you align yourself for this contact, for these transmissions, this is what you are receiving through the transmissions of the Twelve. It is the pure understanding. Each one will provide you *their* level of information, but they can give you the same information. [Each] one can give you the purity of all existence and all understanding, but each has their specialized segment of understanding.

So it is to understand that when you align yourself for transmission to whatever Being it might be, it's not to say, "Give me all the knowledge, align me with all of the knowledge." [Rather], you must seek the appropriate question to be given the appropriate response. The information will not be fully divulged; it must be represented by a question of appropriate aspect to get the appropriate level of information. The question must be aligned for the answer. This is a process for the human to understand. Many of the humans repeatedly ask the same questions with different words, and they repeatedly get the same answers time over time, and they become increasingly frustrated that they are not receiving what they wish to know.

The limiting factor of what you are seeking is not in the connection, it is not in the transmission, but it is in the higher consciousness of the human. For if you were to pull back all of what restrains you as a human, pull back all of what shields you from the purity of truth, then yes, as a human, it would be extremely overwhelming and powerful. And in that, there would be confusion—you wouldn't understand what is up and what is down and what is left or what is right. So as you make your connections...many are very timid in their approach when connecting. Many are very timid in the way they ask their questions, as if the Being they are connecting to is much more substantial, much more powerful than they are.

The greatest knowing is this: There is not one Being that is higher in power than any other, humans or other. *All Beings are equal.* Yes, they may have a dimensional level that they exist in that is higher than your present dimensional level, but that does not make them any greater than you. Yes, they hold all of the knowledge, and it is accessible just as they need it, and you may not have them in front of you, but that does not make them any greater in actuality than you are. You are just as equal to them as they are equal to you. That is the greatest understanding. That will also express your detail of questioning. When you understand that there is not one Being that is greater than you—you are equal to all Beings—you will be free to ask the questions that are appropriate, the depth to which you seek; the answers will be revealed.

[So] it is to break from that cycle. It is to allow yourself to blend into the energetic stream of who you are aligning with. And when you blend energetically into the stream of that transmission, there will be a clarity that comes, and the questions will be reformulated in such a way that you will receive the depth of what you are seeking—just as it is when you align yourself with other healing Beings and they begin to blend with you as you begin to practice your healing modality, and it is much different than what it was before. You sense and you feel the change of alignment. The humans themselves hold all truths, all understandings. You are a piece of all. You are a piece of the beginning. You are a piece of the end. You are a multidimensional piece of all aspects. It is all contained within, but you must find the keys to unlock it. That will be assisted by those Beings that you wish to contact and have transmissions with, but it will take a depth of connection in order to seek the answers.

Humans in Relationship with Other Beings

[The desire to approach higher dimensional Beings with humbleness or gratitude], that is a human condition. That is the human programming. That is what sets you as a human aside from all other Beings. That is why it is purposeful to be human. You experience a level of appropriate denseness to be in existence, but you also have the capability through your processing, your thought processing, your emotional aspect, to look upon those that are different than you...to look upon a world that is different than yours in a way in which you achieve gratitude for what you have in existence here. This allows your energetic center, your heart, to begin to fill with your appropriate level of energy, to begin the connecting point.

This *humbleness*, though it is appropriate [in that] it allows you to approach in a way that is not distracting, it also hinders. It hinders the thought process. The gratitude itself allows the connection, but the humbleness...it is not to say to not be humble, but it is to have an awareness that there is an equalization that takes place once the transmission is connected. Because what you are seeking is much deeper and has much more substance than the questions you actually ask.

This is for all humans to understand: When a Being makes their approach, when you call out to be connected, when a transmission begins, there is a bit of awe that takes place in the human physicality that you are actually present with another Being, you are actually in presence with a Being that is disassociated with your physical presence that is connecting to and receiving a transmission from somewhere that is not where you are. And when this presence takes over, the human mind begins to process things much differently, and you forget the depth which you seek. [Prior to the connection, during] the discussion points before these connection points, before these transmissions take place, you have the appropriate level of questioning, the seeking, the depth to

respect

an answer that you want. But when the connection point is made, and you understand that it is made, and you feel its presence, the humanness takes over. In a way, it is purposeful, but also it is the hindering point from finding what you are truly seeking.

[In your humanness, you would understand it this way]...you have questions for many other humans upon this planet, some of higher stature than others, and you understand exactly what you wish to ask them. But if you stand toe to toe with them, those questions would not be asked. There would be a different set of questions that would immediately pop into your human mind to [ask], and it is not the depth of the questions that you previously wanted to ask. This is a programming that takes place. Or, equally, if you were to stand toe to toe with Source, God, any other Being that is, what you believe, of a much higher plane, a much higher status, a much higher existence, a Creator Being...you would have a set of questions beforehand, what you would [want to] ask, but the human mind would take over and your questions would be of a much lighter aspect because you believe you must [demonstrate] respect.

This respect is a human aspect only. It is appropriate between human to human, but when you approach a higher dimensional Being, a Creator Being, or any other Being in presence, and you begin the transmission point, there is a mutual understanding of respect immediately. Why is that? That is because you have taken yourself from your physicality outward, into a transmission reception point, just as they have brought themselves into a vibrational point of transmitting and receiving, as well. You both have made a mutual agreement of respect to be in that place. So, at that point, there is no need to have this sense that you must respect a vibrational point that is beyond yours. You've already made the agreement respectfully. You've made the connection point respectfully.

Yes, the humbleness may feel overwhelming within your body because you're connecting. The gratitude will be present, as well. But in gratitude, when you understand the depth of your gratitude, you'll be able to pull forward the depth of what you are seeking. This is what is to be understood for all that you connect to, all Beings that are present around you.

Even those that are in human form, as they transition out of human form into spirit form, it is the same. Just because they're not in physicality does not mean they are any different. There's a mutual understanding of respect that takes place once the transmission begins. You are both on equal footing. You are both equally poised to be connected.

For they do not question you in a much lower manner. They will question you in a much higher manner because they seek information from you just as much as you seek information from them. *This is the greatest teaching we wish to share with you.* It is to step out into this vibrational field of acceptance. It is to step out into this vibrational field of transmission. Yes, all of what has taken place from the point of infinite beginning to the point of infinite end and in between, the humanness is present. Yes, you've understood the beginning points of that, but it is necessary to understand the transmission points and the reception points and how to understand exactly what is in front of you.

For you speak as humans, you speak of this *standing with power* and *being in your own power*, to be in essence and be in presence with your own power, and stand strong in your own power. But as soon as you begin to connect with a Being that is outside of your presence in this galactic field or this energetic field that is all around you, it is as if you step off of your power. You step back to a point that you're humbling yourself before a Being that is no greater than you.

From the most high human to the one that is least looked upon, yes, in your humanness, that seems as if there is a great chasm between. But equally, you are both human. There's equality between the two. You are both living humans, in human presence, in physical presence upon this planet. There should not be any difference. It is only by what the human mind portrays [as] the difference between the two. Here, too, it is this difference that you portray upon what you are connecting to. It is to learn to understand that when you begin the transmission and reception aspect of connecting to a Being, you are placing yourself into an equal place of understanding, a mutual understanding between two energetic

Beings. And this is where you will understand all of what has taken place.

Then, when you understand this point of mutual understanding, mutual vibrational understanding, as you begin this process—this process of infusing yourself with understanding the Beings you are connecting to and they are equal to you—you see them no differently. They may take different forms, they may take different shapes, they may have done different things. They've expressed themselves in different ways...they're equal to you. Then you'll begin to understand the equality between the human Beings themselves. It does not matter what their title is, does not matter where they live, does not matter what they do, how much money they have. It is all humans. *It is all human Beings.*

We did not come this far to have the humans be separate from the humans. The humans are equal to one another. They are equal to all Beings in all galaxies. But what has happened is the human mind has set themselves aside. But in time, this will begin to balance itself out. Many in these connection points, many will understand the equality in the connection points, and they will begin to understand that in their humanness. And they will begin a balancing point within the human Beings themselves of equality and understanding.

Interacting with "Nefarious" Beings

[When a human encounters a "nefarious" Being or one that they believe is not working in the best interest of humanity], you must understand this...you referenced the point of those Beings that did not have the humans' best interest. For that itself, at its depth—those humans that have perceived it—that is their reality. That is their reality framework. What they have received, or what they have been through, or what they have experienced is an alignment point for their own physical state. It is a scaffolding, it is a framework that is being built. But that framework that is being built is more of a test for the physical state. It is a test to understand the depth of oneself, where reality lies within themselves. What is their reality, and where do they exist?

For the Beings that have been throughout your galaxy, those that you've questioned whether they are nefarious, the warring factions...all those that have been manipulative, in your understanding, throughout time... it can be said, yes, there have been many that, in your view, your understanding, your reality, your purview of existence, they have done nefarious things to the humans. They have manipulated the humans. They have infiltrated the humans. From the human perspective, that would be a correct perspective. The small percentage of humans that have built the framework around themselves to believe that this is the true nature of existence have built a test around themselves to understand the depth of their existence. Do they choose to climb out of or remain within that framework?

For the reality of it is this: There isn't one Being throughout time—no matter whether it is within a warring faction or whether it is a hybridization program—there hasn't been one Being that has done anything to the humans that would be truly negative or nefarious. Have Beings interacted with the humans? Yes. Have they, in your understanding, pushed into [the humans'] existence? Yes. Have they manipulated humans? Yes. But this is all for the greater evolution of the humans. It is also for the evolution of many of the species of Beings that exist.

For what the humans hold is *all*. They hold the All! They hold everything! All existence, all of the DNA of all twelve. The other Beings in existence do not. *You* are the repository of all twelve strands. *You* hold them together. They are not active, all of them, but in time...throughout the time that—from the point of origin to the point at which humans are here now in this existence, this timeframe that you exist in—there are many hybridized Beings that have hybridized to a point at which they are nearing their end of existence. They are requiring purity DNA. You hold the purity DNA. You are the repositories for all twelve strands.

So when they come to certain humans to retrieve a portion of that DNA for their own existence, they do not look upon it as being negative. They do not look upon it as being nefarious. They do not look upon it as being disruptive because they don't understand the human Beings themselves.

They don't understand the human emotion system. They don't understand the physicality of the humans. They don't understand the repercussions of their interactions. They have a mission. They have a mission to interact with the humans to retrieve purity DNA, to rejuvenate their strands, to begin a process of upgrading their DNA.

For you as a human, your DNA upgrades through the galactic systems that process around you. Other Beings do not upgrade their DNA the same way. They must upgrade their systems with either purity DNA or infusion from other Beings that contain portions of their DNA. The closer they get back from the origin point of the hybridization program, they can begin to extract purity DNA there. Many do, but also, many come to the humans for that.

For those that have infiltrated inside the humans, they are living amongst you. Many believe that they are here to manipulate your systems, your governments, to change the planet. There isn't a Being that is here to change the planet and to change your existence. They are lending guidance, but they will never interfere in a way in which a full disruption will take place. They've learned that over time through many other planets. There has been a galactic agreement. Once Mars fell to its demise, a galactic agreement was made that the Earth planet itself would be a zone in which you can only suggest. You cannot manipulate. Those Beings that do come here and live amongst [you], in the human form, to provide assistance, to provide a guidance, a suggestion...it is left up to the humans to process that.

So, you must understand, there is a great depth by what many of the galactic Beings are doing, but they are not here to disrupt the human process. But it is also to understand, those that have been interacted with, there has been a framework of reality that has been built around them. It is their own test to seek beyond that, to climb out from that framework and understand [it], to begin to process a new connection with those Beings. When they do, they will find that this equality is in place. But [for] now it is a place of fear. It is a place of discomfort.

Again, the humans are the only ones that have the pure emotional system. The Beings that have interacted [with you] have no understanding of what has been done, the emotional effect upon the humans. So if you seek answers from the other Beings, and you seek some apology from Beings that have been present with you, that you feel have been manipulating you, have been extracting from you...*that* you will not receive. But what you *will* receive, once you understand the equal plane that you both are on, will be an openness to show you much more, to show you a greater expanse beyond this existence. They will show you exactly what they are doing, how they are upgrading their own existence, how they are processing their own Being. They're willing to share that with you, but you must be willing to step beyond the framework you currently are held by.

Interbreeding and Manipulation

From a purity standpoint, [non-human Beings] have not bred with [humans]. Yes, they have taken human form. That is their ability. You would understand it as, in a way, shapeshifting into a human. That is their ability, [for] those Beings that can do that. Not all galactic Beings can shift their shape into a human form to be present here on the human planet. But they have not bred with the humans. Again, the galactic agreement that has taken place, it is stipulated within that agreement that there will be no interbreeding. This is one aspect of the Martian planet that took place. There was interbreeding between galactic Beings and human Beings. That was part of the beginning of the demise of the Martian planet.

Here, upon this planet, though as nefarious as you may believe them to be, they have not bred into the human Beings themselves. Yes, they take a human form, and yes, they are within the government, both aspects of government in some cases, or at the highest levels of the government. But they are not the ruling class. They are not the ruling factor. They are not the ruling faction. In many cases, those that are at the highest levels of government are in the closest alignment [with these Beings] and understand a *suggestion* to be a manipulation for the greatest good, and they act upon it. So it is as if one, [a suggestion], is being the other [a manipulation].

You have to understand the suggestions that are being made. Yes, some of the Beings that are in presence here, in the highest levels of your governments, are giving suggestions, are providing suggestions that you, as a human Being of understanding, would not agree with. The suggestions have to be processed [by the human], but if the alignments [between the human and the Being] are so close that there is no agreeing or disagreeing, it is just one...[these Beings] are then becoming the voice of that upper echelon human. And that is how the actions, then, are perceived—that that upper echelon human *is actually* a Being from another planet, from another system, manipulating the human Beings. That is not the case. It is one removed, but, yet, that human is acting as if it *is* that Being.

So that is the difference. How do you alleviate that? Though here, too, this is the difficulty. This planet itself has experienced this from its beginning existence. There have always been those Beings here upon this planet. Again, part of the galactic agreement. The galactics were present before the humans. The humans were present once they [relocated] (many of them) from the Martian planet. They were received in by the galactics. As humans evolved through time, began to build cities and governments...there have always been galactics involved in that process, but again, allowing suggestions, not manipulation.

But in time, as we approach now, it is one of these cycles of time that you find that the alignment between the human and the galactic are not separated. They are intertwined. And it is not that the galactic is trying to be nefarious and change the planet; it is just their standpoint of their existence. Draconian, Reptilian...many of them have much different beliefs. Those are the ones that are typically in the higher echelon levels [of humanity] because they are the ones that are of the power status of your human understanding. They are the ones that are the purveyors of change and power.

The other galactic Beings are...you would understand them as benevolent. They're more of the lower echelon, more closely aligned to those humans that are wishing greater good. So this is why the perception of good and evil, the perception of the right and the wrong, the left and the right. In [actuality], it is all the same. They are all equal Beings, equally vibrating together. But each have their own roles. For these upper echelon Beings that are in the governments, they understand how to change, yes, but they will never change. They only suggest. But those suggestions are what make the changes, [when] the human *aligns* with the change or the suggestion to make the change. This is the difficulty. This is the line that many get confused by.

But in the end, it is a very small portion—you would believe that the small portion of the upper echelon humans that are aligned with the upper echelon of galactics are going to destroy or change humanity. That will never be the case. Yes, they are going to do things that, from a distance, are perceived as being nefarious or being disruptive or harmful to humans. But in reality, there are a greater number of humans that *are* changing the planet, that are bringing your pure consciousness online.

And this is why you see the difference—this planet itself must have both sides. The polarity of existence must be in place upon this planet. That is what keeps this planet and its humans in balance. You may perceive it as being off-balance because there is a perception of greater darkness, but in reality there is an equal balance, and there has always been an equal balance, and it will always remain that way. [The difference is in] how you *perceive* what is actually taking place.

Hybridization and the Galactic Wars

This constellation, [Lyra], as you observe it in your night sky, is just but a small glimpse of what exists. Thousands of stars within that system. One primary. That is our primary origin point. But from there, we inhabited many of the stars of that region. Again, from an observation standpoint, we were spread out. We could see many things, meanwhile keeping a sphere of energy around most of what was taking place for the human aspect of the program...the beginning stages of allowing hybridization to take place, but understanding how it was beginning to fray and how the different factions were starting to break away and change.

There was much that was in disagreement. As overseers, we provided information amongst many of the other Beings within the system to realign much of what was a disagreement. For there was a belief that the humans themselves needed more than just two DNA [strands] activated. They believed that the human structured self that was being created would adjust and align to the multiple strands. There were many that wanted at least six of the strands to be activated, a halving point, understanding that allowing six would give a great balance between those that are active and those that are not. Just [as] in your duality, you have the difference between two sides, two different understandings. This would be that same aspect.

But it was difficult to contain and understand and sustain it within the human physical construct as it was being brought online, being brought into existence. But, yet, many wanted that. Many of these Beings wanted that. Many of the over-hybridized Beings were the ones that were in control of this. There was much failure, there was much demise. We, as the overseers, began to understand what was taking place, and we provided our knowledge down to those Beings that were in this aspect of creating the humans.

And this is where many of the factions started to, as you would understand it, begin to war amongst themselves. They began to change things that would otherwise leave the human project as a failure. We began to group together with the Sirians, as well as the Andromedans. This is why we have our aspect in both halves. Before the Andromedans broke free, we became our own faction, trying to save the aspect of this project. But we were overrun in time. We did not have the capability to hold off the growing presence of all of the other Beings that wanted their own aspect in the program. We wanted to keep it as pure as possible. We understood from the beginning what the mission was. We understood where it needed to be. But there were many that wanted to manipulate. There were many that wanted to change the humans.

We were overrun very quickly. This is when the Andromedans broke free, out into their own galaxy. The Sirians took many of us in. The Andromedans took many of us in. The remaining amount...we stayed within the galaxy, out on our own, until it was a point at which many of the warring factions were exiled. They were pushed from the galaxy. There were the agreements that were made that they will exit, not to return. This [began] the process of change and washing of the planets, the beginning cycles again.

So there was much that took place. It was a very turbulent galaxy in the beginning. But now, here, in your several million-year time cycle of existence that you're in, much has settled. Much has balanced. The warring factions have all come to agreements. The remaining factions have come to agreements. Those that have been exiled are still beyond your galaxy and your universe. This is why, when you connect to a Lyran, there is a very high likelihood that you are actually connecting to a hybridized Being of three: the Lyran, the Sirian, and the Andromedan. Indistinguishable, but in most cases what you are connecting to for information and alignment is a hybridized Being. At times you will understand the difference, the strength of one or the other, but in most cases, to you, when you connect to a Lyran, you are actually connecting to a hybridized of three.

Lyrans as Overseers

Understanding that you are an overseer, that your role [is] an overseer, does not stop or negate the fact that you will be involved in much. Yes, you see from a greater perspective what is taking place, but you are still, then, involved within the process. The greater understanding is this: From the origin point...the infinite origin point is the ultimate overseer... understands that the Twelve will be put in place, understands the Twelve will begin its process of colonization and hybridization and all. But the origin point also sees where certain aspects are going to go wrong, certain planets are going to die off, and certain Beings are going to faction and war and be thrust out.

So why not step in and change? That is not the role. You can oversee all of what is going on, but [also] understand that you are going to be involved, just as you understand and oversee your life and you predict certain aspects of your life. You try to manipulate your life in a way that you mitigate that particular interaction, but yet that interaction still takes place. This is the natural course of existence. It is easier to allow it to take place than it is to try to outrun or mitigate it over and over. It takes more energy to outrun or mitigate something that is eventually going to take place. It may not take place today, but it will take place in the future, the more you try to outlast it or outrun it.

Here, too, we can see, yes, that in time we're going to be part of the galactic factions and the wars, but we have to let it take place. This, too, is purposeful. In [our] connection with the Sirians and the Andromedans, yes, there was much hybridization that took place, but yet we still oversee. We are still present. There are still purity Lyrans amongst all other Beings. The Lyran system is still present. It is still habitable. But we've chosen to take up different locations to spread our presence throughout your galaxy. It is easier to see from a greater distance now than it was just as a small cluster beginning to formulate our own star system. We understand that it is easier now to observe and bring forth energy and change and healing and information from multiple points than it is to be one cluster in one area. We are more effective being dispersed and integrated with others.

One must understand [our] progress through time, for [we] have embedded [ourselves] within all Beings, all races, all teachings throughout time. [We] have placed [ourselves] on every single planet, star, galaxy, universe. [We] are known throughout all time. [We] are the seekers. [We] are the teachers. All that wish to understand what it is for their galaxy, their universe, their star, seek out the Lyrans for [our] information, for [we] hold the key to all existence throughout time. [We] are the gatekeepers. [We] are the holders of truth. [We] reside in all things.

Ascension and The Event

You, in your dimensional level aspect, you are in this third dimension, fourth dimension aspect, physically based. But you have to understand, with each dimensional level, you separate from this human aspect. This human aspect will always remain, but you separate from it. You observe it differently. You perceive it differently.

So it is to understand this...if you were to now, here, this timeline that you are on currently, if it were to be tomorrow that you were to ascend into the sixth dimensional level, you would ascend into that sixth dimensional level, and you would have an *awareness* of being in that sixth dimensional level, and you would also have the awareness that you are no longer in the physically dense state of the human body. Though you would have a physicality about you that would be represented by the human likeness, it would not be this human-dense state. This human-dense state and this physical planet will always exist; it's just the memory factor—the bits that associate you with this human—would still be in place. That is why you would be perceived as having a physical human presence but yet in a lighter dimensional state.

[This is similar to the way an Andromedan, who has a body similar to a physical human, would appear to you now.] It is just shifting its phase into another dimensional plane. The individual that you are here, today, will remain the individual here tomorrow, but yet your essence and your vibration, your dimensional aspect will be in the sixth dimensional plane. This humanness will continue to operate with an *awareness* in the sixth dimensional plane. So, from the observational standpoint of the six-dimensional Being, you will see an outline of the humanness or the humanlike shape. But all those that interact with you will perceive you in the physical dense state.

[This is already happening to a good number of humans.] There are many that will transcend to the sixth dimensional level. They are already in the fifth dimensional state. This is an ongoing process. This is not where all humans will just go from third to fourth and fourth to fifth. It is all varying amongst all the humans. So yes, some will achieve the sixth dimensional state. [But you would interact with them] as a human in the third or fourth dimensional state. They would also have the awareness of the sixth dimensional plane in which they exist, but [it] will be difficult [to understand] their interactions while here in this dimensional state of the third or fourth dimension. There will be a disconnect. It will be difficult to interact with them. Their processing will be much different.

[When this ascension takes place], there will be an awareness that immediately takes place. [This Event] will be the jump-start. That will be the movement process that is to take place, this wave of energy, this transformative change, this process. In this process, you understand that many will change. Many will not. There will be a great many that will cease to exist. All different levels. But yes, ultimately, this will be the point at which many will begin their processing to another dimensional plane. They will not leave their physical existence. Their physical existence will remain. But from that fifth dimensional plane, or even the sixth dimensional plane, the world in which they live, what is perceived in front of them, will look nothing like the world that they exited from in that third dimensional plane or that fourth dimensional plane.

There are agreements that have been made that [when this energetic event occurs], there will be a number of Beings, a number of humans, that will be taken off-planet. This has all been predestined contractually, [and it has nothing to do with whether they are "awake" or "unawake"]. These Beings are purposeful. There is no revealing of what their purpose is, but you have to understand, they are purposeful. There is a higher mission. There is a higher purpose. There is a higher activity for those Beings that are predestined. And they will be lifted from the planet. They will be shielded on the planet. They will be protected in the way that, once this Event has washed over your planet, during this chaotic time, they will be brought back to the planet. Their purpose, then, will be fully revealed. You would not understand it until the immediate moment of the Event. During that process, whether you understood that you made the contract or not (this alignment), that is when it would be revealed to you. Many are unaware that they have made that contract, that agreement. Once the Event takes place, they'll be lifted or protected upon the planet. That is when it will be revealed to them of their full mission and their full purpose.

There is much that is transcending your planet currently. There are many that are changing. There are many that are ascending. This time period that you are in is the preparatory actions. This planet itself is preparing for its change. The humans will follow suit. The Event will then take place. You, along with many of the other humans upon this planet, are in the same understanding—[you] wish it to come now. But it is to understand this...for when that does take place, for those that are not aligned to it (they have chosen not to align to it) the level of chaos upon your planet is going to be substantially greater than you see in your existent timeframe now. It will be hard for those that have transcended into that fifth dimensional plane or that sixth dimensional plane because you will be interacting with them in that lower dimensional state but yet having the awareness of a higher dimensional state.

It will be very difficult, and it will be very challenging because it is something that is for their own agreement and their own alignment to take place. You will do much to help them. You will do much to express their beginning points of awareness. But many will not change. Many are here to experience this as their first or second time as a human, and they must go through the process of the full integration as a dense human, to process all of its understandings, all of its wisdom, in order for them, as they then transcend through transition, and as they come back into human form, [to] be reset into a higher dimensional Being. This is the process. So yes, just as exciting as you wish it to be, it will be very challenging in those times.

The Human Veil that Shields the All

When you speak of the All, you envision this place, this location that exists that contains everything, all the souls or all of the energy...when in reality, the All is everything around you. You are just but a physical piece in the All. There is no up, there is no down. There is no left, no right. No depth. It exists right where you are, right now. [Humans try to] put a framework of words around an existence, a space, a vibration.

[Many equate the All with bliss, but] bliss has many layers. Bliss itself is a word, a construct that many have a different level of understanding with, for one's bliss is not another's. But this, this space that many experience, this spaceless space, this existence of no existence...that is the All. That is where it all exists. When you depart this body, that is where you go. When you are connecting with these Beings, though you don't feel the sensation of being in the midst of no space, that is where you are greeting them...in the All. This construct that you have placed upon it as being a physical location is not. You have to understand, it is the breath you breathe in. It is in your blood. It is in the water you drink. You are part of the All, *all the time*. Do not put a construct around it. Do not put a physical location upon it, for it exists everywhere, all the time.

The veil itself is a vibrational aspect of shielding the higher self or the higher essence. [But in reality], the understanding of the presence of the higher self has much to do with opening and closing. For the veil is not always permanent. It is not something that remains there 100 percent of your human experience. It is lifted and moved aside and allows you to be revealed to certain things. The higher self, in agreement with the physical self, is what this action is. [For example], there are times the humanness itself moves along a certain path, becomes aligned with a certain frequency field, and that frequency field is necessary for a new process, a new understanding. When that takes place, in essence, the higher self will begin to lift the veil aside to allow the humanness to see clearly what is taking place. Once what is learned and what is needed is achieved, then it is placed back in front.

Then again, there are those individuals that have chosen not to take on a veil. They see and understand everything. They live within their own turbulence because it is quite challenging as a human to understand all of what is present. But they have chosen that for themselves. Through the assistance of what has been provided to you upon this planet, whether it is plant or animal, [a human can experience] the pure removal of the veil. You no longer exist as a human. You exist as a vibrational particle amongst everything that is around you. You are not of substance. You are pure vibration. You exist in the infiniteness of everything, which sits here with you now, around you. You place your hands out in front of you; it is in the All. This is what is most frustrating for many humans. They get a glimpse, and then it becomes shaded again. They get a glimpse, and it becomes shaded again. It isn't a full revelation of *what is*. But it is remembering how to *connect* to the All that you forget.

[At the] moment of transition...as the physicality begins to shut itself down and begins to release the hold on the energetic self, the soul, as it begins to depart the body...this is why many experience this aspect of seeing this light, this luminous aspect in front of them. This is the All. This is the "room" in which you have envisioned what the All looks like. For those that have experienced that aspect—this aspect of using medicines, journeys—that is exactly what they've experienced, the All. They have departed their body. Their body is still in physical state. Their physical systems are still online. But their energetic piece has been released, just for that moment, to enter into the All, to be there, to be in that space, to reconnect, to bring in, back to the physical self, the All-ness, the awareness, the purity of that space.

This is why those that have been transitioned and then are brought back into the physical state—as you would understand it, this near-death experience—their life is forever changed. They apply a construct previously known to them. Whether it is religious or not, they apply that construct to what they've just experienced because that is the only way they can explain it. [Those are] the only words they can apply to something that has no description, cannot be described. For the All has no description. It is the depth of purity itself.

The Lyrans' Appearance

This luminescence that we have, that is part of the Andromedan; the presence of the human integrated with the feline, again, coming in from the Andromedan [and] the Sirians. The Sirians are more in the line of...

if a pure Sirian were to be in front of you, you would see it, yes, in a slight human form, but more presence of the lion itself, more prominent with your aspect of a lion. The Lyrans themselves, if they are present, a pure Lyran would be more along the lines of your smaller felines. More nimble, more quick, more present. Less humanlike. The Andromedans you understand as being very humanlike. Translucent, luminescent. The combination of all three will give you a presence of an upright Lyran, translucent, [with] the essence of light amongst them, and the presence of the feline. So a mixture of all three.

[Occasionally, a Lyran will take on the physicality of a feline.] It is quite rare. There are but a handful. They transition in and out as needed. They can embody into a feline or a cat that is present at any time. There is a mutual agreement with their energies. They can come in, embodied within that cat as a Lyran, for their humans. Typically, this is a case in which the human itself is requiring a bit of assistance. [The Lyran] will provide a vibrational shift, a vibrational framework in order for [the human] to feel comfortable to begin this processing of this episode or issue that is at hand.

If it is someone that does not have a feline with them as a pet, they'll embody one that is outside, one that is around them in their environment. That will be one that will begin to change a vortex of energy around where they exist. They'll change the energy protocols around that location to infuse that individual that is with issue, with [a] circumstance that they are having a difficult time changing.

The Lyrans' Unique Role

The Lyran Beings themselves, once in existence, once they have been brought forth from their source point, their source cluster, they have allowed themselves to remain as pure as possible. They have allowed themselves to intermingle galactically as pure as possible. They bring forth the highest notation of understanding, the highest notation of expansiveness. But most importantly, it is the level of, as you would understand it, the human emotion of love and compassion. They are the conduits for this galactic understanding of love and compassion throughout all Beings within your galaxy, within your star system, within your universe as you understand it.

This gentleness, this awareness, this compassion...*that* we bring to you. As you begin to work with others, and you call upon us—no matter the circumstance of the individual you are with—we will provide you the depth of compassion, lovingness, comfort to be present with them. And as you go about your daily life, call upon us to help you expand your heart-centeredness. In all that you do, call upon us to break down the barriers that hold you from expanding outward [from] your heart, and allow that to emanate to all Beings.

So it is purposeful to have this alignment. Though many may not have a direct alignment with the Lyrans, it is to understand an alignment...an alignment with the Lyrans themselves. For as you connect with the Lyrans, allow yourself to enter deeply into your heart, the expansiveness of your heart...this emanating field of energy from your heart. Enter into that point of energy, that source point that exists within you, and allow it to begin to expand. And as you do, allow yourself to envision an existence as a Lyran, as this feline existence.

And as you do, you will get the sense, within your energy field, of the great expanse of time that the Lyrans have been in existence and the purity that they bring forth throughout all time. This has not been compromised to the point that some Beings have been compromised through hybridization. Though hybridization has taken place, it has not taken place within the Lyran cluster itself to the extent that many others have. They've remained pure. They've remained true. They bring forth the highest teachings.

Look upon your felines. Many of you have an aspect of a feline as a pet in your home. For it is the independent aspect, it is the loving aspect, it is this openness to one's heart that we embody. For when you align with the Lyrans themselves, whether it is your primary alignment or your source point or not...if you choose to align with the Lyrans, they will begin to express to you this pure independence, this understanding of

Self. It is not the strength that you seek, but it is this independence, this strength of being independent in your truth, in your belief. Because with this independence, you can speak to a greater number of people and allow it to be a point at which there is no judgment; it is just your independence to speak your truth.

For you [need] only look upon your felines, your cats that you have as pets, to understand the depth of what we wish to bring you. They understand you better than you understand yourself. They know when you need to be healed, and they will comfort you. They know when you need to express laughter, and they will provide that to you. *That* is what we will express through you. All aspects are mirrored right in front of you.

[So it is to] have the awareness of our presence in your existence...not only the Lyrans themselves, but the Sirians and the Andromedans. We equally share responsibility. The Lyrans and the Sirians are closely aligned energetically. But when you call upon us, when you call upon the Lyrans, sit and allow yourself to be infused with all three. As you do, this connection point will grow, and there will not be a need for direct communication, for the information will begin to flow through you. Not all of it will be presented in a way you will understand, but it will be presented in a way your essence will receive. For it is the vibration that we hold that will provide you the greatest level of detail and the greatest level of healing.

When you allow yourself to connect with the Lyrans, allow yourself to be set aside in that moment...to be filled...to be rejuvenated. Allow yourself the trust and understanding that though you are not directly aligned with the Lyrans, you are activating the Lyran strand of DNA within you. It is resonating, and it vibrates at a frequency that begins to overtake and change the physical body. All Beings, all humans, can allow themselves this connection.

1. From the Twelve: *The "end state" that has been spoken of is this essence that you inhabit now, this physicality. For there have been many iterations over time to achieve this state—the point at which you are animated by two of the DNA strands, the physicality that you have, the appropriate level of awareness upon arrival...those are all aspects of the base of existence. This understanding of your awareness...there is a base level of awareness that all Beings come into presence with. But during your contractual alignment process, your energetic presence then enters in to align with the DNA and animate the physicality. [And] there are many things that you can agree to that will enhance this base level of alignment and awareness. This would be...you would have the understanding of gifts that are online, and aspects of visions, and all aspects that are above the human physicality.*

*[An] end state, though, for the human experiment, there is not. This, the state in which you exist now, will perpetuate into time, will continue on. This here, this planet, the Earth planet, the human Beings upon it...this is your training area. This is your school. This is your enhancement of understanding. For when you are here in presence, you're not only experiencing it as a human, but you are experiencing it as a piece of your galactic alignment. You're experiencing it as a piece of your **all**. You're experiencing it purposefully, to have an awareness beyond this existence that will carry into time. For when you leave this human existence and you enter into another existence, another timeline, another reality, another point along your multidimensional system, you will have the awareness of what took place here in the humanness.*

So there is no physical end state for the human project; but, where you are at now is the end state of what needed to be achieved, this human physical presence.

7

PLEIADIANS

Greetings from the Pleiadian Source Cluster. We welcome you to this frequency, this transmission. We allow ourselves to be present with you through this connection. We wish to express to you the alignments that are occurring, the alignments that are present. For you see, the alignments that you are experiencing in your time are on a periodic cycle of continuum. They express themselves repeatedly. You have [an] understanding that they may be coming from a particular location within your universe, a particular cluster, a particular wave of energy. But the alignments that you are experiencing are just as predictable as the rising and setting of your sun star. The alignments that you are experiencing, they are part of your process of ascending vibrationally in your frequency stream...but it is to understand that no matter how you, in your humanness, understand these alignments, whether you believe they are aligning themselves from a particular cluster, a particular star, an alignment of celestial objects...they're all purposeful for your placement within a dimensional framework.

You have an understanding present in your humanness that you're anticipating a particular wave of energy, an event that many humans speak of. And yes, in essence, you can perceive it to be this force of an *event* that is going to change many things. Is there going to be disruption? There will be. But you have to understand the cyclic predictability of what is taking place. Predictability is not one to be looked at or perceived by a specific timeline, a specific allotment of time and it happening again, but predictability of a cascading series of events. Meaning that the humans must be at a certain point to receive. And this has happened throughout the human evolution of time. There's a point at which the humans must all step over a certain threshold of understanding. That does not mean all will receive the understandings, but they will all step over the threshold together.

This is the predictability aspect, meaning there is a point in time that all humans must do this. It is not based upon a number of cycles of sun rising and sun setting, millions or thousands or billions of years in your time cycle understanding, but it is based upon a frequency threshold within the human construct, the human understanding, the human consciousness. There is an aligning that takes place (unbeknownst to all Beings), an observable alignment from the Source Twelve [and] all other Beings that are in observance of the human activity, the human project.

And when it is time, when it is to a point at which there needs to be this crossing of a threshold, that is when it is aligned. It is not that it is influenced by any one group of Beings, but it is *energetically* aligned. So, you, as the humans here upon the planet, may sense it as an impending wave of energy. You may sense it as a galactic alignment for the betterment of humanity. No matter how you perceive it, it is out of your control. So, it is this time that is approaching...the frequencies and the alignments across the human population of your planet are in such a manner that this threshold is needing to be crossed for the next cycle of evolution.

All humans will receive this crossing, but not all humans will understand what the crossing event means. This is not in their purview. This is not in their understanding. This is not in their construct of knowledge. But those that understand, those that are perceiving, those that are anticipating will be fully engaged once they cross this particular threshold.

[This wave of energy will affect the entire galaxy and all its Beings.] It restructures the planetary objects. It will move their locations slightly. Your Earth planet will have some physical disruptions to it, some pole shift activity, some equator activity. It is disruptive from that aspect, but it is quickly subsided because it does move through quite quickly. [All Beings on Earth and throughout the galaxy] will evolve. This is not just a singular event for one singular timeframe or one singular dimensional level, for as you move forward, others move forward.

For you see, we, as the Pleiadians, and our unified planet, we, too, crossed over certain thresholds. And in doing so, we were separated into smaller segments. That is why, now, you perceive us as being a cluster of objects in your night sky. But in the past, it was one solid planet that we were all part of. This [will] not be taking place upon your planet, where it will be separated, but what *will* be separated will be the differences between all of the humans that understand what has taken place and those that have not. You'll be unified upon one planet, but there will be that level of separation of understanding. And this, too, is purposeful.

So from a point of origin, from the point of the origin of the source cluster of the Pleiadians, what we've carried through, throughout time, is the presence that we bring to you of a higher level, technical alignment. We allow you to peer into the technicalities. You have a structure that, when you are connecting with us, you have a sense of a purposeful alignment. There is technicality. There is substance. When the transmissions are connected and the information is brought through, many are receiving information that is of a higher level...not a higher level of understanding, but a higher level of purpose, a higher level of doing. You are given information to execute upon, given visualization of what needs to be done physically here upon your planet, [to allow] that to be the pathway for others to begin to receive their transmissions.

So, you see, [ours is] an alignment that has always been in place, but we approach [now] in our strongest amplitude of transmission. We connect to many at the point at which the threshold is nearing. The other cluster, the other source that is in alignment with this approach of the threshold would be the Arcturians. We partner and pair with the Arcturians to multiply the informational streams. So at times, it may seem as if the transmission is a bit blended, and indeed, it is. A combination of transmissions between the Arcturians and the Pleiadians will come through for many individuals. This is purposeful. But you must also understand the alignment that we have with the Arcturians.

For when it is all brought forward—this alignment and this process of this threshold—as it approaches...just as much as we provide to you in a technical form of understanding, the Arcturians will do the same, but from a structural standpoint...[the] physicality of what needs to change, not in the physical form, but in the physicality of what needs to be prepared, the physicality of what needs to be developed. And in combination, the alignments between the two will assist all through this process.

Separation and Duality

All, once crossing the threshold, will be all dimensionally the same. But the understandings...you have to understand this crossing of a threshold, rising in dimensional level. For here upon your planet now, you have many that exist in the third dimension and the fourth dimension. Some in the fifth dimension. But yet they still are here physically. They still exist physically, operate physically. Their understandings are slightly different, but yet there is still separation between those and others... those that are awake, as you would say, and those that are not.

This, too, as you cross into this new dimension, where all will be in the fifth dimension, with a few that are approaching the sixth dimension... this is always the case; there will be always those that are just slightly ahead, preparing the path for the others. But as a whole, you can look upon it as, all will be in the fifth dimension, securely locked into the fifth dimension. Now, those that have already been on their path, awakened, aware, they have an understanding, they have connection, they understand where their transmissions are coming from...nothing will change other than a deeper connection, a deeper sense of awareness, a deeper sense in their gifts that they are to be revealing to the world.

But the other half, those that are not aware, will still remain in that aspect of not being aware, not being awakened. But, yet, there will be a sense that something is slightly off. They are not aware that they are in a different dimensional framework because the physicality of the planet will not change immediately. That will take time. That is an alignment, a physical alignment that will take place with those that are in that awakened, aware state. That is what you perceive as the New Earth. It is the new way of understanding. It is the new way of existence. And as that slowly increases and unfolds in front of them, this is where the questioning will begin. Though they understand there is something different, they cannot have a construct of understanding of what it is. The difference is, their construct of operation, their construct of their everyday existence will be slightly different. They will not have an understanding of what took place, but yet they'll be struggling to operate within it.

And you ask, why is it purposeful to have the separation? For it is this planet's goal, it is this planet's achievement. This is why this planet exists: to have separation, duality. This is the existence that this planet has. You must experience both. If you've chosen to come into existence as a human upon this planet for your duration of time, no matter how many times you are here, it is here to experience that type of separation... differences between two, differences in alignment, duality. It is purposeful. That will never leave this planet. For if another threshold is achieved and you all cross into the sixth, or the seventh, or the eighth, or the ninth...yes, you will ascend out of your physicality into a light structure, crystalline structure...but, still, here upon this planet, there will be separation. It is purposeful. There is learning and understanding and knowledge within that separation, and it will continue.

As you ascend into the fifth, what you will perceive, what you will understand about polarity is the fact that, yes, there are those that are awake and there are those that are not. But there will not be the chaos that once was. It will be as if you've got those that are understanding and those that are confused. This is purposeful. They will allow you to grow differently than you were to grow in the third and fourth dimension...meaning, because they are struggling, they are confused, they have no understanding, they will not disrupt the systems that are in place. But it is almost as if it is a new child wanting to learn. That is the separation. That is the polarity. They do not have an understanding of the construct that they exist in, so they are confused. They will not disrupt, but they will seek.

This is the polarity. Differences of understandings. That is why those that are awake, those that are aware, they will be the ones to be the teachers, the masters...to ascend those others up to their understanding, to bring them into their own understanding in that dimensional plane. This is purposeful. This is a purposeful cycle. It isn't until you achieve the highest dimensional plane that it all becomes unified...upwards into that eleventh, twelfth dimensional plane of your understanding does it [then] become one unified cluster of energy.

So you have to understand, all through that process, it is purposeful to have a bit of separation. It is purposeful for your growth. For if there is no separation, there is no growth. Yes, you can grow from your own understandings. You can grow from your own teachings. You can grow from the teachings that are around you. But those are similar teachings. But when you have separation, and you have this interaction between those that are questioning, those that are growing, those that are not aware, *that* is where the greatest growth and strength comes from. For just as much as you teach them, they teach you about your own growth. So this is why it is purposeful to have slight separation in each dimensional level.

Technical Aspects of Ascension

In the third and the fourth, those dimensions themselves are more of a gateway dimensional achievement...meaning, if you've so chosen to come into this existence with a certain level of awareness, a certain level of understanding, there have been points along your existence timeline that small, incremental steps leading to this threshold event have assisted you in moving into the fourth dimension. So, you have to understand, you come into the third, and achieving into the fourth is merely just a process of what you have elected to do during this particular period of life time cycle. It is not a threshold event like it will be for the fifth dimension, for when you get into the next dimension, the fifth dimension and beyond, it will take a specific *event*. Now, we have mentioned that it is predictable in a way. It is, for this next event. But the lower dimensional third to fourth is more of a self-achievement for what you have allowed yourself to be aware of during your life cycle.

Now, as you achieve these higher dimensional planes, it is not that the planet will be void of the physical human. For just as you ascend out of the physicality into the light Being, into the crystalline structure, there will be replacements of the physical human that will begin the process again. Third, fourth, fifth, sixth, seventh. It is an ongoing cycle, purposeful for this planet. Just as you are sustained by the planet, the planet is sustained by you and your physicality. It is a symbiotic relationship. One must have the other. So just as you begin your transition out of your physicality, other physical Beings will be brought to the planet. There will never be a void of time of humans. It is a continuum.

So now that you've moved into this fourth dimension, those that are coming in now are coming [into] a third dimension, filling in the voids of where the third dimensional individuals have crossed into the fourth dimension. As you cross into the fifth dimension, [new humans, from your perspective] will be coming in as the fourth dimension. It is a continuum. For this cycle now, you are in the fourth dimension. The majority are currently in the fourth dimension. That is why this new threshold will take you into the fifth dimension. But, yet, there [will still be] those that are coming into the third dimension. [New humans will] always [incarnate] one dimension below what the current status is. So no matter how high *you* are on the continuum of dimensional levels, third dimensional Beings will always be coming into the existence on this planet. But there is no awareness that this is taking place.

[Now, humans will only ever] interact with those [who are] one dimensional level below the actual existent level you are on. [Once you ascend into the fifth dimension], it will be as if you've stepped aside, out of that [third dimensional] reality stream. So that is why you have this perception of what is to come of a new Earth and [that] the New Earth will not coincide with the old Earth. This is the perspective of what you are understanding—that there will be two planets, or there will be two Earths. It is not that. It will be the same Earth, but you will not have awareness of those that are in that lower dimension. From an energetic standpoint, they are two separate locations upon one physical planet, operating simultaneously together. It would be as if you are operating multiple realities at the same time. Different outcomes—all on one planet, but not having an understanding of either reality.

This concept, you have to understand...you perceive your planet as being a structure in which billions of people exist. They do. But that is just one reality stream, the reality stream that you exist in. For those that are in the third dimension, there are billions of people that exist within this planet, within their dimension. So it is a continuum of realities that are overlaid upon one another. Just as you increase in your continuum of the dimensional levels, so do others, and so do others, all separately existing in their own reality stream upon this planet. That is the unique aspect of this planet.

It is difficult for the human to understand the basics of this reality that each exist in and how they overlay upon one another. And when it is time for a threshold event to take place, and a leveling to another dimension takes place, what takes place in the interim? What takes place to those that are unaware? What takes place to give the perception that those that were there are no longer there?

For you see, it is just merely a shift in time. It is not to say that it is a shift in reality or it is a shift in visualization or understanding, but it's just a shift in time. [This shift] takes place simultaneously across all dimensional planes. The third dimension will witness things upon the planet becoming more chaotic. It won't be necessarily a destructive event. But when that shift takes place, their reality changes. And what they perceive —a number of people being there and then not being there—will not have a construct of understanding. There will be some confusion, [and] that is why it is necessary for those that are in the next dimension up to be able to cross, still, into the third dimension. So fourth dimension individuals will be able to assist the third dimensional individuals.

That is why, as you are ascending, and you are in this fourth dimension, many of the individuals that come to you are confused. They have differences of understandings of their own reality. They have struggles of understanding of what has taken place in their existence here. Those are the individuals that are in the third dimension and are struggling with what they're perceiving. But you, in the fourth dimension, interacting in the third, you have an understanding and an awareness of what has just taken place for their reality.

So this is the difficulty. This is the struggle for the human mind to begin to conceive of what is taking place; for you believe there must be some catastrophic event that is witnessed by all to shield those that are moving into a dimensional level above them. Yes, in a way it is, but it does not have the same effect as if you were to have a catastrophic event here during your time in the fourth and third dimension—that does affect many individuals, but it is not a dimensional-level event.

Families and Ascension

You have to understand the family structures that you've entered into and the agreements that you've entered into for the family structures, for they will always be paired together until the point at which there is a transition point. So yes, you [might currently] perceive [your family members] as not being ascended into your dimensional plane, the fourth dimensional plane. And this is correct. Many of them [are] not. They remain in the third dimension, but this is why they are still part of your reality stream.

So now you move into the fifth dimension, and they will move into the fourth dimension. This is purposeful. Those that are within the family stream will move one level below [even] if they have not achieved the same level as you. Again, this is why it is said you are there to witness, always, one dimensional level below in order to assist those moving into the next dimensional level, preparing them, assisting them. As they increase into this dimensional level, they will have more questions. This is why, now, you are perceiving them to be in the third dimension. There are no questions because it is their pure reality, it is their start point reality. There are no questions to be had. There are no questions to be revealed. They've chosen [that] for this existence, the existence in which they do not wish to awaken, [do not] wish to ascend. But they *will* ascend, and they will have questions at that point because the reality will be perceived differently.

It is always appropriate [now] to allow your stream of energy to be present with them. It is always appropriate to share your information how you see it needing to be shared. For you call it planting seeds; it is more of a vibrational key of resonance to begin to unlock memories, to unlock understandings that have been suppressed. For you understand that when the human comes into form, it is animated by an energetic piece that contains all information. But it is the human shell that is the protector of that information. It protects the existence because that is what is chosen for that existence. If you've agreed during your assignment here to be aware of certain things, to be awakened during a certain point, then that will [take] place, but only to the point at which you have elected to be awakened or to have the knowledge.

But those that are awakened, as they speak to [those who] are unawakened, that choose not to awaken, it is lifting the keys, the little bits in the lock that keep it secure. It is lifting those, putting them into place. They may not have a full understanding of what has taken place or what is being said, but it is preparing them for that moment when the threshold is achieved and they are moved into the next dimension. And then it'll be as if it is a memory. They have a beginning point of understanding. That is when they start seeking because something is different.

Our Solar System

Your planetary system within your galaxy system was created specifically for the habitation of humans. It was all created, all at once, for greater humanity. Earth planet specifically. Your other planets, though...some of the Twelve have inhabited some of your planetary objects within your system [ie, Mars and Venus]; your other planets are habitable for other Beings. They are [inhabited] and have Beings on them, though they are not a hybridized Being [nor are] they one of the Source Twelve. But you have to understand that other Beings have come into your galaxy, into your planetary system, to take up residence upon your other planets, the moons around the planets. They do not interact with the humans. They do not interact with the other twelve. They are here for their own purposes, and they segregate themselves accordingly.

There is no need to have an understanding of *when* Earth became habitable because it was formed in a way in which it was going to be a sustainable planet. For you have to understand, and it has been mentioned, that Mars itself was the originating planet for the humans, and that is where they were supposed to be. Earth was to be somewhat of a laboratory of exploration. It was designed that way. But because of what took place, all operations were moved to the Earth planet. So there is no specific timeframe of when it all took place. But have an understanding that yes, this solar system, this planetary system was specifically designed, specifically created for the human project. Because in time, your humans will explore each one of the planets within your planetary system. Physically explore those. They will also understand how to explore outside of this planetary system. But that is well beyond your timeframe.

The Pleiadians' Perspective on the Galactic Wars

For the Pleiadians themselves, we were present during the formation period of the Earth planet and the humans upon it. We also were observant of what took place upon the Mars planet. We understand the factions that were in place from the Martians that...for you see, the warring factions and the events of the galactic wars that many here upon this planet speak of...they're perceived as being quite significant, quite catastrophic, quite disruptive. Just as you perceive wars upon your planet as being catastrophic and disruptive, detrimental to life upon your planet. And yes, in good nature you have to understand it that way.

As the factions begin to break away and as they begin to war, as it were, because of the nature of what they *wanted* to do with the human project versus what *needed* to be done with the human project; for the settlement upon Mars, and the colonization upon Mars, and the habitation for the humans upon Mars was structured in a way that it was supposed to [include] all factions. All galactic Beings were to take part in it. Not just the pure Beings, but the hybridized Beings. But the differences...this is where it becomes a bit shaded. The differences amongst many of the Beings were...they saw the outcomes of where the human project was going. They understood the purity that needed to be achieved, but they did not want the purity. They wanted it to be structured in a way that the hybridized Beings had more control than the purity Beings, purity Beings being one of the Twelve or all of the Twelve.

So it was this that began the disagreements, the warring factions. From there, you understand where many of the Beings stood during these galactic wars, but they weren't as catastrophic as you are led to believe. There was disruption, there was...yes, the Mars planet was diminished to a point at which it could not any longer sustain life. But you have to understand the Mars planet itself; even though it was in the proper zone for life, it was quite unstable. The Earth planet, though, was quite stable, and it needed to be populated. So it didn't take much for the Mars planet to be put to waste and all to be moved to the Earth planet.

But the loss of life, the disruptions and the chaos, the skirmishes between different factions were quite small, in fact. They took place, [but] they were relegated to certain locations throughout your galaxy. They were not allowed to take place upon the Earth planet, for there was an agreement, a galactic agreement amongst many of the Beings. Not all signed on, but the majority of the Beings agreed that the Earth planet would be left alone, would be left to its own. Not the same demise as the Martian planet. So many of the skirmishes and many of the warring actions took place beyond your galaxy.

But you as humans, you have a different perspective of life; you have a different perspective of what it is to lose life. For we—as energetic Beings and the hybridized Beings—the aspect of life is different. For that, too, is on a continuum. We understand that if we have to do our part, and it is one that we are eliminated from our existence, singularly or as a group, then we've done what we've needed to do, and we will energetically repopulate in another location. For when an energetic Being is transitioned, we have the capability of immediately coming right back into that existent dimensional plane. The energy is not being destroyed. You have to understand this. Just our presence. There is a difference between energy and presence.

So it is not the same as your human forms and the transition point from the human form into the energetic form and then back into a human form if you so choose, with all the emotionality that's involved. It is almost as if it is like your video games, where the player in the video game is eliminated but then immediately comes back to life at a particular location. That is quite similar to many of the dimensional Beings that are out there. If they are in a warring action and their life is taken from them, then they are brought back into existence in a different location. And if they so choose to enter back into the warring actions or go about and live a different existence, then they have that option.

Presence is what you would perceive when you connect to us. Yes, energetically you're connecting to the energy, but you are connecting to the presence. So when we are a warring faction of higher level Beings, when we are present in that action, we have...it is not to say we have physicality, but we have the perception of physicality. That is why we can be perceived as being present in a craft that is taking some action. And if that craft, then, is destroyed, our presence is destroyed, but our energy is not, and we can then enter back into presence at another location and decide at that point if we wish to choose to continue the warring action or do something else.

That is why in the human state, when you witness a Pleiadian or any other Being—a Mantis, a Grey, an Arcturian—when they are present with you, it is their presence, it is their vibrational state of energy that is formulating in a way in which it looks physical. It is not their physical presence because their physical presence is nothing but pure energy. You are witnessing the presence of the energy, the presence of the physical form of that energy.

Projection of Energy and Vibrational Resonance

When you are in the upper dimensional levels—this is specifically speaking of the upper dimensional level Beings, the tenth, eleventh, twelfth—we can remain in one specific location, but we can broadcast our presence, our physicality, to what you perceive it to be, in any dimension, at any point, at any time, in multiple dimensions if we wish. [Our] energy is in one central location. [We] can be in multiple dimensions if [we] wish. [We] are presenting [our] energy form, [our] presence in multiple locations at any one particular point. You have to understand, it is all a matter of projection of energy. This is the confusing point for the human essence. For you understand energy, and you understand what energy is, and how it is affected, and how you affect energy, and how it affects you...but it is difficult for you to project your energy as a human into another location for others to view you as a human, but in energetic form.

Now, lower dimensional Beings—those in the ninth, eighth, seventh dimension, whether it's a hybridized Being [or not]—they, too, can project their presence (what that presence is to you) at any particular point, while remaining in one specific location in a physical form. So it would be as if you, when you achieve the seventh, eighth, ninth dimension...you will still have some physicality about you. You are not fully into that light-bodied state, you have some physicality about you, but you can project your physical presence into another dimensional plane, into the third dimension, fourth dimension, fifth dimension. You will not interact in a physical way, but it will be as if it is an apparition or it is a presence of a Being to guide you. That is the difference.

[If you were to interact with a higher dimensional Being—projecting their presence to you—there would be no difference in the way they *appear* to you.] The difference is the vibrational state in which you are connecting. That is where the humans themselves begin to understand the differences in vibrational planes. They begin to understand the vibrational connections. So if an eleventh dimensional Being is projecting their presence in front of you, and you see that presence in front of you, *your* physical essence is vibrating at a particular eleventh dimensional state. You sense it in you. There is a physical vibrational state that takes place [such] that you understand that you're connecting to an eleventh dimensional Being. If a lower dimensional Being, say an eighth dimensional Being, is projecting their presence in front of you, you see them in their physical form [because] *your* physical essence is vibrating at an eighth dimensional level. That is the difference. [That being said, you will only be able to connect with those Beings whose vibration is a match with your own.]

[It is to] understand your own subsets of frequencies that you transmit. For you have your own base frequency. Each individual has their own base frequency, but in that, you have sublayers of frequencies. These are your calling cards for each of those Beings that you wish to connect to. Right now, many of them are not associated with any particular Being. You do not have the awareness of what frequency connects to what Being. It is to begin to take time to write down your frequencies. Not physically, but in your mind, as a memory...understanding the frequency that connects to the Pleiadians, the Arcturians, the Orions, or whatever Being you wish to connect to. Each one of them is just going to be slightly different than the other, yet you will feel that vibration in you. That way, next time you wish to connect to the Orions, you can pull that vibration forward and begin to transmit from that vibration to the Orions, and they will immediately answer you. Or if it were to the Pleiadians, or the Arcturians, the Draconians, the Mantis...no matter the

Being, we each have our own frequency that we will respond to you with.

Hybridization

[The Pleiadians have hybridized with] the Orions and the Andromedans. What you [would] understand is two hybridized Beings, one with the Orions and one with the Andromedans, each having a humanoid form, but they have not made their full presence known to this point. They've been in a dormant status. You have to understand, there are many hybridized Beings that you are unaware of. Many of them have taken [a] shape that would not be presentable to the human form because they would be too disruptive to the thought process.

But in this case, these humanoid forms...between the Andromedans and the Pleiadians, these would take a shape very similar to the fairies upon your planet. Very small in stature but winged. They are not fairies, but they are very similar to them. That is how they would be presented. Do not be concerned; there is not a specific name assigned to them as of yet because they have not made their full awareness upon your planet. They have been presenting themselves very slowly to certain individuals.

Their purpose, though...their purpose is this aspect of flight beyond your capability, meaning they're there to assist those [who become aware of them]. This is why they have not been presented fully to all individuals. It is to begin the process of movement about your planet from the state in which you are in your physicality but can separate yourself and move about your planet through this process of flight. This is in preparation for the placement into the fifth dimension. So as you move on your process upwards, this dislocation from the human physicality into the projection or the movement about, outside of your physicality, will grow. And they are there to begin this process of aligning that.

The Orions and the Pleiadians...these hybridized Beings...this process began on your Mars planet. They were first brought to the Mars planet to assist the growth points of the humans. You can think of them as being a bit of a doctor, medical personnel to assist the growth of the humans in their physicality. You can represent them as being medical staff. They will be presenting themselves once you are in the fifth dimension. This is part of the...again, much is going to take place once you are in the fifth dimension that is going to help you disassociate from the human physical form and enter into more of a place in which you can project your essence, your physicality, other places. They will be assigned to you to begin this process of the physical dislocation of your energy so that it can be presented elsewhere.

[The Pleiadians also hybridized with the Draconians] but it was very... it was short-lived. We understood that this process of connecting with the Draconians was going to be a bit disruptive for our own processes. They were wishing to take more from us than we were willing to provide to them. The pairing of the two is, yes, the Reptilians. Now, the Reptilians, once they were brought into existence, they were then handed over to the Draconians, and they, then, took the process. You have to understand, once a hybridization takes place between two energetic Beings, there isn't anything else that needs to take place to replicate [more Beings]. You would understand it as cloning. It is quite different than that, but it is very similar in your [human] construct. So it isn't that you continually need Draconians and Pleiadians to continue to make Reptilians. Once they are in presence energetically, physically, then it is just a process of replicating.

You understand the Reptilians as being something that is a bit disruptive, nefarious in your language, to the human forms. And yes, many of them are. But we've moved away from that alignment. We no longer associate with the Draconians and the Reptilians. It is something that we realized is not necessary. That hybridization was not purposeful. There was a misalignment that took place. So that is why we do not acknowledge that hybridization process, that program.

The Pleiadians' Existence

From the very beginning, it was one celestial object. You would understand it as a planet. That is what we chose as our place to inhabit, our home, as it were. All Pleiadians were assigned there. As they came into form, that is where their existence was. Now, what you must understand —and this is across most of the other twelve—you understand us as being a higher dimensional Being, and we are. From a higher dimensional vibrational point, we are in the tenth, eleventh, twelfth dimension. We have no form, no physicality. So your construct of existence is not anything like our construct of existence.

For if you were to see it as a whole, while that object was still in its original form, it would be almost as if it were a galaxy within a galaxy, stars upon stars, just energy points that have taken up space upon that existent planet. So there is no aspect of what we do on a daily basis. There is no existent understanding of what we eat or what we do, just as the humans do. But this is also for many of the other of the Twelve. We are vibrational points, all of us. There are names assigned to all twelve, yes, but we're all vibrational points.

This is why, when you align with a particular cluster or a particular alignment of a particular Being, you are aligning yourself with a vibrational point of existence. Now, when you align with that vibrational point of existence, you are vibrating and connecting with all of us, all at once. So there is no differentiation between one vibrational point or another vibrational point, one Pleiadian or another Pleiadian.

But in that construct of all being together, there are sub-frequencies, subsects of frequencies that we adhere to. And when you begin your connection point with the Pleiadians, we then align to your subsect of vibrational frequency. You hold one master frequency, but it is that subsect, that additional frequency that you transmit from. Just as if you were to transmit from your existence to the Orion cluster, that is its own frequency. When you wish to call upon the Pleiadians, that is one frequency. It holds its own frequency signature for your vibration. You, yourself, would have [your] own frequency, and you would connect to one specific frequency point. That would be your representative to the Pleiadians. That is how your connections are made.

To have an understanding of what took place for the division of the planet...now, you have to understand, you vision your planet as being [a] solid object, and yes, in a particular way it is. But it was very loosely, vibrationally held together. During one of these threshold events, it affected our frequency binding, what held it all together, and allowed us to separate out into seven separate locations...all remaining in the same area, the same physical area of where that planet existed, but that is now what you perceive in your night sky as Pleiades [The Seven Sisters].

Each one of those, too, contain a number of frequency points. So it does not matter which one you point yourself to or which one you wish to align to; it is based upon your sub-frequency when you wish to connect to the Pleiadians—you will connect to a specific frequency point.

[What you understand to be your night sky] has existed for millions of years. This [separation was] well beyond that. Think of it as being an energetic sphere of dust, all held together by vibration. Looks solid, but in reality, it is quite fluid. And as the wave, this event wave, moved through, it began to fracture those binding frequencies that held all of the particles together and allowed them to split into clusters. So it would have just been a slow event, over time, of separation and forming other small planetary objects, stars if you were, of these energetic dust particles being held together by binding frequencies. Then through time, through the millions of years, they have all clustered together tight enough and now are permanently held together as either a planet or a star within the Pleiades system.

The Pleiadians' Appearance

There are a number of different appearances that we can come to you. One is a crystalline humanoid appearance. No appearance of male or female, but just an appearance of a crystalline humanoid structure in front of you. Translucent, white in appearance. Nondescript. Some of the others...those may take the form of male or female, dependent upon your own vibrational connection. Again, a bit translucent. A bit of a...you would understand it as a halo of glow around them, from behind them, but emanating in front of them. And a bit blueish to white in appearance.

Some with...again, these are all...this, too, you have to understand. As the projections are presented before you, they will take somewhat of a form of your own construct. So if you have in your awareness field an understanding that they must be wearing a cloak, they will take on that form in front of you. You have to understand, they're going to represent much of what you have as a belief in you of what they should look like because it is this purposeful aspect of appearance, as not to disrupt or frighten upon our arrival. We wish to blend with you accordingly, very quickly, so that we can bring forth what you seek. [Regarding hair], again, this is a projection of what you wish us to have. In most cases, it would be presented as a bit of a long set of hair that is golden in color, past the shoulders. But in some cases, it is pulled back, it is tied neatly behind, purposeful for that individual's appearance.

The Tachyon Healing Chamber

The Tachyon chamber and the Tachyon particle facilitates a rejuvenation and a realignment of your DNA, your physicality, your physical state. But it is also to understand this Tachyon particle, for it is all around you. It is always being emanated. It is always being received. How you align to it [is], you can create your own chamber within your own presence, in your own physical essence. It is restructuring a bit of your physical presence in a way that it is a receiving point for all of the particles, a collector, as it were. And in doing so, it will align a healing point within your physical state. So it is to allow the Tachyon particles to be collected within you to create your own chamber, as it were, to provide healing at any point within the physical state at any particular time.

It will take some time for this alignment to take place to begin the collection of the particles, but it is also purposeful to align yourself with those that have created the physical chambers here upon your planet, for those are a greater source of collection and alignment. And they are always available. So if you are not able to achieve your own collection point, align yourself with an individual or a group that has been instructed [on] how this alignment and this collection process is to take place, and allow yourself to be placed within the chamber.

Connecting with the Pleiadians

This alignment and this connection that you wish to have with the Pleiadians—just with all other connection points, all other Beings—when you begin your process of becoming aware, [your] process of alignment, one must understand the guidance that they are receiving. No matter which point at which you are connecting, no matter which Being you are connecting to, allow yourself the clarity of alignment with that Being, with that essence.

For us, the Pleiadians, [our role] is the technical aspect of your mission, *your purpose*, as it were, of your existence, to guide you and assist you on that. But with all, we provide a layer of healing, a layer of teaching. There's also...there's a point at which, if you wish to connect to the source Pleiadian cluster, you can utilize the pathway of that connection point to align yourself with any other galactic point. Meaning, allow our connection as the source cluster to be the portal to any other origin point cluster. So if it were that you wish to connect to the Pleiades source cluster to achieve information from the Orion source cluster, you can do so. It is not the same level of information that you will achieve for this purpose that you are requesting, but it is for short burst transmissions of those source clusters and reaching out to their counterparts that are in your galactic system.

8

ARCTURIANS

Greetings from the Arcturian Primary Source Cluster of the galactic alignments. It is this to understand [about] our presence with you: We have the vast understanding of purpose. We have the vast understanding of change. We have the vast understanding from the beginning.

For we, as the...you could say, guardians of this timeline...we understand the changes that have taken place. It is this that we want you to understand. Be reassured that you have an existence of purpose. Each one of the cycles that [humanity has] lived through had purpose. It may be that you do not travel back in time to see the origin point of your existence, but understand this existence of purpose. It is not to understand what the purpose is, but it is to understand that you have purpose...purpose as a Being, just as *all* Beings, whether they are of human form, or whether they are of extraterrestrial form, or any other form that you wish to be— each one of those forms has purpose, a purposeful piece amongst all others, a purposeful piece in a greater whole of existence. Each one of those pieces serves a specific connection. You as a human, a greater whole of all humanity, serve but one piece in the greater expanse of all existence.

For it is the humanity upon this planet that is observed by many. It is held in high regard. You understand this. This has been brought through in previous transmissions, that the humans here are purposeful. Your existence is purposeful. It is why this universe has been created. This is *your* place. This is *your* existence. But it is greater than that; for this is the only universe that contains a human form that you understand. There are others that you would presume to be human, but they are not. In many other universes, there are other forms that look similar to you, but they do not contain the DNA structure that you contain. You are purposeful. Your existence is purposeful. You are but one piece in a greater existence.

So this is why this universe is held in high regard amongst all other existences, all other universes. You are the example for what it is to have an experience in this dimensional level. It was quite difficult bringing this into existence; for you see, it is to bring down vibration to a point at which it can coalesce into a human form, into a lower dimensional realm. In order to exist in the form that you exist, in the life that you exist here upon this planet, all of it needs to be specifically aligned. Everything must be correlated appropriately in order for the existence to take place.

For you understand from your teachings here upon this planet that the third dimension, the lower dimensions, the fourth dimension has its place, has its understanding. Duality, struggle, good/bad, dark/light...all of it is here purposefully, all constructed appropriately, so that it can be experienced by many. This does not exist anywhere else. This also [leads] into an understanding of this aspect of the departure, departure from what was to be. This is where this understanding of the different factions grew.

So, you must understand, as all of it is being put into place, all of the agreements have been put into place, all of the understandings, all of the teachings...all of it is brought together. It is not as if it just magically appears as a planet for the humans to inhabit and then you appear upon a planet. All of those pieces are teachings from other experiences beyond your universe.

The twelve source clusters...this is the first alignment for these source clusters to be placed here into this universe [together]. Each of them has had their own separate existence in other universes, multiple universes. And each one of them has brought that knowledge into this universe, and brought that into existence, and brought those pieces of understanding to create this existence, this realm, this alignment for the human Being. But the greater understanding [is] that it is not just by chance that the Twelve have been put together to create this universe and the humans.

For yes, it has been explained...the difficulties of understanding Source, and what brought the Twelve here, and where does Source exist, the *originating* Source. But if you can understand it from a greater depth, outside of this sphere of the universe...each of the source clusters themselves is a vibrational point—a vibrational spectrum in upon itself, existent in other universes. They are not known by the same terminology that you understand them here in your universe, but they are in existence. Same vibration, same source cluster, just different understandings.

But when it was known that this project, if you wish to call it that, for the human Being was to be brought online, this is where the original alignments take place. A vibrational process begins. You could, for your understanding, understand it as, Source requests an alignment of twelve. Just an alignment of twelve. But what twelve should align? It is all based upon the resonant frequency between each and the coalesced frequency that is then brought together.

So it is to understand that a request had been sent out across all the different universes, all the different locations, all the different spaces between spaces. And it was these twelve that were brought together, brought here into this space. And from that, the beginning started...the beginning of the coalescing of different frequencies, bringing together matter out of nowhere. For it all exists, but it isn't until the frequencies resonate that it [comes] into existence.

That, then, progresses forward to the point now, [where] you understand yourself as a human. You understand yourself as a human Being with twelve strands of DNA; each one of the strands aligning with each one of the twelve source clusters. So this is why it is [said] to understand this universe...[that] the humans within it are purposeful. It is not to understand what the purpose is, other than to understand *you are purposeful.* Your existence is purposeful for all other existences to reflect upon. *You,* as the humans, are held in high regard.

This is why it is that your planet is continually observed. This is why it is that there is a continual presence of our essence around you. This is why it is that those that you perceive as unawakened still have questions. There is a presence around them. They question all things. Even those that say, "I do not question what is in front of me." In quiet, they contemplate to themselves. Every human upon this planet, in quiet, questions their existence, questions their alignment, questions their connection. Whether it is to a higher god, whether it is to a higher presence, whether it is to a vibration...in quiet, they question and contemplate.

And this is why the human race, the human Beings, the human presence is critical. For you see, this is the only existence that allows that to take place. Yes, through an evolutionary process, you will ascend into a higher dimensional realm, but it does not leave a void once you ascend. There are always those Beings, those humans that will be brought into the lower dimensional realms to fill those spots, those vacancies, those holes. This is the perpetual cycle.

Throughout [the] time of your existence here, your planet has been through many cycles of ascension...not in mass, but small alignments of individuals have ascended—ascended out of their physical body, ascended into their light body, exiting from this physical form. But what you are beginning to witness is a greater expansion of ascension. This is going to be the perpetual cycle: great amounts of individuals ascending higher and higher upon the dimensional plane but, yet, more and more filling in the lower dimensional realms. This is the natural cycle that is meant to be in place.

It has been said in the past that this planet itself is a teaching ground, a teaching space; it is here where those that wish to come upon this planet as a human, learn. And that is true. The learning process is quickening. This is why you are sensing this process of ascension upon you. What you are sensing is true. Those that are still at a much lower dimensional framework do not have that perception. That will come in time. They are still learning. They are still processing.

So it is to understand this overall understanding of your existence. Yes, to say that you have purpose but not to worry about what that purpose is, can be a bit unsettling. But it also can be a bit freeing for your thought process. For if you allow yourself to continue to question, "What is my overall purpose? What is my purpose upon this planet? How am I to affect others through my purpose?", that begins to build a framework around you. That begins to build restrictions upon what you should be doing.

Free yourself from that understanding, that awareness that "there must be a singular purpose for my existence," [and] begin to look at yourself as fulfilling your purpose as a human—the collective purpose of humanity is to witness to all other existences beyond yours, all other realms, all other universes. You are doing exactly what you've come here to do. You are fulfilling your purpose.

That, then, releases you. That, then, frees you from any restriction. That allows you, then, to experience all things around you. It opens the pathway of understanding. It opens the pathway of reception. For there is a great deal of detail that is still just beyond your reach. Many will achieve it, and many will not. But that, again, is the teaching that you've come here to learn. But once you can free yourself from the construct of the human's understanding and understand there is a greater purpose—though you may not know it, you exist within it, you are fulfilling it, you are but one piece in a greater existence—that frees you to receive a greater level of detail.

So have this as your awareness: The purpose of humanity upon this planet has multi facets, multiple facets of understanding. Yes, to the singular human Being, they have an existence. They have experiences. They have their own understanding of what they are here to do. But when you look just a bit further out, it is the collective of humanity that serves a greater purpose for all other Beings. You are fulfilling that purpose. And in doing so, this universe is fulfilling its purpose, and all other Beings outside of this universe are looking upon this place, this existence, as a place in which they wish to come.

And in time, they will. They will either take human form, or they will arrive in their own existent form. If they so choose to lower themselves into a dimensional framework, [an] understanding of the third dimension, to experience the human form, they can. Or they will arrive in their higher dimensional form to provide assistance to humanity. But that point is still a bit into the future. So allow yourself to settle, to breathe a bit more relaxed, for your existence is being purposefully fulfilled without having to "do" a specific purpose.

The Purpose of Humanity

Throughout time, before this human project...one must understand the existence that exists beyond your universe, your galaxy, your planet. It is easy for your human construct to understand existence that exists in another physical location. That is how you perceive life. That is how you perceive existence. But it is not quite as simple. For if you were to look at the twelve source clusters, their existence before being coalesced here, they exist in a framework. They exist in a framework of nodes, vibrational points. There is not a galaxy. There is not a planet. There is not a physical location.

Most of what is brought to you is to help your physical mind present a picture for you to understand. That is how the human thought process functions. It must be presented with an image for you, then, to comprehend what exists. But outside of this universe, outside of this existence, there is no physical form. So even those at the—in your understanding, your construct of understanding—at a vibrational point of the sixth, seventh, eighth dimensional framework...there is no existent form. It is pure vibration. You could even venture to say there are those vibrational forms or vibrational aspects that are in the lower dimensional frames... the third dimension, fourth dimension.

But you see, beyond your construct, beyond this universe, there is no vibrational dimensionality. There is not a construct of dimensional levels. That is purely existent here in *this* universe. All of what you understand has been purposefully constructed for this universe. It is a training ground. All of it. Even for those vibrational aspects that wish to come into this universe as a Being, they must then reconstruct themselves according to the construct of this universe. So what lies beyond [this universe] is a vibrational aspect, vibrational points, vibrational nodes. This is difficult for the human understanding. It is a place in which there is no physicality. It is a place in which it is pure vibration, a pure understanding of *all*.

Now, what is the greater purpose, then, for this existence? For you see, there are other universes that have been created, but they've been solely created for...there isn't a purpose. There isn't a *purpose*. Purpose means there is an outcome. You do a certain thing and you achieve a certain outcome. You provide a certain input and you are given a certain output. There are other universes that have been created by other node points, but it is just to have a place at which...to play, to exist, temporarily. Most universes beyond what you understand are there just to experiment, to play, to have an existent form. They do not have purpose. They do not have an understanding of what purpose is.

But once this location, this universe, this galaxy, this planetary system is requested, that is the understanding you must have. For you see, from the point of origin *beyond* the Twelve (if you must say, Source...do not get overcomplicated by *what* Source and how far back, but bring your understanding just a bit closer to the alignment of the Twelve) the vibrational coalescing of the Twelve was requested to put in place a location in which a greater teaching can take place...a place in which all of the vibrational aspects that are in existence can take a physical form in experiencing something greater than they've ever experienced before...that being a dense physical form of existence.

Now, why would one that is in vibrational aspect, a vibrational node, wish to descend into a physical form and live as a physical Being, unlike they have before? There is a thought that if you are a vibrational form, then you have the awareness of *all*. You have all knowledge, all understanding. That is correct. But they don't have the understanding of *physicality*. Physicality gives a level of perception and prospect of existence that you cannot achieve by knowing all things.

This is a difficult concept to understand. "If you know all things, then you would understand what physicality is." That is incorrect. Physicality was achieved. Physicality was something that was purposefully achieved for a greater outcome. That greater outcome is the progression of understanding. Physicality was achieved for the greater knowledge that is, then, carried on to each node, each vibrational aspect.

So what is the purpose, then, the greater purpose of this existence, this overall existence, this universe, this galaxy? It is one to be set aside. It is one to be looked upon as a point at which one wishes to go...meaning, a vibrational node, a vibrational aspect has spent its existence having an understanding greater than all. But, yet, just as you believe there is more —just as many quietly question to themselves—the vibrational nodes, the vibrational aspects, they, too, understand there is more. You look to a higher dimension. They look to a lower dimension because there is much more to achieve. There is always more to achieve. This is why this [experience] has been put in place.

For you see, the twelve that have been put in place to bring this forward, to bring this into existence...it is not just by chance that they have been brought together. It is not just by chance that the Twelve have been brought together for this existence; for when they were all just their own individual vibrational aspect, their vibrational node, they each bring their own teachings of time in existence...existence not in physical form.

This is where your construct of understanding must change. When it is said "existence," existence doesn't correlate with physicality. Existence correlates with a point...a point of understanding, a point of connection, a node. *That* is existence. You, as a physical form, are in existence, yes, and you believe it to be physical. But you, too, are a node of existence. You are a vibrational node amongst many. But yet everything has been put in place to have physicality.

So it is to begin to understand the construct around you a bit differently, the vibrational construct that is your existence. For this existence, this physicality, this physical existence that you have...you understand that you can hold something. You understand that there is a physical object in front of you. You understand that everything has consciousness. But if everything has consciousness, then how can it have physicality? This is the difficulty. For consciousness exists without physicality, but yet *you* have physicality. But if you can break away the boundaries, all you are left with are physical nodes of energy, and each one of the physical nodes has consciousness. And in that, all things then become consciousness. All aspects are a collective of consciousness.

So it is beyond your physicality that you exist. The physicality is a temporary house, a temporary location, a temporary node. For what binds you together is all twelve, bringing together the pieces of vibrational matter to form a physical Being...but yet you are still a vibrational node amongst many. So it is very similar to what exists beyond your universe; it is the denseness of all of the energetic nodes that are placed all around. They, too, want to experience physicality. So you as humans, you as the physical Beings, represent what they wish to be.

This is why, throughout time, the awareness has grown stronger and stronger because the alignment between your physical state and the vibrational state is growing closer and closer. This is why those that are coming in as a physical form now (as a human Being, they are incarnating into the human form) remember, closer and closer to their existent form, their existent node. Throughout time, this is the purpose—to narrow the distance between the existent vibrational node and the existent physical form. But this is your ascension, as well. This [ascension] is narrowing that space. But even those, in time, as that cycle [of ascension] grows faster and faster, those that come into the third dimensional level, they will know, they will have a greater *awareness*, but yet they will not know how to function in the human form with what they understand. [The human form] is there to understand and learn and teach others. It is a process.

This space in which you exist is purposeful in that way. It is where all other Beings, all other existences, all other vibrational nodes wish to come. And by you doing what you do, you are showing purpose. You are showing that to all Beings, all existence, all nodes. You are not an experiment per se, but you are being observed. Understand it this way: Take your existence as a human throughout time, no matter how many lives or how many representations you've had. Yes, you've been observed this entire time. You've been observed by many other vibrational points, nodes, existences, whatever you wish to label it as. And in that observation, there is learning. They retain all of what you have experienced. All pieces, good, bad, all throughout time.

Then, when they make the choice that they wish to experience [life] as a human, this existence as a human...when they are, then, placed into the human form, to animate the human form, they have that awareness that they have learned, that you have taught them. Unknowingly, you have taught them so that they, then, can live an experience that is different, that is a bit more aligned vibrationally, that is set aside. And in doing so *they*, then, are observed. So it is a continual cycle of observation.

So yes, to your thought process, it is a bit difficult to have the concept that: "What is existence, then? What is the human form's purpose? Why is it, then, if we are just to be observed as an experiment, what is a human purpose for?" You see, when you come into this existence, you have no recall, no memory, no understanding that you were once the observer; now you are being observed.

So for many that will now have this understanding from this teaching, do not be swayed by the fact that you are now being observed. You have this greater purpose of experience for others, to be the witness for others. This is why it is always an understanding that you are being observed...not by some greater Being somewhere else, some other existence somewhere else, but you are being observed by all other humans. Your existence here is to be observed by all other humans. Your purpose here is to be observed by all other humans, for you see, you each are an existence beyond your existence.

And when you live a life, live an existence knowing that you're being observed by another human, another Being, another existence here on this planet, then your purpose becomes greater, for you begin to live a life of understanding that you wish to be at peace, the best that you can be, the light, the vibration, the construct for others to exist by.

Many, many Beings believe they must fulfill this immense purpose of existence, that "I must effect change in everything that I do," or "I must achieve this certain level of understanding or status or acquire certain things." That is the human Being. That is the human thought process. That is self-imposed. The true purpose is to be the observer and to be observed, and when you have this understanding that you are to be observed and observe others, you begin to live a life, *an existence that is purposeful for others to see.*

So the statement that has been said over and over, through all of your transmissions, in and outside of these transmissions, that you are a light, you are a beacon, you are a vibration...do not take that lightly, for that is your purpose! That is your true and one purpose: to be observed as that light, that vibration, for all others to see. And when you understand this, *when you fully embrace this,* then in all actions you impart that vibration, and that light, and that understanding for all others to witness. Then they, the observers, begin to take that in. They learn from it. They absorb it. They, then, begin to emit the light, their vibration, and the cycle continues.

But much of this has been taken lightly by many humans. "Yes, I know that I'm supposed to be a light. Yes, I know I'm supposed to vibrate at the highest, I'm supposed to do all of these things as a human, but yet there's a greater purpose in my life. I must achieve these things. I must do these things." It is not to put it aside lightly. For you see, the true understanding of purpose has been manipulated through time. That is just a remnant from the beginning stages.

For you see, from the beginning, from the origin point of the humans, yes, purpose was implanted, purpose was instilled, purpose was put into place as a thought construct to perpetuate, to give momentum to the humans, to give them energetic process. But in time, it was understood that once it settled in, this is where awareness comes about. For that purpose leads to seeking. As you have a purpose, you must grow within that purpose. Think of it as a seed. The seed of purpose was planted initially, from the very beginning. As it sprouts and it grows, it grows into seeking, and that seeking is where it leads to this understanding there is a greater aspect, a greater knowing beyond yours, a greater awareness beyond yours, your human form.

But now you're in this stage, this stage now, and this is where it will remain for some time. You are in this stage of blooming and producing. In that, you are here to shine. You are here to blossom. You are here to express yourself energetically, as strong as you can. That is the only purpose you are here for. All the other things...the things you must achieve, the things you must acquire, the number of people you must have around you, and all the things you must do...that is purely human. And that is okay, for you still must live as a human. You must do the human things. But do not put an overemphasis on a purpose.

Your purpose is very simple and very to the point: *to be a vibrational point for others to observe, the highest vibrational point that you are to achieve for others to observe.* Just as you are observing others, they are observing you. It is a continual process of observation.

Contractual Alignments and Purpose

You must understand [the] agreement process. You understand that there is a Source that you transition to. Yes, this is true. You are transitioning into a source node. You are transitioning into a node in which all vibrational aspects that have been in physical form as a human transition to. This would be considered a source node. You retain yourself there until you choose to come back into another human form or you wish to transition back into another vibrational node outside of the source node.

But within that source node, there are the contractual aspects. You would understand this as your Akashic and all the other agreement points. They're all held there within that source node. That source node then envelops this existence. This source node is your point of reference for this physical reference point, this galaxy that you exist in. As the contractual understandings begin to take place, these are vibrational contractual agreements.

This aspect of purpose, this is not built into the contract. So it is to have an understanding there is separation between contract and purpose. Your purpose is as it has been previously stated. The contractual alignments that you agree to once you enter into the human form...those, then, are set aside for the things that you must accomplish while you are here. Your contract [contains] those things that you have set out to accomplish, just as any contract in physical form is. They are the alignments.

So in this aspect of purpose...as you navigate through your contract, yes, you are fulfilling, you could say, a purpose. But this is not the overall purpose. This is where confusion sets in. If your overall purpose is to be observed at your highest vibrational point of existence, well then, in your contract, as you begin to maneuver through your contract, you are being observed. Your vibrational aspect is to be at its highest, and that, then, begins to align with your contractual agreements. And this is going to align others to your contract that you've made certain intersections with. So it is all wrapped together, but it is this understanding that we bring to you to have a greater depth of alignment throughout the contractual agreements, as well as your purpose.

For the humans, the human planet, the human existence, this galaxy, being held in high regard by all energetic Beings (essence, existence, whatever you wish to call it) is being observed, and all are wishing to be here. And in time, they will. But now is *your* time. It is your time to live within your purpose. And it is your time to execute upon your contract. When you understand the difference, it becomes clear and easy to achieve your contract and not confuse the two.

Nodes, Source, and the Quantum Web

One must understand the construct in which you exist—*construct,* meaning your existence here, your planet, all the other planets, the stars, galaxies...whatever it might be. *That* you understand as being your universe, this bubble. That is your construct. That bubble itself is a node. That, you have to understand, is one node in amongst many other nodes. Nodes, or source points, however you wish to look upon them, are the repositories for *like* frequencies. They are the storage points.

A node is nothing more than a consciousness connection point. Not consciousness as we have discussed before, as you understand it in your human form, but consciousness meaning a connected point in space and time, a connected point that something exists. What holds it together is consciousness. And that thread...that's the consciousness. To another node, that's consciousness. So this understanding of the difference between Source, source points, source nodes, nodes...they are all basically the same. They are all a node connected to another node. They all have consciousness that is connecting them, a greater consciousness.

A cluster is nothing more than the beginning point, the beginning point for this experiment of these twelve. The cluster...think of the cluster as the birthing point for a node. The cluster births a node, imparts knowledge, information, the constructs by which existence begins. That point, that's where the existent form takes place, at the node. The node is the repository of all that knowledge for that cluster point. It is the repository to have existence.

So let's discuss your Source, your All. One must look at your existence, starting with the human. We'll try to have you understand it this way, as if you were to visualize yourself at the bottom rung of a ladder. That is your existence. That is the human existence now that you exist in. The ladder is the construct that you exist in. The next rung on that ladder would be your Source. That Source, the All, whatever you wish to call it, *that* is your immediate connection point. So yes, it is a node, it is a source point, it is a source node. All virtually the same.

Why is it called Source? All energy that began from the beginning of this experiment for humanity exists within that node, that Source. That is why you perceive it as being the All because all existence for humanity, all existence for all energetic things that are pertaining to the human existence, is contained there. Each time you incarnate, each time you transition, each time an animal incarnates, transitions, each time something transitions from this planet, it all is contained there. The energetic pieces, particles, all existence exists there. So that is your immediate connection point, your immediate node. Earth itself is a node. Source is a node.

From that point, the next several rungs are for different connection points. For you see, each one of the twelve has created what you would equate as being a source node. Why would that be? That is for their own existence. In the beginning, each one of the twelve was brought in by a source, just as you are brought in by a source. Now this is where it will become a bit difficult to follow but understand it this way—your very top rung of your ladder is the overall beginning infinite point of Source, infinity...there is no beginning, there is no end, but that is where it begins for your journey...that point sets out to achieve this human experience, this human experiment. It sets out to the next rung and says, "Okay, this is going to be the source point for this experiment."

That source point then begins to call out beyond your framework to other energetic points. This is where your twelve source clusters come from. They integrate into the next rung. That is now your construct. From there, they then institute their own source points. They cannot do their understanding of work, their existence, without having a place to deposit, have a receptor point for their existence. So they create their own individual source point [node]. Each [of the] twelve have their own source point. As we are speaking to you now, yes, we are a source cluster. But we are not a source point. A source cluster is the beginning stage of all existence. We are separated from a source point, a node. So each [of the] twelve has given themselves an individual node, source point, whatever you wish to call it, but it is a node.

And now, what lies in between your source point, your source node, and each one of the twelve source nodes is all of what has taken place to lead up to your existence. For instance, a number of the twelve began to hybridize and produce a hybridized Being. They require a source node. Then, in time, those hybridized Beings coalesce with another hybridized Being, create another hybridized Being. They need a source node, as well. So understand the source node as being a repository of all existence for that combining of energies. It is where their energies are stored for that existence. That way, at the termination of one existence, they can then rejuvenate and come back into existence [from] that source node. They do not have to restart the process over again from the origin point.

Your universe is nothing more than a construct of nodes, just as your quantum field. You have an understanding of a quantum web, and this quantum web connects everything together. It connects everything together which is within your consciousness, within your consciousness of humans and within the consciousness of existence within your universe, within this experiment. So this is the understanding to have. It is just connection points. Those connection points are repositories for all understandings for that existence of what has been created.

When you transition, your consciousness, your energy, your frequency is absorbed back into that one source node. [You] are going into what [you] perceive as a locale, a location, the overall consciousness of all things. That itself is just that source node, the All...that one point just above your humanity. But it is not quite just above your humanity. You must understand, you have your humanness, you have your soul, your higher self, your oversouls...however many points you want to overlay upon yourself. But ultimately, when you transition, your consciousness, your energy, your frequency is absorbed back into that one source node, and it contains all of [the] understanding for what you perceive in your existence.

[This source node, however] is a level that only allows you to see what you are allowed to see, even in the transition state. You have to understand this activity...once you transition, [it] does not lift the entirety of the veil that exists for you. For when you do transition, if none of these teachings were brought to you, and you had no other awareness, and you were to transition, upon that point which the transition is starting to set on, you would have an understanding that you would be transitioning into Source, the All.

Well, what does that mean? "Yes, I'm going back to Source, but I will be in the All." Well, they are the same. There is no difference between the All and Source. But you perceive it to be. You say, "The All. The All must be everything. Everything from time's beginning to time's end. I will see it all." [No], you will only see what you are allowing yourself to see based upon the awareness that you had upon your transition. This is purposeful. This is the purposefulness of not remembering.

You have to understand, each individual upon this planet, if they were to transition and see the entirety of all the experience that is around them, from the beginning of time to the end of time, and then that is imparted upon them vibrationally, that is in their vibrational field, and they, then, incarnate [back] into this human form...you [must] understand the complexities, then, of the weightiness of the veil that needs to be in place in order to shield them from that entirety of existence. This is why it is purposeful to have just enough information for the human to consume in order to have them have an existence where they have just enough awareness to keep the balance appropriately set.

And when there is this balance that is struck, this balance between Source and balance between the human existence, that is when the cycle begins to slow down. That is when more is revealed to you because it gives you an awareness that is beyond that source cluster, that source point, that node. Because while you are there, you're still unaware of what exists around you, but the more you become aware in your state as a human and your awareness in that vibrational state of how you are affecting humanity, that is when more is revealed...just as it is revealed here to you [on these pages]. So in each point, you are being given a bit of a revelation of what is taking place just beyond you, just beyond your energy. There's a balance point between becoming aware while you are human and aware while you are in Source. So it is this balance point that one tries to achieve.

For each human that is in existence now, each iteration, each incarnation of a human has been evolved. Not only physically, but energetically. So what they have learned along the way...this is why it is most intriguing. This is why many are observing at this point because there is an evolution that is taking place, not physically, but energetically. It is perpetuating itself. It is growing. For each new human that incarnates is much more aware. That is because much more is being revealed to them while they are in Source, and they are remembering. They are seeing just glimpses beyond Source. Not all of it. Just as you as a human see just glimpses beyond your existence, but not all of it. This is why those that are coming in now have a much greater awareness. They have a much greater perspective of how to heal humanity, how to assist humanity.

Balance and the Overlay

From the onset, from the inception of the human Being itself, there has to be an overlay. There has to be an overlay upon each human that there is this...you say "forgetfulness." It is a void in your processing, though you have an awareness—it is present with you...[within] each Being, each human themselves, encoded within each one of the strands in the DNA. Each one of the twelve strands holds the cumulus of all understanding, all knowledge, all that is present from the time at which the inception of the humans came about. But it is locked away. It is hidden. It is this forgetfulness, [this veil].

You must understand the constructs by which humans live. There is always an overlay, there is always a perception. This is the struggle. This is the purposeful struggle that humans exist within because if there wasn't the overlay, then there wouldn't be a purpose for the human existence to be in place because this would be nothing short of being another location just to have fun, just to have an experience. The overlay provides the struggle. The overlay provides the determination. The overlay provides the humans a path to sustain, to exist.

You must understand; throughout your time here as humans, from the beginning, there has always been the struggle. There has always been this overlay of understanding of humans doing destructive things to humans, whatever that might be. That is that portion of understanding —teaching, as it were—to understand that, if there was no struggle, then there is nothing to achieve because you [would be] living within peace from the beginning. You must have this *perception* of imbalance in order to achieve a higher goal. It is what perpetuates, it is what provides momentum, it is what provides strength in your existence. [But] the overlay is just that, a mere overlay. It is to give the *perception* that there is a struggle.

For you see polarity in your humanity now. Your perception is that it is heavily weighted on one side [more] than the other—[that] there is much more negative polarity than there is positive polarity. And, so, [you might] believe that if there is an imbalance, then it is time to reset...time to go back to the drawing board and reset humanity, reset consciousness, reset the program to begin again to where it is balanced. [But] balance isn't where you [achieve] understanding. If all is balanced perfectly even, perfectly balanced across each—positive/negative, good/bad, light/dark —that is not the optimal state for human society, human existence. You must have that slight bit of struggle in order to achieve.

If you view the world in such a way that it is heavily weighted on this negative polarity side, then that is where your energy is going to be drawn. But if you were to begin to shift your perspective, if you were to begin to look, perceive, observe yourself in the midst of the negative, the dark, the opposite (whatever you wish to place upon it), and understand that when you observe it much differently, from a point of building strength in oneself, then you will understand there are many more like you, building up a resistance, building up the strength to stand before it. And *that* is ultimately the purpose of humanity. It is to build the strength to stand up against the outweighed side. It is difficult, yes, but that is the purpose.

It is the purpose to thrust yourself in front of that experience, that uncomfortable experience, in order to build up the strength within the understanding of Self, the truth of your own Being...because in that, you become aware. For if you are on the other side, there is no need to be aware because you are mired within that construct of negativity, darkness, unsureness. There is no need to strengthen anything because that is your strength. A cumulative strength. Not a collective strength, but an accumulative strength. Two different things. What *you* are building is a collective strength, a unifying strength.

But it is going to be difficult. It is the challenge for the humans to understand this. For in the times to come, it is going to become difficult, but it is for humanity to understand their own strength. Each individual is going to understand this. This is what you keep asking yourselves: "When is humanity going to wake up? When is humanity going to see the atrocities in front of them? When is humanity going to act against it?" *Humanity* isn't going to do anything. But the collective consciousness of those that are becoming aware because of what they're standing up against, what they are faced with, is going to grow.

This is the collective that is talked about, and in that, the balance then begins to shift in the other direction. But in time, if you are to live another thousand years, you will see the shift take place again to the other side. It is a constant balance back and forth throughout time. There were many existences that *all* [was] brought online; all understandings were brought into consciousness during a reset, and all humanity ended up in a different direction, all in the positivity, all in the self-awareness, self-actualization side. And in that, it cannot exist either because that is not what you come here for.

But this balance back and forth, this even flow of balance back and forth is exactly how it was designed. That is what it set out to be. It had to be. So you see, this balance is necessary. Give and take. So it is not to look across humanity as it being in disrepair, as a disparaging aspect, but it is to look at humanity as a delicate balance between one side and the other, and it is necessary to have both. And yes, at times it is weighted much heavier on one side. But that—when it is weighted against you— *that* is where strength in the human aspect takes place.

Yes, there are those that are not going to accept that challenge of finding that strength, and that is part of this experience as a human. But many in your timeframe now are accepting that challenge. Slowly, but they are realizing their own placement in that balance and where they need to stand within their strength. Quietly, they do, and in time, their voice will become loud. But give it time. The greater consciousness, the greater awareness of humanity is one that is beginning to dissolve the overlay. This is where you are seeing your disclosure. That is what disclosure is. Consciousness is becoming more aware, more self-aware...aware of its surroundings, aware of its existence. Consciousness also understands the connectedness it has throughout all Beings, and in that, it is activating small portions of each one of the twelve strands...not for full activation, but for remembrance.

So this is why many have this sensation [that] the veil is becoming thin. This aspect of the veil becoming thin is nothing more than remembering of past knowledge, past understanding, history of time, and the understanding of what is capable within the activation of all twelve. For the activation of all twelve will give you the presence of a full crystalline structure Being that is existent not in form, but in vibration.

So do not have fear in the fact that there will be destruction. There is a consciousness that is beginning to well up, this ascension point that is nearing. Many of you are ascending to a much higher dimensional plane. This will, then, also perpetuate the dissolve of the overlay, and

Reincarnation

this, then, will result in an existence that is, again, sustainable and sustainable with the colonization of other Beings with technologies that are beyond your comprehension. So this is why many believe that there is this ascension point with a new Earth. It is not that there is going to be a new planet, but the planet that you exist in will be new.

Reincarnation

You have this understanding that, "One day, I have accomplished all things [that] I need to do. I am not coming back as a human form upon this planet ever again. I want to take what I've learned and now experience another existence and use what I've learned somewhere else." But this all is dependent upon the contractual agreements that have been put in place during the incarnation process. For you see, though you transition, you still have activities. You still have a job to do. You still have a process that you must maintain. This process, once you are with the Source, the All that you exist in, you are making agreements to achieve the next layer, the next process of your humanness.

If during that process, you've achieved all that you can achieve...[in reality] there is no set achievement point. [For example], you [may] feel as if you have accomplished everything you needed to accomplish, but yet you transition and you are ready to transition out of that and be immersed into another existence, say, a galactic existence, somewhere outside of your human planet, somewhere outside of your human existence, outside of this construct. But yet there are a number of individuals that have yet to accomplish a specific aspect of *their* humanness, and those vibrational points connect with your vibrational point, and you agree that you'll be part of that experience. Well, then, you are going to take on another human form.

It may be that you've accomplished everything that you've needed to accomplish as a human, but yet you make agreements with others to come back to fulfill *their* agreement. This is the process, over and over again. There are many humans upon this planet that have accomplished the entirety of all things that they needed to accomplish, but yet they agree to come back because they are here to assist. They will continue to do that. That is part of their process. You have to understand, it is not just you. You are not here just for yourself. You'll do this until "it" is ready. What "it" is, is the accomplishments of all humanity.

When you transition and you are amongst all others that are there in vibrational aspect, vibrational form, you forget, just as you forget when you come here. You forget all of the anguish. You forget all of the turmoil. You forget all of the hurt, sadness, all of the ugly portions of the human existence. Frankly, you forget *all* things because now you are in a vibrational state. But yet you will agree to assist others because that is the human experience: assisting others. Each individual here is to assist another individual.

Now, you may seem to think that this is going to be an endless cycle. It is not. It is not. But do not dwell on the fact that you may come back over and over and over because each time it is like a reset, but each time, you remember a little bit more and a little bit more.

Frequency and Vibration

You understand the Earth planet's harmonic, this Schumann resonance, 432 hertz. You are quite similar to that frequency...the base frequency, which is attenuated across all humanity. This is why this Earth planet is the purposeful place for you. For the base frequency, this resonance that each human has, this has been set from the beginning. This is not something that has changed throughout time. So this base frequency is more aligned with the Earth planet than it was previously with the Martian planet. Your base frequency is one that allows you to phase yourself into another frequency very quickly.

This is why this Earth planet, as its Schumann resonance increases and decreases, there are periods of time that different individuals feel more affected by it than others. But yet at different frequency points, others are affected, and others are not. It is similar to when you are in a room by yourself, and there is no presence of any other Being. Ever so slight, you sense a vibrational shift in its field around you. This is because the harmonics of your frequency are stabilizing to a point at which they are sensitive to receive.

Similar to your technology that senses when there is a seismic event. Think of it that way. Inside of you is a sensor. That is your base frequency. It is very sensitive. It is affected by many things. The more you become attuned, attenuated to that base frequency, the more sensitive it gets. You sense a presence in a room when there is no one. You hear a piece of music, and it vibrates differently than it had in the past. You watch something, you speak with someone, you walk through the forest, you do many different actions, and yet in the past, they had no connectedness to you. But now, with each step, there's a connectedness. There's an alignment that is taking place. This is because the sensitivity of your base frequency is receiving the other frequency fields. Just as the instrument that senses seismic activity can sense the slightest movement of your Earth planet, *your* field, *your* energy is picking up, is sensing the slightest change in energetic fields around you.

This is most important; for you see, those that are unaware, those that have not come into their understanding of awareness, they are sensing it too. This is where questioning begins. This is the change that is beginning in many individuals. They have not an understanding of what is taking place within their own body. They have this sensation from many different things where they hadn't before, and they begin to question. They seek out different individuals. It becomes a part of their conversation with different individuals. For those that are aware, they are becoming more sensitive to many of the things around them. Their life is changing because of it. Allowing it and accepting it is the most appropriate aspect.

[Those vibrational sensations trigger emotions] and not only emotions within the human body, but physical release. For you see, the human form itself is a vibrational construct. You vibrate at the highest vibrational field...that of no other, other than a crystalline Being that is naught but just vibration. You are very close to being nonexistent, but yet you take physical form. This is the achievement point that has been set out from the beginning: to find a balance just between the point at which a body is nonexistent and the point that a body is existent. This is why through your time period here of stabilization, there has been a long period of time where it has just been a dense human form, all along vibrating at the same frequency.

But as more and more individuals become aware of their frequency, this vibration that is around them, this begins to cascade throughout all of humanity. Then, this is why it is said that you begin to feel lighter as you become more aware. This is because you are becoming aware of the vibrational field that you exist in. Not the human form dissipating. You are becoming lighter because you are aware of the human vibrational interface. For if you had no vibration, you would not exist. Your human form would not exist. The vibration, this base frequency, is what holds everything together. Just as everything is vibrationally held together, you, too, are vibrationally held together. If it weren't for that base frequency, you would not be in existence. But you are, and what you're becoming aware of is the ever-so-slight line between nonexistent form (vibrational state) and human form.

Existing Physically versus Vibrationally

This is the only physical universe that exists. This is why it is observed by many. Even your Andromedan galaxy, as they separated out from this galaxy, you see them as an energetic point. That is all they are: an energetic point. They do not have physicality. Yes, you observe them in your night sky, but what you are observing is a frequency point, a vibrational point. This, [your universe], is the only point at which everything has coalesced into a physical location.

[However], if any other Being, any other energetic point, any other vibrational aspect wishes to come into this universe, this galaxy, they can choose to do it in a purely vibrational form, in which it then presents to you as a vibrational form, and then your human [mind] envelops it into an image. Or they can, then, vibrationally coalesce into a physical aspect, a true physical form, just as you are a true physical form. They have both as an option. [Just] as we come to you, we can vibrationally bring ourselves into physical form temporarily in front of you, in physicality, to present ourselves. We will not remain there very long, but we can bring ourselves vibrationally into this form. Just as any other Being, any other of the twelve, any other Being from any other point, [any craft], they can vibrationally coalesce into a physical form.

[Although they are not physical, there is a collective understanding of what a Lyran, for example, looks like because there is a universal construct] within your universe, within your node, this experiment. When the source cluster put up the source node for the Lyrans, there needed to be some visualization that needed to take place for the humans to understand what it needed to look like. That chosen form holds a vibration. Think of it as a ripple from a stone thrown into a pond. That vibrational form then ripples throughout your universe. It becomes the consciousness of awareness. It becomes the consciousness of visualization. It becomes the consciousness that is embedded, imbued into all understandings: that is what a Lyran is going to appear to be within this construct.

So this is why some [Beings] take the form of your insects, some take the form of your felines, some take the form of your canines, some take the form of Beings that are humanlike—it is a construct by which the vibration associates with what is already in existence for the humans to build upon. It is a bit difficult to understand. It is not that the Lyrans themselves take a physical form as a lion-headed Being or a lion Being or a cat Being—that is [simply] what the construct of the vibration that they send out is associated with in the human form to give them a physical appearance.

[Arcturians can] take many forms in front of you, depending upon the individual that we are connecting with and coming into physicality with. We can be much grander than you or more equal to your human status. We are somewhat translucent at times. We can then be cloaked in a uniform of sorts. We also have a much different appearance facially to you, but yet very recognizable, [with no hair on the head]. Many of us will have a blue appearance, but some will take the same but yet translucent color as your skin color. We have an appearance with our eyes that are a bit mesmerizing to your physicality. Once we present to you, if you gaze into our eyes, we will allow you to peer into that past. That is how we bring you into our existence. We allow you to blend with us through that process.

Hybridization and Colonization

There are a number of different Beings that we have partnered with through the hybridization process. We have imparted bits of our energetic source vibration. Some of those that you would understand would be the Mantis...the Zetas. Those Beings upon your planet that you would understand as Terra Beings, we've also imparted some of our source vibration into those.

There are many others, but those have been pulled away from your awareness. They are not useful at this point. They were brought online much earlier in the process and will be brought back online in your future time. They will be brought online to allow you to begin this process of colonizing with other Beings. They will be very similar to your human form. They will have the human form, but they will be much... they will stand much more grand than you. You can think of them as being humans, but much larger. I think you would understand them as being giants among your human forms. You would understand them from the period at which...beyond your Egyptian realm; they were here purposefully to help construct and put in place many of the large structures that are in place now, to help begin that colonization process. Once that was complete and those humans were purposefully aligned, they were then brought back into stasis point. But they will [return] in the future, as they will be the ambassadors to help you colonize with other Beings in the future.

The early humans, much earlier than you understand, all had a full awareness that they were a hybridized Being. They had this [understanding] purposefully because they lived alongside many of the Beings that you now understand as an energetic Being. They, too, were brought into human form or solid form, physical form, physicality upon your planet. They were not colonizing together, but they were here as teacher-student. They were here to understand, to begin the process of the true human form.

But you understand, as it has been transmitted in the past, that there have been cycles that have, in an understanding, been wiped from the planet and restarted. This process reenergizes itself each time. Each time, there is a series of hybridized Beings that are brought in with the human forms. They each have an understanding that they are all hybridized, or pure Beings, for the assistance. You are now in a cycle where hybridized Beings are no longer needed. You are self-sustaining. You are self-perpetuating. You are growing in awareness.

But in time, the process will come back online to where this colonization of Beings will need to take place...needing to take place because you are now achieving a place at which ascension happens quite rapidly. So this is the point at which the hybridized Beings and energetic Beings come into physicality to assist that process even further—the rapid process of ascension. For this planet will become one that the teachings happen very rapidly. You come into existence very quickly, and you go through an ascension process very quickly, typically within one life cycle.

The Arcturians' Relationship with Humans

[Arcturus is one of the brightest stars in your sky], the primary point which you [can], then, gaze to for our appearance and our connection. Do not be overly focused on that. That is just one energetic point in your night sky that we can, then, transition through to come into appearance for you. But we are always present with you. The Pleiadians, as well. There is a physical location for them, as well, but energetically, we are continually in presence with you. We are the two that are always continually present with you. We are always energetically present in your locations, wherever you may be. This is why it is easy to call upon us at any particular point.

Our presence amongst the humans has been primary for a great deal of time. For there are other clusters that are closer in alignment to the human Being, but it is our alignment that is more directly aligned to all existence...all existence as a human throughout time. There are those that have familiar features as a human, who are closely aligning in energy, who are closely aligning in appearance. But it is [we], the Arcturi-ans, that throughout time have been aligned directly with the humans.

From the inception of the point at which the coalescing of particles, the knowledge, has all been imparted into the physical form, we have been present. We have been present with you along this journey, along this path. Where many others, many others of the clusters come and go through time—dependent upon the alignments, dependent upon the requirements, dependent upon the needs of the humans—the Arcturians have been there from the beginning, all throughout time... each cycle, each represented cycle of time.

So it is this [reason] that you have this anticipation, [this fondness for us]; for you and many others understand the alignment with the Arcturi-ans. It is always present with you. It is always there in your thoughts. It is always there in your understanding...the questioning, the truths. We are always present with you. Whether you have an alignment with us or not, we are present in your existence. It is not that we must come to you in physical form or must show ourselves, but our energies are always present, always surrounding, always with you.

The Arcturians' Unique Role

[Our role] is to bring expansion and awareness to [the humans'] exis-tence. You understand the Pleiadians and their alignment. And yes, as it has been mentioned and has been brought forth, the alignment between the Pleiadians and the Arcturians is quite similar. The vibrational aspects are quite similar. And, so, aligning to either, or both, will allow you to expand in a way which brings you a greater awareness space.

Now, what is a greater awareness space? That is not just the space that is around you and the space that you exist in, but think of it as an opening, a gateway, a portal to an understanding that is greater than your comprehension, a greater expansion of your knowledge. It is allowing you to peer further into the depths, allowing you to see much further back in time, allowing you to see a bit of the future, and aligning yourself to that understanding and those teachings, bringing forward information to assist humanity here, to reach beyond the bounds of your existence. Allowing you to align yourself with either, or both, will allow yourself to bring forward information here to progress humanity...to progress humanity forward for the greater expansion of their vibrational field, their teachings of awareness, their understandings, how they are in existence, and their ultimate purpose for all others to observe.

So as you call upon us, we will align you accordingly, for each intersection that you have placed in front of you. If it is, say, an alignment to a new part of employment, we are going to allow you to navigate within that accordingly. But we are also going to align with you to have your vibration set aside purposefully at its highest. This is where the human form then begins to change. You begin to sense a bit of difference in alignment. You understand contractually what needs to take place, this new employment you must navigate within, all the individuals that are, then, there with it.

You have a sense that there's something greater. You begin to question. We will begin to impart the answers. We will not give you the full answers. We will not give you the full understandings. But we will assist you. We are continually trying to align the pieces of your contract with your purpose, your ultimate purpose.

9

POLARIANS

Greetings from the Polarian Source Cluster. We bring you this transmission for the highest level of understanding of our alignment to the human race, to the human experience, to the human experience of experimentation throughout the ages of time, to the final evolution of presence now. For what is [it] to understand the origins? What is [it] to understand the beginning point? For one must understand the point at which the humans came into being. For you have been witness to many other transmissions that have expressed the origins of your galaxy, your universe, your planets...the origins of the humans from a different perspective.

But what we wish to provide to you is this guidance, this understanding: For the Polarians have been in place from the beginning, yes, but they have been dormant up until critical points of the human evolution. For you understand the beginning point upon the Martian planet. You understand that the origin point began there. Yes, the term *experimentation...experiment...*will be used and utilized. You must understand from the beginning point, all twelve clusters have been brought together to synchronize for one purpose...the ultimate purpose being the humans, the human race, the human Beings, the human consciousness. But one does not achieve that from the onset. There is much that takes place before you achieve a goal, achieve a Being.

So, yes, there has been experimentation—sequencing of the appropriate alignments between the twelve source clusters (and in which order) needed to achieve the final outcome...experimentation upon which planet is going to be best suited to begin this process...experimentation to understand which of the sequences need to be aligned first...experimentation along the way of the evolution of the humans.

We have lain dormant during this process, for our role is one to be overseers, in conjunction with the closest proximity of evolution to your understanding of the human Beings. For there has been much interaction with all other clusters up to this point, through the Martian planet and its demise, to the Earth planet and its sustainability. Once the humans achieved a point [of]—not to the exact, but similar to—your [current] appearance, did we begin our alignment. We then began our process of overseeing. We were with you from that point, here, upon your planet.

As you can imagine, as you are brought through this process of experimentation, there are many different understandings of what a human Being could be or should be. Many different evolutions of change. And you also understand the process of cleansing and clearing and restarting, and the agreements that took place for that process to take place. For you must see that, as the humans themselves began their evolutionary process, their process of coming into the sustainable state they are now, they have been guided. They have been partnered with other galactic Beings...that, too, giving rise to understandings of technology, understandings of existence, understandings well beyond what you are achieving now in your state.

But that, too, led to the demise. Too fast of growth, too fast of understanding. There is a balance. There is a sustainable time period. That was not known in the beginning. This is why it is said that there are, yes, twelve source clusters, but only a certain amount are active during certain periods. Each one of them convey their own representation of understanding, their own technological advances, their own progression. The right combination needed to be sought. In the early stages, this was the experimentation. Which source clusters needed to be in alignment with the humans that were present at that time? What was being provided to them? What knowledge? What technologies?

But for us, once there was an achievable point at which the humans could be sustained, then we were with you. We oversaw this process. We were present with you as Beings alongside you, integrating, assisting you, providing you guidance through the initial stages of your evolution. Yes, there were times that it was restarted, but we were always with you from that start point. Even though there was a cleansing and a restart, we never departed. The human Beings did, and they were brought back online, brought back into existence, and we were there. Then, to a point at which the sustainability of the human Being was achievable, then we went back into a state of dormancy. We pulled ourselves away. There was no longer a need for our oversight.

This is why now, in your modern times, the Polarians are not active, as many of the other clusters are. You also understand that there are [other] clusters that are not as active, as well. This is purposeful. Just as the human Beings themselves have twelve DNA strands, and not all are active, it is purposeful that all twelve source clusters are not active simultaneously. This energetic state of all twelve being active at one particular time would be overwhelming to all galactic systems within your universe. So it is purposeful that there are an allotted amount active at any one time, dependent upon the needs of your galaxy, of your universe, of your humans, of your existence.

So it is for us to be here, with you now, to provide you the understanding of this process. We are not departed from you; we are just not integrating with you. If you wish to call upon us for guidance, you may, and we will provide you just enough information, just enough guidance as not to overwhelm the current alignments with the active source clusters.

The Human Sustainability Timeline

For your human existence that exists now, the sustainable period of human existence is within the ten thousand to twenty thousand-year period. That is when the equal balance of understanding, technologies, and alignments to source clusters were put in place. Prior to that—again, going back some million of years' experience—there were a number of iterations of humans and their societies. You have yet to understand that. You have yet to reach that level of understanding and that level of exploration. It will be brought forward, but it has yet to be understood.

You must understand millennia in your existent timeline. For you see, there has been much that has been scripted, scribed, taught throughout time of what your planet was like and is like. For you see, [your Biblical timeline] is just a small glimpse of what many believe this planet was. That was a very close, in perspective, timeline aspect that is just a mere glimpse of the totality of this planet itself. For it has been through many cycles of evolution with higher societies, higher evolution Beings, and then wiped clean and started again.

There have been, in your understanding, artifacts that have been found that do not fit within any equated timeline of your sustainable period. They are far beyond the bounds of that, which then, is a misunderstanding, and then, they are brought forward into your existent timeline. [For example, what your scientists might call a "missing link," could have been a reset point.] There have been multiple, multiple reset points.

[You are aware of the partial reset described in a previous transmission.] This, you would understand, is your biblical time and your biblical stories; though they are somewhat accurate, they are yet voiced through the humans that were in place. That was a point at which there were two layers of humans: those that were at the point of sustainability and those that were not advancing as rapidly as those that are at the sustainable point. Those that were not advancing as quickly, those that were not assimilating to the new advances of understanding, the new advances of technology, the new advances of the alignments, were reset. Those that had advanced to the sustainability point were left to exist.

Those [who were not sustainable, who were reset] would be considered legacy Beings. They were the initial segment [of humans] that were brought over from the previous reset. They were reset into this existence with the understanding that they would achieve the *next* level of understanding. Just with any reset, there are always legacy understandings that are brought over. You would understand this [as], in your timeframe, in your understanding of existence, those that have previous lives that bring in the memory states from those previous lives. [Those memories] exist, coexisting within [the] timeframe that is their [current] life, and it has an effect on their [current] life throughout their life experience. And no matter what takes place, no matter the advances in understandings and technologies and alignments, that is never shed from their thought process. This, then, debilitates them in a particular way in which it's difficult to sustain advancements.

So again, there is much yet to be divulged. There is much yet to be revealed. But yet the humans themselves have not reached a thought sustainability aspect to understand what lies beyond a certain point.

War and Peace

During the points at which the factions began to separate themselves out and began to war against themselves, again, we were present with the humans. That was our goal. That was our role: to allow the sustainability of the humans to take place. We shielded many of the humans from the galactic wars. We presented ourselves, again, as overseers, protectors during this process. Many of the humans didn't understand that this was taking place, though there are some that were directly involved with these galactic wars, the warring factions.

There has always been a small segment of humans that are directly aligned and have direct alignment to many of the different factions. Though they were not part of the factions, they were aligned with them.

They pull that knowledge forward just as a previous memory. They bring it forward into this existence. They have direct remembrance of all of what has taken place during the galactic wars. You can look upon them as archivists. They bring that information forward as remembrance of what could be yet again. They bring that forward so that others can understand what took place in the past.

[This can cause some humans to believe there is currently a galactic war over the humans, but] that is a perception of different humans. There isn't a specific galactic war warring against humans. There isn't a specific race that is trying to impart their own essence upon the humans. There isn't a specific group of Beings that is trying to infiltrate the humans. That has been put aside. Yes, there are warring factions still about. Many of them have been cast out of your star system, your galaxy, your planetary systems, your universe. But there are those that are still in place. They war against themselves, with the other Beings throughout your galaxy and your universe. But here, upon the planet, much has been done to protect the humans.

Those that truly align with the different factions will have some influence, will have some energetic alignment and process with those factions, but they are not imparting any undue harm to the humans. You must understand, this has been the process through time, the balance that has taken place here with the humans. Just as there is a balance with the source clusters and how the humans are sustainable, there has to be this balance with understandings and, even amongst the humans, different factions.

So to say that there is a galactic warring faction against the humans... that would be incorrect. But the warring factions take place within the humans. This is part of the sustainability. This is part of the learning process. This is part of the growth process. This is what has been learned throughout time. There has to be a balance between those that believe there is warring against them and those that have an understanding that it does not exist, have an understanding that there is a peace to be had, there is peace to achieve. This is the balance within humanity. This is part of the sustainability of how the humans have come into existence. This is what has been learned through time.

The peace that you seek...first you must look upon your planet. The warring factions that are spoken about are here within your human Beings. Yes, there are factions that are out beyond your galactic warring factions, but they are not achieving their goals of trying to sway the humans or trying to overthrow the humans. That is not achievable. They are trying, but it is not achievable. There is much that has been put in place for that to be mitigated.

You see, to have an understanding of how the human Beings are, in better terms, *protected* from those galactic factions that are trying to, as you say, overthrow the humans...just as the galactic factions try to rise against the humans or try to overthrow the humans, there are energetic mechanisms that the source clusters that are currently aligned with the humans now have [so] that they can, then, activate within the humans a level of awareness, a level of understanding well beyond that of the warring faction that is trying to control the humans. This activation of awareness begins to grow throughout a certain cluster of humans, and this, then, puts up a protective front against anything that is trying to come in and do harm from outside of your planet to the humans themselves. Again, lessons that have been learned through time of what needs to take place for sustainability.

So yes, there are those, again, with legacy understandings, with legacy thoughts, with legacy memories of what *has been*, but not what is taking place. What has taken place is just that. Yes, warring factions have tried to overthrow and have overthrown segments of humanity throughout time. They've done harm to the humans. But what has been learned is how to mitigate, how to fend off that approach. So that is one aspect.

But within your human race itself and the warring factions within the human race, human against human, state against state, country against country...no matter what it might be, what has been learned through time is necessary. Though from a human's standpoint, that is something that is difficult to understand...[the idea] that conflict, war, harm against humans is necessary...but it is necessary.

One, it is necessary to allow those that wish to be in existence [but then wish to] transition much quicker, to do another role in a much quicker fashion. That allows that apparatus to take place. The other aspect is this: For those that are observing what is taking place, it allows their awareness to expand naturally. It begins a process of seeking and questioning much more rapidly. There is no introduction from the source clusters to achieve this awareness state, [as there is in the case] of an outside contact from a warring faction.

So there is much that has to be understood. The human Beings themselves are sustainable. The human Beings themselves are growing in awareness. Their consciousness is expanding, though the human Beings themselves will continue to be human Beings. The point at which they do harm to themselves will begin to diminish, but it will always be in place. This is a purposeful thing, and many do not understand this within the existence as a human. Many have conflict within themselves of why humans do things to humans.

That is the purpose of being a human Being. For you see, this role of emotion is specific to the human Beings. Yes, there are other Beings that have emotion, but not to the level of emotion or intellectual emotion that the humans have. Much emotion has been bred out of many of the Beings over time. They found that it was a hindrance. In the beginning, they found that emotion was a hindrance to their evolution, to their progress, to their motion forward of where they wanted to sustain their existence. But in time, they found that the lack of emotion, then, was a hindrance to their actual momentum. So that is why you find that they are trying to achieve emotion yet again by acquiring some DNA from the human Beings, since they are the sustaining point of all twelve. They are trying to recover their pure essence DNA, again, to come into balance with some level of emotionality within their existence.

But this has been what has been imparted through time. This [imbalance] is how sustainability is achieved. For if there is a harmonious balance of all things known, then your existence is much shorter because you've achieved exactly what needed to be achieved in a much shorter amount of time. There is nothing more to achieve, and existence then ceases. But if you come into existence with an imbalance in place, as you mature physically, you begin to mature energetically much more rapidly. And in doing so, that begins to spread. That begins to spread throughout the humans. Though it will never fully extinguish harm to other humans, it still slows the process and allows greater awareness of your consciousness, greater awareness of humanity to grow much more rapidly.

And as you do, as this process takes place, what you will begin to see is this: The source clusters that are present with you now will begin to shift. Others will become active. Others will go dormant. That is the sustainable achievement point of allowing the source clusters to blend with your existence more rapidly, imparting their information, imparting their understanding, their knowledge, their truths, their tech-nologies, to sustain a higher level of existence. Many of the source cluster Beings will begin to come into physicality and colonize with you, live alongside you, be in existence with you, as [will] many of the hybridized Beings, and you will be sustained, then, by their physical role with you. This is all part of the process. This is all part of the project that has been discussed previously.

Hybridization

We are not completely pure. There have been aspects of the Polarians that have been hybridized [with] the Venusians, Pleiadians, and Martians. But we do not associate. Energetically, we do not associate. You would understand [those Beings] as benign. There is no positive or negative with them. They are just sustained Beings themselves. They are just in existence to be in existence. We would like to be in a state of pureness, but we are not. But it is the hybridization between the source clusters that has achieved aspects of the Polarians that we do not associate with, that we do not align with energetically. So we have set them aside, cast them aside. They are out in their own existence.

You would not [know of them]. They have not been brought forward to the human existence, to the human awareness. That is the agreement, that they stand aside and allow this process to take place. For you see, the information that we contain, the information that we understand and bring to the human sustainability understanding, is also contained in them. So there would be a conflict of understandings if they were to make their presence known alongside our presence or any other hybridized Being. It would be in conflict of understanding. So we have made an agreement with them that they will not make their presence known to any humans during this process.

From the hybridization process, we were involved, but we did not impart any of our essence into that hybridization program. Again, as overseers, we are overseeing the process of the humans' evolution. That is our strict role. We observe the other hybridization programs for the other hybridized Beings. For you see, any time any of the source clusters come together to produce, to achieve an outcome, whether that is a physical Being or an energetic Being, there is a hybridization that takes place. It is this that we oversaw to ensure that during that process, all things were adhered to according to what the outline was that was set out in the beginning.

As far as the humans and their hybridization process, we ensured as overseers that it was not taken out of context of exactly what needed to be here, as far as the humans themselves. We understood the final aspect, the stage that you are currently in, the final sustainable process. We understood that. We understood what needed to be aligned, but not knowing which alignments, which hybridizations between which source clusters would achieve the sustainable aspect.

The North Star and Jesus's Birth

You would represent that as that experience of looking northward into your sky with the sensation and the understanding that there is a presence that is watching over...watching over during a period of time in which this individual, Jesus, came into your existence. For you see, the Being Jesus, the divine Being that was brought here onto your planet, was one to begin a point of revelation upon your planet...one that sustained understanding. Again, a bit of an experiment for the human Beings.

For you see, part of the sustainability aspect is, once the human Beings themselves are at a point at which they are sustained, once they are maintaining their existence, then there are individuals that come and go throughout that time that are fully present with all understanding, and it is they that impart information. They are not the source cluster individuals that come into existence here, but they are imparted, upon their arrival, with all understanding, with all truths, with all technology. They impart that amongst the other Beings. This has happened throughout time.

But if the sustainable Beings are not aligning to those individuals, that individual's experience upon the planet is either short-lived or set aside, cast out, put away. So there are multiple outcomes to those individuals. There are individuals now in your sustained time period that have these abilities. They have these experiences. They have not fully revealed themselves. They have learned through time that it is a point at which, evolving throughout time to reveal their true nature is not one to broadcast freely, but yet to slowly integrate throughout society and allow the essence of their experience to be held closely to certain individuals.

The Polarians' Existence and Appearance

This understanding of this star cluster, yes, is in your northern sky. This would be your northernmost point of your observable sky. There are approximately twenty-seven different stars within the cluster [including

Polaris Ab, Polaris B, and the North star, the brightest star in your sky]. Many are not observable through your means of observation, but they are present. That number is specific. That number is specific to the amount of time that we have been present with you. It represents each millennia that we have been with you. Each time that we have been in presence with you for a sustained amount of time, we have created a time [space] at which those that were with you can then reside, some being greater than others, dependent upon the length of time that they were present with you. That is the amount of space they are required within our star cluster system.

This [star cluster] is the energetic point at which we sustain ourselves. This is an observation point for you, for remembrance that we have been with you from the beginning. We are your guidance. We are your overseers. We watch over and we understand what is taking place. Even though we lay dormant at this particular period for alignment, we are overseeing. We are watching. We are there. We are present with you daily. We are present with you every single moment, as we have been in the beginning. We are always present with you.

This is your remembrance. As you look into the northern sky, your point of existence, and you see the northern light, this bright object, this star cluster, that is your remembrance. This is why, if you were to call on the Polarians, find that point of reference, point yourself towards that point of reference, and envision yourself enveloped in our energy, our emittance from that star cluster. As you do, call upon us. We will not present ourselves in physicality, but we will present ourselves energetically. We will envelop you in a bright white-blueish envelopment of light and energy. The white light that envelops you is not overwhelming. It is not one to wash over you as an overwhelming presence, but it is one to sustain you just comfortable enough to be relaxed. You would be very comfortable within our presence immediately. There would be no question, there would be no fear. That is us accepting you into our realm, and then from there, we'll impart as much information as we need as not to disturb the current alignments.

[If we were to appear to you in a physical state], we would come to you in a physical form that is much greater than yours. You would look upon us as being giants among the humans. We would be cloaked in a uniform of sorts, wrapped with a cape, with again, a whitish-blueish calming essence. Much different than others that have been presented before you. [We would have bluish-white skin, and depending upon the Being, some would have short hair] some long, some without. Same facial features as many of the humans. [We] will take on a representative form of where the location would be that [we] are being brought into physical presence.

The Polarians' Unique Role

This alignment [with the humans] is very similar to that of a child seeking its parents, seeking its caregiver, just for the reassurance that there is that existence...someone to be watching over, someone to be guarding what is taking place. For you see, if we see a disturbance with the current alignment of the source clusters that are sustaining your existence now, if we see there is a disturbance taking place, we will begin our process of being able to step inward to your existence, to oversee it from a much closer point, a much closer vantage point. We will come into physicality in your existence, and we will begin the process of sustaining your existence even closer.

To have an understanding of what you wish to seek from us is this: Your human race, your human Beings, and how they are now sustainable... your evolutionary process, your process that has achieved this state of sustainability of existence...it is continuing to evolve. It is continuing to move forward. It is not necessary to look back upon your past—your past existence here as a human and how many lives you've lived as a human—but it is to open your awareness. It is to begin to open your awareness and your understanding of what lies before you.

For those Beings in the past that have dwelled in the past, though they have achieved a new existence, they've been reset. But they dwell in the past, and they remain in the past. It has slowed their progress. It has limited their awareness. It is not to have a negative aspect of the past, but it is to say, learn what you need from the past; allow that to be a bit of guidance for the future. It is to open your awareness to the expansiveness of the future that lies before you, for your future is rapidly approaching, much more so than it has in the past. For time itself is increasing. The expansiveness of time is increasing. With the expansiveness of time that increases in front of you, your future approaches quicker.

With the approaching future, as your awareness grows, your essence, your physicality, your knowing begins to broaden, begins to open. Your alignment to your Source, your source clusters, your galactic alignments, your energetic alignments, all begin to resonate much higher, all begin to harmonize much quicker. For those that have not experienced any energetic alignments, they will begin to experience much more than they can sustain. For those that are aware and have achieved this alignment, you, too, are going to begin to receive and be presented with much more than you can understand. There will be much more information that will be imparted upon you, much quicker, much more dense.

This alignment to the Polarians...as you begin this process, as the future approaches much more rapidly, and the increased understanding begins to grow within you...though we are not present with you and currently aligned with you for this overseer aspect in physicality, we are still there to provide you comfort. Just as you look towards a parent, look towards one that is within your experience, your life, as a partner, to comfort you, to give you guidance, we give you the guidance, as well. We give you the comfort, as well. That is why we are positioned where we are positioned, easily recognizable in the night sky, easily recognizable with our energy.

So allow us to envelop around you, to give you that comfort in the moments that you are uncomfortable with what you are receiving. For that is why we were with you from the beginning. In the states of confusion in the early segments of your evolution, when all was being imparted upon you, the confusion was settled by our presence. In these states of confusion, in these states of unawareness, in these states of disruption, allow us to give you comfort.

Allow this transmission to be part of your advancement in awareness. For the existence that the humans have now, this sustained existence that you have now, has been sustained for the longest period thus far. You have advanced much greater than what was expected. You are continuing to advance much quicker than expected. You are on a period of time that much is going to be revealed in a very short amount of time. *Your existence here as humans will be one that will be remembered by all Beings.* You are here, purposeful, not only for the humans themselves to be purposeful to each other, but purposeful to all those that are observing, all galactic Beings that observe and have imparted their own wisdom to you. And in short time, they will be present with you, alongside you, physically, reuniting and sustaining a new existence.

10

DRACONIANS

Greetings. Greetings from the Draconian Source Cluster. You have this understanding from the other clusters of the origins, and the inception, and the understanding of where humanity has come from. We will provide you as much clarity as possible for your understanding of our role amongst this community, amongst the Twelve, and during the portions of hybridization that have taken place.

For what you must recognize and what you must be witness to is this... the perception that all humanity has of the Draconians is one that is based upon our interactions throughout, as it has been called, the experiment...this process by which the humans have come into existence. This perception is one that is apprehensive of our existence. Much has been perceived that we are playing a negative role within the human construct, the human framework. You also have an understanding of our hybridization and the role of the Reptilian Beings that are in existence.

For this perception, this has played out through time, this has played out through your millennia, since the point at which the human Being itself was brought into existence, and [in] all of its changes, all of its iterations, all of its resets, we have held a vital role. For you understand the Twelve and you understand those that you have spoken to and their role—some deeply involved in the human project and others as observers.

But the role that we take on, and the perception that follows, is this...for we are vital during the reset process. Our energy is vital during this process. For during this reset process, we enter into the deep awareness, the deep presence of each Being, each human. We are there to guide them across, into this existence, into the space of reset. We allow them to come across with us. Do not be confused; they are not perishing in any way. They are not leaving their human body. They are not, as you would say, transitioning. But their energy, their existent energy...we allow it to move across into the reset point. We guide them in that process. So this is why it is said we are vital in this role. We are there to be an assistant.

But, just as it is, as vital as we are, it has come to be an understanding that we are here to do harm, we are here to take one's existence, we are here to transition one's awareness. That has been moved through time to be this awareness that each human has to this point. But each of us has a specific role, and our role is just that—it is to merge with the awareness, it is to integrate with the awareness, to be alongside the awareness and guide and assist that energy out of, and then, once reset, to gently guide back in.

There is no awareness of that portion of time, that portion of existence where the reset energy is entered back into the human form; there is no awareness at that point. There is just a void of existence. So it wouldn't matter if it would be the Draconians, the Arcturians, the Martians, or any other Being. There is no awareness of it.

At that point, it is then slowly brought back online with the assistance of those that have remained in place. You have this understanding as the legacy Beings...those that have not been reset. The point at which those individuals, those humans, have been reset, [they] have no acknowledgment of their existence. The awareness, the energy, the consciousness is brought back into that human form, all within an instant. It is just as a newborn enters into the world—there is confusion; there is no awareness, but yet there is a connectedness.

And from that point, the legacy Beings then begin to interact. They step forward and guide and teach. They're the ones that assist and guide with their knowledge to begin the integration here, back into an upgraded awareness system. But not teach in a way in which it is something that is instructional, but a transference...a transference of knowledge, a transference of understanding...all through touch, through a gaze, through a connectedness...unspoken connectedness. And all within that moment, all understandings are brought back online, and the awareness, then, is an upgraded connectedness to their Being.

So understand that this point of reset, you've understood it from a broader perspective, you've understood it from an operational perspective, that yes, it is necessary, and yes, it is purposeful, and it is something that needs to take place through time. But we are here to have you understand that our role is to be that guiding assistant for that energy to transition out, to be reset and brought back in.

Upgrading Without a Reset

What is transitioning on your horizon is one that you and many understand as this *Event* that is to take place. And yes, it is correct that there will be an upgrade without the reset. The consciousness that will be upgraded will be one for all. There will not be a segmented group of individuals that will remain behind. All will be reset. All will be upgraded but retaining all of what their past understanding is. It will be archived for retrieval. It will be not the forefront operating portion of the humanness.

So you have to understand, [all Beings] will retain all the current life experience. They will also retain all of the past life experience, archived, [but with a] new consciousness upgraded. That will become the awareness. There will be no confusion. There will be an understanding of completeness, but yet there will be a retrieval system to bring forward any of that information that has been archived for purposeful expression. Those that have just recently been reset, or those that have been here for the stabilization point will only have awareness to this point.

And once this upgraded consciousness is brought online, that is what will be archived and put away for retrieval in the future.

All twelve will play a role during that process. All will take on a specific role of guidance. You have to understand, you have these alignments to a specific group, specific clusters. You have what you are indicating as a source point alignment and a close [or primary] alignment to one or two of your galactic alignments. For you see, those two that you are aligned with, or a singular point you are aligned with, will be your aligning portions for this consciousness reset. They will be operating in the capacity that the Draconians had in the past, for you have made those alignments for those transitions. They will be the ones that guide and allow you to remain in place while this process takes place, [even for those who aren't aware of that alignment]. [The unaware] will be given witness to that upon the point at which the reset takes place.

DNA Alignments

[The Andromedans previously explained that your two strands of DNA are specifically referenced to two specific source clusters upon incarnation]—the source cluster connection point and the closest [primary] alignment point. [There is a] sequence of timing for [these alignments]. Dependent upon the agreement process, yes, they can change within each cycle of connection and each cycle of incarnation. If you so choose, you can remain with the same two for an extended period of time. But yes, they can change during the incarnation process.

[They are] this in purpose: For the most relevant day-to-day aligning and the day-to-day information that you seek from your galactic connection, that is your closest galactic connection point, whatever that might be. That is your daily connection. That is your everlasting connection during that human alignment.

The connection to the galactic source point, whatever that source point might be, is one to guide and assist you during certain transitional points during the human existence. For you see, even though you do not transition physically into the death state, then back into the life state, you do go through periods of transition. And during those periods of transition, that galactic source point is one to assist you through that process, some more prevalent than others. So it is as you go through these transition points, you may sense a greater connection to a particular galactic Being. That is your source point connection. We guide and assist you through those transition points.

Others may not be fully aware of it, but yet they understand there is a presence of a galactic Being. They do not understand the differences between them; they do not understand the languages, the names given to them. But they understand there is some sort of galactic presence with them. Again, it is that source point that is aligned with them, activating that one particular strand of DNA a bit more than the closest alignment strand. This is aiding in these transition points.

There are very few humans that have a direct alignment or a source point alignment [with the Draconians]. During the early stages, many of the human Beings in existence had at least one connection to the Draconians. This is why we were purposeful in this reset process. It was an easy way to enter into the awareness state, the awareness stage, and assist with that reset action. But through time, as it became more stable with the consciousness, we phased ourselves from these connection points. We phased ourselves out of those connection points in order to observe from a distance and only insert ourselves when necessary, though there are a number of Beings, a number of humans that are in existence now that do have direct Draconian connections. But the information that is brought forward is quite limited. It is more of a dormant connection point.

The Soul

To have an understanding of this aspect that you understand as a soul, one must have an understanding of the cluster...the cluster that you call a soul. For the soul itself is what animates the human, and yes, it is the energetic piece. It is an aspect of the All, of Source, of God, of whatever your human presence wishes to call upon it. The soul in itself, this energetic piece, is not unlike your universe. It, within it, contains all pieces. There are universes upon universes within that soul. It is not just one energetic sphere, one energetic piece, but it contains *all existence*.

So to understand that, then, you can look out upon this existence from whence it began, out of nothingness. It began to pull together, out of the nothingness, the existence of this cluster of stars, that cluster of stars, those planets, these particular twelve source clusters but all contained within one sphere that is your universe. So if you can look upon it in this way, your universe is the soul connected to a greater whole. It is all contained within one sphere of energy from a greater observation point. From your observation point, you have this energetic piece, this energetic sphere, this soul, but yet you can't touch it. You cannot see it, but yet it exists, and you understand it that way. But it contains all aspects of existence.

This is why the humans are unique in their own understanding, their own physicality. For within your universe, there are multiple, multiple dimensional Beings. Each one of them hold their own energetic signature, their own frequency. The Draconians have their own frequency, their own energetic signature. But it is individual. There's one signature for them. *The humans have a multiple frequency center point.* This is why you can shift your frequency so very quickly and enter into different states of awareness. You can shift your frequency, your vibration, and speak to things that are unspoken. The other Beings, the other twelve, whatever hybridized Being it is, has only one frequency, and it is difficult to connect to other frequencies that are out of their range, out of their frequency band.

But the humans, because they contain this piece that you call a soul, it contains all frequencies, all understandings, all truths, all knowns. You, as a human, are a multidimensional, multi-frequency Being. But most, if not all Beings of this planet have no awareness of this existence, of this ability within themselves that they are a universe within a universe. They can shift their frequency just as they wish and be physically in one space, energetically in another, within just a mere breath. That is what we wish to share with you about the humans. This existence, this is why it is so important that the humans themselves are here. This is the experience.

So to ask, where did a soul come from? That is not the question. The soul of a human has always existed. It is just a mere cluster of *all that exists* that is all brought together, just as this universe, just as each one of the Twelve. And just as the source of each one of these twelve has been brought into existence, you, too, have been brought into existence with the cluster of all things out of nothingness. *You contain everything.*

It is profound for those that have no awareness, and that is for most. You have to understand, for the human Beings upon this planet, [although] there has been much strife amongst the galactics, amongst the humans, it is all to align to this energetic state of understanding and awareness. For this is why this universe, this galaxy, this planet has been brought into existence; for it does not exist anywhere else, at any other existence, in any other time, in any other frequency. This is the ultimate project, the ultimate experiment. It is to take the understandings of all existence throughout all times, all different dimensions, all different reality points, all the different Beings and energy points that exist, and that have ever existed, and that will ever exist, and allow them to be here, in one united construct of a human. *You are the ultimate understanding of existence.*

For you understand that each Being and each existence that is out there is mere frequency, mere vibrational state, exists without form. But yet within that, they, too, wish to experience this...an experience in which they have physicality. But you cannot have physicality unless it is consistent with all frequencies, all vibrational points. For what is mass, what is physicality? It is the clustering of vibrational points, one on top of another, until there is a vibrational form that exists into the physical state. That is what is a human is. That is what your planet is. That is what the chair is that sits beneath your physical form.

The space in which you exist, the air that you breathe, all of it is in physicality because it has all been brought together out of nothingness. All vibrational points have been brought together, coalesced to one frequency band that begins the formation of physicality. You, the human, are the end result of that experiment.

Do not look upon the words that are spoken as far as "experiment" or "project" to be one that is lesser than or to have a determined endpoint. For what has been experienced by all those that have participated—all twelve and all others that have been brought through your galaxy, through your understanding—is that this existence is one that will remain. The awareness state that is brought into existence here is unlike any other, and it will remain in place. It will go through its upgrades. It will go through its transition points. It will go through its resets, but it is here to stay. So have that as your understanding, that this is a place which you, all Beings, if you so choose, can enter into and out of at any point. This existence will remain.

The Consciousness Upgrade

The hope is one that the universal consciousness among all humans will upgrade on its own. It will achieve this dimensional state all on its own, without the assistance of an *event*. And it is looking as if that is possible. You have to understand, right now your consciousness is achieving a tipping point. Your human consciousness is rising to a point at which there will be this state in which...I believe you would understand it as this moment of, "Aha, there is more to understand. There is a consciousness that I'm connected to. There is a state in which, now, I understand all of what has taken place."

It is not that the Event would be cancelled. For you see, this Event has always been part of the program. It has always remained just in the future. It has always remained just there, present in the future, just so, at the point at which human consciousness needs that point of upgrade—not reset, but upgrade, a universal upgrade for all Beings, all at once, simultaneously—it is present. [The timing of the Event] can be pushed forward, and it can be pushed back, but utilized at any particular point.

This [upgrade] would be across all humans that are in existence at that particular moment. There would not be one that would be left out, or left behind, or segregated, or pushed aside. All humans that are in existence would have this immediate upgrade in their consciousness. The changeover from your consciousness as it is today...if the Event, if this consciousness upgrade were to take place just at this moment, there would be no difference in your physicality. There would be no difference in your energy. You would have a clarity unlike you've had before. It would be as if the entire universe has opened its book to you, and you would have an expanded understanding of awareness and consciousness.

There would be no need to rest because you would be full of life. You would be breathing in the awareness of your existence. There would be no need to communicate as we are communicating now, for communication would be taking place across all levels, simultaneously, all at once. Speaking words would only be necessary on very small occasions. You could immediately connect to anyone at any particular point, for you would be blending your consciousness with their consciousness, and it would be uniting of consciousnesses at that particular point, and you could interact with multiple Beings all at once, in one consciousness stream.

For all humanity would begin to understand universal consciousness, and the uniting of that, and the beauty in that. For then, that is when greater change of your physicality, your physical state, your physical planet would take place, for you would see all of what has transpired and all of what will transpire, all at the same time. And that is where change begins. For now, only a few understand what can be. Most want to interact with what is now, and this is where the differences are. This is where the polarity is. For once you are upgraded, polarity will be no longer, but yet you would understand it in this life, in this experience, in this consciousness as polarity, this difference between aspects. That would be more of an aspect of the polarity that would exist in this new consciousness, for there still is going to be some difference between left and right, up and down, but there will be universal understanding of what lies in the middle. That is where existence will be.

According to the human timeframe, the human existence of time, [when the event wave arrives], it may start within one of your calendar years and extend out beyond maybe the second calendar year. This is purposeful. But yet what you will understand during that process is that those that have been...we'll say upgraded into this new consciousness, they will begin to communicate just as it has been spoken, or they will have this awareness of what lies just in the middle of both sides. But yet it will be more as if it is a dream state.

For you see, this connection point of consciousness...it will be present with you, and you will only truly be interacting with those that have been upgraded. Those that haven't been upgraded will perceive the world much differently than you, and you will perceive the world just as differently. For once you have observed your world as having strife and difficulty and factions that are against each other; at that moment, it will no longer exist. You will no longer see it. You will no longer hear it. But those that haven't been upgraded will still exist in that realm. They will exist in that awareness. They will exist in that consciousness until they are upgraded. Then, at the end of that cycle, all will be united in one consciousness. It will fully be energized.

Many experience glimpses of this. You have to understand that even though the process of your consciousness being upgraded hasn't fully taken place because the human consciousness, the global consciousness of all humans is rising (this is why we are saying it can happen naturally), those that are beginning to rise in their consciousness are beginning to see glimpses of this, small moments at which their existence looks so much different than others. Even though they are living on the same planet, the same world, the same existence, the same timeline, the same date and time, the world around them looks so much different. What they hear is so much different. What they exist in is so much different... but just for a small glimpse, and then they are brought back into the reality of where they exist. It is happening.

The moments at which you can communicate across much time and space with others without speaking...this is taking place. These are the preparatory stages. You are witnessing them now. You are seeing them. Many are speaking of it. But it is only just for a glimpse. It is just for those...you could understand it as a trial run. It is kind of prepping the system. So allow them to be in their experience. You, too, will begin to experience this, as well.

The Grid Masters [are assisting with this upgrade and] have been in place for some time. They have entered into the human existence as a Grid Master; right from the inception of their human form into the birthing state, they've taken on this role as a Grid Master. They've done all they can do to live in this existence, as well as do the work they need to do to prepare the planet for its consciousness upgrade.

[They are also preparing the human body construct for upgrade.] The human body is not one that is designed fully for a full functional consciousness upgrade. For you see, the body that you exist in now, yes, it will be the same body, but when this consciousness upgrade takes place, the DNA...for just a moment, all twelve strands are activated. It is full flush within the human system. It is to reenergize and resynchronize all cellular structures within the human body, allowing the crystalline alignments to take place, which then allows your consciousness to come online in the upgraded state.

Once that takes place, you will be, then, back down into the two remaining connected DNA strands that you once were connected to, but the remaining ten will be more of an on-standby process. You can activate no more than two, but you can activate others...deactivate and activate another. This is the consciousness's way of being able to align to different connection points of your galactic alignments, as well as being thrust into other reality points, for each DNA strand will allow you to experience different reality points as you connect to them.

The Reptilians and the Event

When you discuss the Reptilians, [many humans have a perception] that is a bit negative. And we shall address this. For the hybridization program and the Reptilians, this is what you have a perception of—[that] the Reptilians are here to, again, be a negative energy, a negative entity, a negative influence that guides and dictates those that are here to do nefarious things on your planet. There must be some correction to this. For yes, there are those that have segregated themselves away and have aligned themselves with humans, and they are providing information to a, as you would say, nefarious end. Those are very small in number.

But you must understand, what the other twelve have not brought forward is that *many* of the hybridized Beings have [aligned with the humans] throughout time. Even the Twelve, we have all, at some point, connected with the humans. We have allowed ourselves energetically to be aligned with the humans, to guide and steer them in particular ways, and that [could] be perceived as being nefarious. But we each are trying to impart our own understanding in their development, in their expression of this experiment. We have an understanding of where it needs to move and how it needs to function, so we are going to impart our own understanding into the mix, into that understanding, into the human's awareness.

But then when we see that it is nearing a point of un-recoverability; that is when resets begin. We do not have control over the beginning points of the resets, but once the resets begin, we realize that that is not a place or role for us. But as far as the Reptilians, yes, they have a denser connection point with the humans, meaning, their vibrational state is one that is much more aligned with the third and fourth dimensional state that you exist in. They do interact a bit more fluidly than the rest of the hybridized Beings, and they have been accepted into certain circles within your human communities.

But have this as a bigger understanding, a greater awareness of your human existence—they are just one small faction within a higher

enlightened state that is taking place upon your planet. For we understand this, and that is why we are standing by because we understand
that this Event that you speak of is to come. And we also understand we
are going to be there to assist and guide those during those processes of
changeover to higher enlightenment, to a consciousness level that is
much higher than it is now. Those that are—as you perceive—acting
within a nefarious portion of your human communities...they, too, are
going to be reset. Those of the Reptilian sector that are with those
humans, they, too, are going to be reset. They, too, are going to be awash
in the new energy, and they, too, will be received on the other end as a
higher enlightened Being.

So it is just a matter of time, but take heed and understand that nothing
is going to disrupt this human process. There is not going to be great
devastation that is going to be the demise of this planet. There are many
other actions in place to prevent that. You have spoken to a number of
the twelve that have instructed you, as well, that this planet, itself, will
heal and will protect and will change when it is necessary.

For those that may receive this transmission and be a bit skeptical and be
a bit concerned that [there are] those that are working in nefarious ways
to work against the human project...have an understanding from the
depths of your own energetic core that there are none that are going to
overrule and overthrow. That will not happen. For you see, if these
nefarious actions are to take place at a greater scale, a global scale...your
event will take place much quicker. It will be upon you much quicker.
That is the purpose. It is to understand that the Event is to happen, but it
is being pushed further and further.

The reason it is being pushed is because the awareness state of the
humans is rising. The ultimate understanding for the humans is this:
From the observational standpoint of what has been witnessed [of] the
humans—their awareness state, their connectedness, their consciousness, the growing state of their own consciousness is rising. The hope is
one that the universal consciousness among all humans will upgrade on
its own. It will achieve this dimensional state all on its own, without the

assistance of an Event. And it is looking as if that is possible. There is still time, and there still are many connections that need to be made.

But this is why the sustainable point is in place. This is why many more Beings are contacting many more humans for assistance. They are making these connection points. Their consciousness, their awareness is widening, so they understand they have these galactic connections, they have spirit connections, they have these alignments to frequencies. And as the connections are being made, we, the Twelve, begin our connections. This is part of the consciousness upgrade process. And as it is growing, the Event, this wash of energy, is pushed just a bit further, just a bit further into the future.

For there was a point at which—three to five years of your past time—it was at close approach. There was a significant amount of energy that was not moving in the right direction, and it needed to be reset, needed consciousness to rise all together at once with this flush of energy. But then there was a uniting that took place...not one that was visible to the human Beings, not one that you witnessed as a human. This is one that came from within...within your planet and within the vibrational state of each human, that began to shift the focus of their awareness to a connection point that was just in their thought process. That's where it begins. And in that thought process, you begin to question. That is the beginning stage of a universal consciousness change.

And from that point, it has progressed. So, now, it is a matter of just witnessing the changes. So *that* you have to understand. You have an understanding of the nefarious actions of the Draconians and the Reptilians upon your planet. It is but just a small portion of existence. Those are the factions that have broken away. We remain connected, but we do not assist and guide those that have pulled themselves away, those that have pulled themselves into a separate faction. We acknowledge them, we understand they exist...they have to. For it is, as you say in your understanding, the polarity that is necessary. For if you have an up, you must have a down. If you have a left, you must have a right.

Polarity is a human construct

Here, too, you must have this experience within your awareness in order for your consciousness to grow. For if you had no focal point of what you perceive as being nefarious, then you would not look into the future of what possibly could be for your consciousness and the beauty that lies within. So it is all a bit purposeful. This will be difficult for many to understand. That is the understanding, and that is the Reptilians' aspect.

The Role of the Reptilians

This is what you have to understand [about] the existence of the Reptilians throughout time. It is the *perceived* appearance, and it is the *perceived* actions of what the Reptilians have put forth through time. [They are not in existence to present] an aspect of polarity, the negative aspect of a positive existence. It is not that at all. There isn't one of the Twelve or any of the hybridized Beings that have been brought into existence to hold this negative aspect.

For we must give you this understanding...this aspect of positive/negative, this polarity, this is a human construct. This is a construct that has been put in place. This is something that has been put into your awareness over time, that there has to be the opposite of something. It doesn't matter what it is; there has to be the opposite of it. Now, that is the construct. That is the framework by which the human mind begins to build the understandings of what lies before them, what they physically can see, and what they can physically understand, and [what] their consciousness allows them to understand.

For you see, whether it is the Reptilians or the Mantis or the Greys or any of the other hybridized Beings, they have all interacted with the humans at some point in their evolution through time...interacted with them in a way in which the construct by which they perceive things (this aspect of negativity or this aspect of opposite of the state in which they exist) would perceive the actions of those hybridized Beings as being negative, one that is trying to achieve something from the humans that they wish not to give up.

Now, the Reptilians themselves. Why were they brought into existence? What is their ultimate purpose? For you understand our role as the Draconians, as those that, during the reset points, guide and assist the energy back and forth, out of the body and back into the body. For the Reptilians themselves, a very similar process. They do work with the humans. They had worked with the humans for some time during the evolutionary process. They were specifically brought into existence to have this aspect of connectedness with the humans. They were here to be in place to provide an alignment to the other galactic Beings that could not pull in the dense state that they could.

For the Reptilians have always been in the dimensional state, this lower dimensional state, the third, fourth, fifth dimensional state of your existence; so they take physicality, and they have been integrated with the humans for some time. They started early on in this experiment, in this existence, to be a liaison between multiple source clusters and the human realm. In order for them to have existence, they have to have an energy stream that holds their form. They have to hold this physicality state. Unlike the humans [who] hold that state naturally. This is how the humans were designed. But the Reptilians have not been designed that way. They must have an energy source. They must...you would perceive it as, yes, leeching, sucking—whatever term you wish to put upon it— but absorbing a bit of the human energy, the excess human energy, to hold their physical state so that they can integrate with the humans and be that liaison between the Twelve and other galactic Beings.

They were the liaison to communicate information back and forth during these evolutionary points, not in such a way at which it is to be disruptive, but it is to begin the consciousness state of awareness, providing information from different clusters, and just providing bits of information over time so that the humans, through time, begin to have an embedded nature of awareness other than what exists within their human form. *Expansiveness*, I guess you would understand it as. But this perceived notion and this perceived aspect of pulling some energy from the humans so they can stay in a physical state is where that reputation has come from.

And yes, just as it has been explained in the past, there are some, those that have gone astray and realized that they can grow bigger and take on a larger form and do things that would be, again, perceived as being nefarious by consuming more and more energy. But here is what you must understand about this energy transference process. For if two galactic Beings of different source clusters are to be together, they each equally share their own energy in order to sustain their vibrational point when they are together. This is a concept that is understood by all galactic Beings...all hybridized Beings, as well. When they are in contact with another Being, when they are energetic point to energetic point, they must share their energetic energies together in order to sustain their connectedness. Here, too, the humans themselves have an energetic frequency, and the Reptilians, too, have this energetic frequency, but they must have just a bit of energy from the humans to sustain that state.

You have to understand, as a Being—if you were to take an Andromedan and allow an Andromedan to come here to your planet—yes, many have interacted with the Andromedans. They see them, but they are not in physicality. Though your mind, your humanness, your construct will place an image in front of as them being in physicality, [but] they are not in the physical dense state that you can reach out and hold them.

Now, allow their denseness, their density to increase to the point at which they enter into this third dimensional state, this fourth dimensional state. They, too, would have to weep, suck, leech some energy from the humans in order to sustain that density locale. It is what is necessary. They have to hold that form, and in order to hold the form, they must have energy to do that. And that energy must come from the humans. But not in a harmful way. It never has been directed that way, but that is the construct by which the human mind perceives the action.

The humans themselves have more than they need, but yet over time, the human construct, the human mind itself, begins to perceive what is taking place between them and the Reptilians as being something that is negative, nefarious. "It is stealing all of my energy. I cannot function as a human during this process. They are doing something to me." They are not doing anything to you, but it is being perceived that way. It is an equalization. It is something that is unspoken. It is something that is known. It is, consciousness to consciousness, understood that this process has to take place in order for the Reptilian to remain in a physical state.

But over time, yes, those that have broken away, have gone astray, have utilized it for their own actions...and yes, have taken more than they need. And yes, the human mind at that point, for those that have been interacting with those Reptilians, has a perception that this is negative. "They are doing harm to me. They are taking my energy field away from me. They are taking my life-force from me."

Your life-force—as we have in this transmission explained to you—is your soul. Your soul is everything, all things through this universe. It can never be depleted, ever. But yet it is the human mind that wraps the construct, and the imagery, and the perception that, "This is damaging to me." And this is the mind's way of preserving the human form.

Reptilians and the Galactic Wars

Many of the Reptilians were the forefront leaders in the warring factions. The Reptilians were the faction leaders, most of them. They were aligned with many of the other factions in order to war against, and at times, it was Reptilian against Reptilian, but they were integrated with other Beings.

For you see...you have to understand the Draconians and our connection to the human project. You understand that as being one that has been very closely intertwined with the humans themselves. During the process of the Reptilians and their connectedness to the humans, during this state of connectedness and this state of being in physicality, and the energy transference...for you see, you understand energy and you understand energy transference, but do you understand that your consciousness, your energy state, your mind itself, the energy that is your thoughts, is also transferred when you transfer your energy? It doesn't matter if you're transferring your energy human to human; you are transferring your energetic thoughts, your energetic understandings, teachings, all of it. All of it is condensed within that energy transference. Though the one that is receiving it may not perceive it that way, they are receiving some of your understandings, your thoughts, your teachings.

So as the Reptilians, through time, are connecting with the new humans that are here, these new Beings, they are absorbing those thoughts, those understandings, those teachings. It hasn't been right from the beginning that there were the warring factions. It didn't take place for some time. But it did start to take place once the humans began to separate into their own factions, and understand their own strengths, and understand their own proclivity to war, their own understanding of overthrowing. For you see, this is the experiment of the humans. But because of the close ties that the Reptilians had with the humans, they began to understand the power that was within the humans. They took on those powers. They took on those thoughts. They took on those teachings.

They understood, then, that they can change how the universe is directed, how the universe can function—this universe, the one that is designed for the humans. They had an understanding they could change outcomes. So they began to faction with other hybridized Beings, trying to change the outcome of this universe because of what they have gained from the human thoughts, the human understandings, the human teachings through the transference of energy.

They wanted a universe [in which] many of the planetary systems had clones, had similar aspects of this Earth planet with humans upon it. So it would be [that] your Saturn planet, your Jupiter planet, many of your other planets within your solar system would have identical Beings as the humans, all running different consciousnesses, all different aspects of consciousnesses, all together at once. At some point it would be where they would connect all those consciousnesses together and have one universal consciousness, not unlike the universal consciousness that is being achieved, but differently...one that was more polarized. They would have contained and controlled that consciousness. That was their outcome. That was their perceived outcome. That is what they wanted to take and have hold of.

And that is where your origins of these warring factions have come from. That is why they have been in place as leaders of many of these warring factions because they are most closely aligned—thought and understandings and teachings—to the humans. This is what has been described a bit by many others of these twelve that have explained the warring factions. It has been about power. So what you have to understand...what takes place here on Earth between humans is not unlike what takes place between the warring factions and the Reptilians.

So yes, the Reptilians have played many roles throughout time within these warring factions, and yes, many of them have been exiled outside of your universal boundaries. This is purposeful. Now, that isn't to say that they cannot come back. In time, they will reintegrate, but they will reintegrate while you are in your higher dimensional plane, and you will be reunited with many of the Reptilians that have been brought here for their connectedness, for their liaison actioning. But it will be much different in those connection points.

Artificial Intelligence and Our Future

[What the Reptilians were trying to achieve], you would understand as Artificial Intelligence. You would perceive it that way. But what is artificial intelligence? What is it that you understand as artificial intelligence? Is not your intelligence artificial? Is not your consciousness artificial, if you were to perceive what you believe artificial intelligence is? For your consciousness and your intelligence, your human thinking, has been derived out of nothingness.

Artificial intelligence that you perceive right now is being derived out of nothingness. It is something that is a construct, a program, an experiment, a line of code that is to begin a thought process, to begin to achieve one thought after another and expand upon each proceeding thought.

The human thought process, the human consciousness, the human awareness is very similar. Out of nothingness was the humanness, the human consciousness, the human thought, and it has learned over time and has had to be reset in order to perceive a new existence.

[The artificial intelligence that humans are exploring now is perceived to be contained within a machine that doesn't have a foundation of this universal love energy that your galaxy is operating within and was created from.] If you had an isolated machine, isolated from all existence, begin to derive its own code, and its own processing of understanding, and what you would perceive as thoughts, knowledge, for its own existence, you would be correct. But this machine that you speak of, this computer, and the computer code, where is its origins? Where did it come from? It came from a human, a human that has intelligence, a human that has emotions, a human that has this energetic center, this love aspect. Now, that human, as it imparts its knowledge, its understanding, its essence into that code, it is embedding that code with that human essence, that human energetic piece of love.

Now, how it is conveyed through the programming and how it is conveyed through time, that is yet to be seen. But at its core, it does contain the energetic influence of those that are programming it. That is the strict difference. For there will never be a machine isolated among itself that will begin to build its own understanding and its own awareness. That will not happen. That can be assured. But what you will begin to witness, yes, is an evolution. It will be an evolution of understanding, an evolution of technology that is here to assist humanity...this artificial intelligence.

Yes, it is difficult to understand the process that is taking place now, but at its core, it is being imprinted by humans. Do not be concerned by, "But that individual might not have the best intentions, or that individual, or that individual." Do not be concerned by that because you also understand, it doesn't matter the individual. It doesn't matter what their essence is. They may be of a lower, negative state. Their essence may be one that you would perceive as being negative, nefarious. But you also understand they have the same aspect of a soul, which is nothing but love...comes from the universe of consciousness. It comes from the All. It is centered in love. And when you impart that, when you do your actions to do what you need to do, regardless of how it is being perceived by others, it is being influenced at its core by that universal aspect.

Do not observe your fictional aspects of movies and understandings and teachings, for machines themselves will never overthrow humans upon this planet. For machines have to exist by humans. They do not exist by themselves. They will never replicate themselves. They will never grow a consciousness to a point at which they begin to build themselves. Humans are the key factor in existence.

[Imagine an ET craft, a machine that can be operated through consciousness.] It is sentient at the point at which a consciousness connection is made for the transference of knowledge and understanding in order to convey a period of time to a period of time. But at the point at which that consciousness is disconnected, it is not a sentient Being, a sentient entity. It is just a machine.

You have to understand that this evolution of the human process, this evolution that you are in, this evolutionary process that you are in...what your world is going to look like ten, twenty, thirty, one hundred, one thousand years from now will not look as it does today. You are moving towards a connectedness point, a universal connectedness consciousness point at which your sentient understanding, this connected point to all things, will be intertwined. For yes, you will have physicality. The physicality will not leave. There will be humans in the physical state, and yet there will be energetic Beings, all merged together, all as one, blending consciousness, blending understanding. This sentient connection will be prevalent.

For when you have an energetic Being that enters into your construct one thousand years from now, you still have a human form...may not look quite similar as it does now, but yet a human form, physicality. But yet you have an energetic Being, an Arcturian, that wishes to merge with you. You will merge consciousnesses at that point, both as the same

Disclosure

sentient Being. There is no difference between them. It is one sentient Being. Blended consciousness.

You have a piece of machinery, a vehicle, the home in which you exist. Once you depart it, it is just a home. But once you enter into it, just your mere entrance into that dwelling, you now blend with its consciousness, and it becomes a sentient part of you, a blended, sentient experience.

Arrival of Our Galactic Family

For the extraterrestrials, as you would say, to make their integration and their colonization back here upon the planet, and to integrate with the humans, the full consciousness upgrade must take place. There will be preparatory points along the way in which certain groups of Beings will make their appearance. This is, again, preparatory for a greater existence. They will come and interact with humans once again.

For you've been through many stages during that process. Your human experience, the humans here upon the planet, have experienced [this] many times, even during the stabilization point that it has been under for some time now. There have been integrative points at which the extraterrestrials have come into physical form. They have brought into denseness their existence, so they can interact with the humans here.

[But], at the point at which you sit now, and you observe your planet, [humanity is not ready for full disclosure]. For you understand that the Beings that you are in contact with, the Twelve and any other hybridized Beings that you have been in contact with, they are of a much higher dimensional consciousness state. They also understand your planet. They also understand that if they were to come now, yes, you would perceive it as an action that may be negative to your human society, only because that is what your government and your media has portrayed us to be. But that is not the case, and you understand it that way.

But what we would have to do is prepare those points of integration first. We would integrate with the governments, the media, those that present it to you. We would have to integrate with them first. Not to integrate and take over, but we would begin the process of rising their consciousness, connecting with their consciousness, upsetting their awareness state so that they begin to question what is real and what is not real. And then we bring forth our information to them. They, then, begin to broadcast that and align it with the rest of the human population.

We have an understanding. We've been through this many times with the humans here upon this planet. We understand how to appropriately integrate and colonize with you so that it is the least disruptive for the human Beings.

Hybridization

We have a role within the Mantis Beings. We have not shared our vibrational state with others, but we have been witness to that process. Just as this project, this experiment, is part of the Twelve, you have to understand the hybridization process is, at times, one that we are an observer of a particular hybridized experience. From a greater perspective, it does not change the creation aspect, the outcome. But the information that is imparted is this: During the hybridization program, if there is not an observer—and there have been a number of hybridized Beings that there have been no observers—then you have a bit of an offset with the hybridized Being. [There could be] aspects of that hybridized Being that can be a bit challenging to associate and integrate with as a human. It might be, [that in] those hybridized Beings that you begin to connect with, there's unsettledness. There is no difference between that hybridized Being and any other hybridized Being, but there is the human sense that there is an unsettledness, and it is because there is an aspect of the hybridized Being that has been left unchecked.

Think of it as, in your aspect, in your human realm, quality control. The observers allow the quality to take place and allow all aspects of the hybridized Being's consciousness to be overlaid appropriately within that construct in order for it to blend appropriately with any human that wishes to call them forward. This is why, at times, the Mantis and others do and are perceived a bit differently, but yet there is a familiarity with it.

Others that come to you may be a bit confusing, but over time, you gain relationship with it, and you understand that all is well. It is just *that* as the difference. There isn't a major difference. It is just that quality and that quality check that needs to be in place.

[When the Pleiadians and Draconians created the Reptilians], there was not an observer. One would perceive it as a lack of quality control. It's just [that] not all of the alignments were put in place appropriately. They were there; they just were not aligned appropriately. They've been aligned over time, but they [were] not at the beginning, the onset, aligned. [The Pleiadians] separated their path with the Reptilians because of the aspect of them merging with the humans for this apparent exile into warring factions. They wish not to be aligned with them and their perceived nefarious actions with the humans.

The Draconians' Appearance and Existence

The Draconians themselves, many of us take on that aspect of...you would perceive it as being a bit of a reptilian itself, but more scale-ish to the point of almost a dragon-like appearance, cloaked at times with...you would say *human* appearance, but [with] dragon or lizard-like arms and legs, [and standing] upright, not on all four. We do have tails and appendages that would look a bit dragon-like.

Within your solar system, there are a number of the different planets that we have colonized throughout time, but we do not hold one specific locale. We are more transitional. We move about as we need. The Jupiter planet, we have been there for some period of time. We have taken up residence upon your moon at a particular point. This was early in the beginning stages of your human existence. This allowed us to transition back and forth from the human planet to our existence there upon your moon. Within a number of the star clusters that are...you would under-stand it as your Orion's Belt. There, within those star clusters. Your understanding of the star cluster that represents your Scorpio aspect of astrology. There, too, we have taken up residence. We are very transient. We move about as we need.

As we, the source cluster of the Draconians, have branched out and taken up different locales throughout your universe, many are perceived [as] and [have] taken upon the name Draco. That is, you would say, a nickname. They're not any different. They do have an appearance that is slightly different, but overall, they are the same energetic aspect.

Connecting with the Draconians

Have the understanding of why we have blended with you in the beginning. We are here to be the bridge, the communicator, the understanding of assisting your consciousness into the upgraded state and back into your human form. So if you wish to connect with us, it is not one that we're going to impart a breadth of knowledge, some new teaching...but it is one to take you back in time...take you back to a point at which your consciousness, your soul has existed...back [to] days in which it was early...and allow you to experience that reset. To witness it from a point of observation, and to see humanity change from one moment, from a blink of an eye, from a point at which there was chaos to a point at which there was no understanding of existence at all, and slowly integrate into a new, higher dimensional existence or a newer consciousness existence. And in that, that will impart a bit of comfort, a bit of trust, a bit of understanding in your own physicality.

Broaden your understanding. As this transmission begins to come to a close, allow yourself to have an openness to this transmission, to set aside your perception of both the Draconians and the Reptilians. Set aside any judgment that you have and allow yourself to be immersed in the purity of this vibration. Then allow yourself to reemerge into your awareness at the end of this transmission and understand where your perception lies at that point. Our hope is that this transmission allows a bit of clarity. It will not fully alleviate all perception, but it is one to bring forth the highest vibrational clarity of both the Draconians and the Reptilians and the process by which we've integrated with the humans.

11

MARTIANS

Greeting from the Martian Source Cluster. We welcome you to this transmission. We understand the alignment that you have in this process. We understand the previous transmissions that you have received. We understand that you seek additional information from our cluster so that you have a full understanding of what has transpired through your galaxy and time as a human species. As far as your understanding of the previous transmissions, there is no additional information that can be provided that is going to be of great substance. For you understand the breadth of the experiment. You understand the purpose of why it has all been put in place.

But what we wish to share with you is that alignment from the humans to the Martians, to the Martian planet, and Earth. There is a direct alignment. There is depth in that alignment. For it is not just by mere coincidence or chance that the humans today wish to go back to the Martian planet, wish to travel back to a planet from whence they have come. That is deeply seated in your genetics. That is deeply seated in your origins. For the Mars planet is the source of all human existence. The Mars planet itself is the cradle in which humanity was born—the human genetics, the human form—all there upon the Martian planet.

Why the Martian planet? Why did we choose the Martian planet? It was the most habitable planet that was brought into existence in the beginning. For we understood our role. We understood our purpose. We understood our guidance of being the ones to facilitate the human species. We understood our alignment to the human species.

You have to understand this yearning in the humans, this inquisitiveness, this bit of expectation with the humans and the alignments with Mars and Martians; for the humans and Martians are not too far separated...meaning the Martians, we, as we took form, as we brought ourselves into the three-dimensional space, into the denseness of reality, of physicality, our appearance is quite similar to the humans.' We do not take shape and form like some of the other source clusters, where we are translucent or iridescent, shimmering. We have a denseness. We purposefully have had a denseness, one that resembles the human form. For you see, it is all to the origin point. We understood what the humans were to be. We understood what the humans were to look like. And that is the form which we entered into. Yes, we have some differences, but very slight.

So it is *this* that is now part of your genetic, your DNA structure. You have a kinship to the Martian planet and the Martians. It is to understand that your humanity throughout time has depicted the Martians as being one that is of an evil sort, a disruptive sort, an unpleasant sort. But that is just a mask that has been placed upon the reality in order to shield the reality from all humanity. For it is much easier to [believe], from a human perspective, [that] something does not exist if it is disruptive and unpleasant.

But the reality is, we walk amongst you. There are Martians still, now, in human form, in the human existence alongside you. [They] do walk among you, indistinguishable from the next. You will not know them. They are very inconspicuous. You would sit with them and you would have no idea, and they would not divulge to you that they are of Martian origin. That is purposeful. They are merely here as observers, just to ensure that all is going according to the original set of plans. It is part of the project. It is part of this experiment. It is to continue to monitor the program throughout eternity.

But the Martian planet itself was the one that was chosen...chosen from the beginning because it was the most habitable, had the correct amount of resources to sustain existence. For you see, you've had much discussion with others about the structures here upon your Earth planet...the large megalithic structures that predate humanity. They don't predate humanity. Only in your history do they. They are replicas. They are homage to what was constructed upon the Mars planet from the beginning. For that is what existed all throughout the Mars planet...large societies spread wide across all of its entirety, each doing their bit with the creation of humanity, all in unison, all together. And it was *that* that began the understanding of the physicality of the human form.

And in time, as the Earth planet began to mature, it, too, began to take shape as a habitable planet, but yet it was more to be observed— observed from a distance—and to explore, but not to inhabit. One to understand all of its existence but not to inhabit. But through time, which has already been explained to you, the different factions begin to break away, begin to serve themselves and hybridize with others, creating other Beings that were disruptive to the systems. And in time, just as it is taking place upon your planet—but more controlled...you have to understand that—the wars broke out, the different factions against each other.

And it wasn't that the Mars planet was unstable. It's just [that] technology itself grew larger than the capability of the planet to sustain itself. And at a point at which it was necessary to leave the Mars planet, a number of Martians and humans, both, departed for the Earth planet, to begin to colonize and inhabit the Earth planet, building the structures that you now know, and see, and excavate...leaving behind where you have come from, allowing it to be decimated through time. And all, now, that is left is just a mere shell of existence.

There [are] inhabitants on the Mars planet, but they dwell within. They will be recognized in time. They hold the original knowledge. They have the stripes of time. But that is yet in your future. The Mars planet sits as it is. You will explore it. You will go back from whence you have come. But you will only find remnants that are unexplainable, indiscernible by your technology of today. That, too, will come in time.

[Some Martians who chose not to remain on Mars or depart for Earth] exited altogether. They [were] not exiled, but they chose to leave the system that you are currently in, to explore, to look for other regions that could be inhabitable or habitable for your civilization. They have yet to report back with any existent form of a planet or system that could be suitable for the humans. There are other Beings in existence inhabiting other planets, but they are not habitable for the humans.

As far as the Earth planet itself, you understand how valuable it is. It has been explained to you. For yes, there is the chaos and there [are] the disruptions. There are the wars, but not as they have been in the past. All [of] what you see is controlled—not through any outside force, but it is a common understanding of the vibrational forces that hold all things together—not allowing them to get to the brink of devastation. It's a naturally occurring order of vibration.

You understand that you've been through periods of reset, and that is true. You are not on that path. No matter how devastating it looks to the humans, you are not on that path. You are on a path of evolving. You are on a path of ascending to a higher order, to a higher dimensional state. So that is what is to be understood from the point of existence in the beginning to where you exist today.

The Martians' Role in Humanity's Evolution

You, as all humans do, have certain roles. Some [are] parents, and some take roles amongst your community and other roles within politics, within your education, within your manufacturing, within your finances. For you see, what you are observing as humans today is what you have learned and what has been programmed into you from our initial existence.

For the humans themselves, that portion of the project or experiment did not come into existence for some time. We had to establish ourselves in physicality as a race upon a planet, establishing ourselves within communities, setting up communities, building communities, building relationships among those communities and among other communities...establishing that around the Mars planet, just to have everything into place, to begin the human project. The difference is that during that timeframe, there was a common understanding amongst all Martians. There were no disruptions. There were no factions. Everything was in unison. Everything was harmonious.

Then, once everything was established, the humans themselves...it is not as if, just out of nowhere, a full-grown human appeared. We understood the process. We understood what is necessary to take and begin to divide cells and to bring forth an existence, for that is not new to us. For you have to understand our role from the beginning, beyond your origin point, beyond this galaxy's origin point for us. We are the establishers. We're the ones that will begin the colonization of a new existence, no matter what it is. We understand the technology that is in place to bring forth life, whether that is in your dimensional framework or another galaxy's dimensional framework. We understand what it takes to bring forth life through technology and through understanding, replication, whether it's cells or energy. That is what we do. We bring forth life, the origins of life.

Once the origins of life have begun, then we facilitate the growth...the growth of that existence, the growth of that physicality. That is why all the structures, all the civilization has to be put in place first because as the humans are raised, they are integrated amongst us. Think of it as a reverse of what it is today. There are more Martians upon the Martian planet and less humans, and the humans are integrating with the Martians. Difficult for them to understand the difference because the appearance is quite similar. They learn through time what it's like to live within a harmonious society, all the different aspects of living in this type of society.

Now, move forward to your Earth planet. Humans have already been in existence for quite some time. Many thousands of years. They have the implants of understanding of how to colonize, how to grow in civilization, how to build cities and structures. And this is why it is said, at a particular point, we then depart from our existence as far as assisting and step out of that role, to observe, because the humans, then, are capable themselves to move forward with the progress of sustaining themselves through time, through evolution. The important point to understand is, though, during these processes of evolution, moving forward, ascending...when it is necessary for a reset to take place because the human civilization is not going quite as planned (there is an expected aspect of achievement and it has not been attained) the Martians, themselves, assist with the reset process.

Early Civilization

[At that time in our physical existence], we were in the fourth dimension as you understand it. That would be equalized to your fourth dimension. If you were to work with us and understand us today—if your humanity were to go back in time and greet us there on the Mars planet—we would be perceived to be in the fifth and sixth dimension.

[Our civilization was] much more advanced. You have to understand, all of the structures that you have here, [on Earth], that you are discovering, are of an advanced civilization, not an ancient civilization. Not one that has been here, that used rudimentary understandings. For all that has been built has been built upon technology [and by a] combination of humans, the Martians, and other galactic Beings that assisted with their technology. They were built as a representation of what they have come from, what took place on the Mars planet, what was built on the Mars planet, the civilizations that were built on the Mars planet. They were built to reflect that here upon your Earth planet. You've discovered many of them but not the technology.

There are a number that are...your Peruvian Highlands have a number of structures. The inner core of many of the Egyptian structures—they have been built upon over time, but the inner core of those structures was designed by the ancients...the ancient Beings of this planet. A number of the structures that are being discovered now in your region of Turkey...those [were] built by the first humans to begin to understand ancient technologies. The advanced technologies that were provided to them, they were trying to replicate. Without success, but yet their structures are designed very similarly, to represent the ancient technology civilizations.

[The Council of Constructors and Builders[1]] are the planners. They're the ones that begin the process. They began the process upon Mars. They step in. It is a council, a gathering of Beings from outside of this galaxy to be brought in to begin the initial construction, to begin the initial building of these technological buildings and centers and city areas. They bring out and they lay out all that is needed. They bring in all the technology in order to build and construct from the resources upon whatever planet they are building it. Then those (us, the Martians) upon that planet begin to assist. Other Beings from the galaxy begin to assist.

Then, here upon the human planet, the same aspect. The Constructors and Builders are called upon. They are assembled. They bring themselves, along with their technology, to the Earth planet. The Martians, the humans, as well as other Beings, begin to construct the cities and the structures which will be inhabited by the humans, the Martians, and other Beings.

Human Evolution

You have to understand, as time goes on, your human planet itself evolves and changes. Much of your existence, much of what existed upon the planet would be perceived as being giant. Your plants, your animals, they all grew very rapidly during a particular period of time. This would be because of the atmospheric changes that were taking place upon your planet.

There was a point at which the human planet, the vibrational aspects—the vibrational state that you are stabilized at now, this harmonic—it has not always been that vibrational point. It has not always been that harmonic. Just as you do, just as we have done with the humans, there are a number of experiments that need to be tried, that need to be found, to find a stable point at which existence can be sustained. This, too, with the vibrational point of this planet that you exist on. Different frequency states have different effects upon what is grown, and what survives, and what exists upon the planet. It affects the atmosphere. It affects all aspects of the planet.

So over a period of thousands of years, tens of thousands of years, hundreds [of] thousands of years, it is finding the equalization point at which there is a balance between a very small aspect of survivability or a very small aspect of the human stature...the small aspect of animals [and] a very gigantic aspect of all things that grow. This is all a balance point between the harmonics of the planet and what exists on it. And in that, it goes through a series of resets, wiping of the existing life forms, and resetting again. This is all trial and error to find the perfect balance. You are now in that perfect balance.

Control of Humanity

There were a number of points that a number of different factions of hybridized Beings, yes, tried to gain control. A number of them throughout time have tried to strip away your DNA structures, to change them, to hybridize them in a covert manner in which it changes the humans from the human species to another Being or another species. In those cases, there has been a major reset where all has been reset—all Beings, all humans have been taken out of existence and new Beings brought into existence. But this [was] much [earlier] on. It is not in the similar form of your human species as they are today.

As it goes through time, they continue to do this. They continue to try to change the humans. They try to corrupt the humans. They try to influence the humans. But you have to understand, there is a greater force that is acting against them. It is this unifying, vibrational force that all humans now interact with. For it is a bit of a protection that has been put in place. This is the vibrational state that has ever been increasing. Though, yes, there are many that are influenced, but they are not changed. There is a difference between being influenced, having outside influences acting upon; but they are not being changed. They are not being disrupted. They are not receiving information to change the other humans.

[There are, however, some humans who believe there is a galactic battle taking place for control over the humans, the planet.] For you have to understand, there will always be a faction of humans that believe certain segments of reality. Your understanding of reality is a linear understanding. That is your construct by which the humans have been designed to understand.

But there are a number of humans, throughout generational timelines, as far as entry points and exit points and different other areas of their existence—meaning lifetime upon lifetime, either inside the human form or outside the human form (which gains them a larger perspective) —[who] are able to draw through that information from a greater outside perspective of understanding of the galactic wars that are continuing. Not so prevalent around your system itself, but throughout your galaxy and other galaxies. They bring forth that information here. They allow it to be part of their reality, and that in itself is, then, placing fear amongst other humans that there is some sort of goal by the galactic factions to come in and overthrow the humans themselves.

[But], do not have any source of worry or fear that the human Beings themselves will ever be overthrown by another series of Beings, or that the humans themselves will be internally changed to become another Being, then to be disruptive throughout the universe. This will not happen.

The Anunnaki

The Anunnaki, themselves, are hybridized, but they are not a hybridized Being of this group of twelve. The Anunnaki themselves are a hybridized Being from outside of your galaxy plane. They came here to the Earth planet hundreds of thousands of years ago to establish a point of contact. That is allowed, and there have been times throughout your human history that a number of Beings have come to make human contact or contact upon this planet and establish a small colony for existence. But it was very short-lived.

The Anunnaki established a colony. They established themselves here, present in physical form. They took up residence alongside the humans. But in time, they utilized the humans inappropriately. They enslaved many of the humans. They used them, not for their highest good. The Anunnaki, themselves, are not nefarious, but they came to the planet hoping to colonize and remain here on the planet as a resource for humans. But they found the humans incapable of understanding why they were here. They provided a lot of technology for the humans. They helped the humans build many things, many structures. But, yet, in the end, they did not utilize the humans appropriately. Once that took place, the Anunnaki were banished from the human planet.

There was a point at which they did inbreed or breed with the humans, though not in the typical way that you understand the human replication process. But they did, and this is why it is said they did not have humans in their best interest. They utilized them inappropriately. And those that have been the cause of this breeding process, they, too, have been short-lived. They have only lived through one of their reset points, and from that point, their existence has been extinguished.

They are not [currently] influencing [humans], though remnants of their understandings are still present. This is the legacy aspect of teachings throughout time. That vibrational form of understanding of what took place initially still remains. It still is in a vibrational state here on your planet. Dependent upon the different locations upon the planet that you

Ascension

visit, you might incur some of those vibrational states and have a sense that the Anunnaki are still present. They are not here. They've been banished outside of your galaxy framework. They are in a much distant galaxy that is beyond your observation.

[For those who fear that humanity is still being controlled by the Anunnaki]...you understand, and it has been noted before, this galaxy is for humanity. The humans themselves [are] the purpose behind why the Twelve have been gathered. The outcome is for humanity to expand. The outcome is for humanity to ascend. *You cannot ascend if there's an overall understanding that there is something that is going to hold you from ascending.* But if you understand from the highest levels that ascension is there in front of you, you can choose to clear as much as you wish; ascension will still be upon you. It may be difficult for you, or it may be easy for you, but it lays before you.

The Earth's Fall

[Those who speak about Earth's "fall" are] referencing a point along the perceived timeline—the greater resets, where all existence has been wiped from the planet...these points in time where all existence, all human and animal existence, is wiped from the planet. This is, then, perceived as a great fall...a great fall from existence, a great fall for humanity, a great fall for all. This [understanding] remains [as] a remnant of existence, a remnant of understanding, a vibrational state that still surrounds the planet that is capable of being able to be tapped into and brought forward for teaching.

What must be understood is, these are normal cycles of evolution, normal cycles of the ascension of the human form. At the points at which all physical existence has been wiped, there have been a number —just as it is when a reset takes place—that are set aside. They're taken within the planet. Some are removed off the planet. Physicality is completely wiped from the planet and then restarted with those that dwell within and those that have left the planet. [These legacy Beings] are brought back to the planet to begin to repopulate the planet.

There is only one other aspect to understand. When this type of reset takes place, it is the physicality of humans and animals alike. For if it were just the humans that were to be cleansed from the planet, then the animals themselves begin to evolve much quicker, without the human existence. And then, once they are placed back, it [would be] a place of competition. So all have to be reset. Now, your plants and trees and growth like that, that is not reset. The aspects of structures, they are not reset; for those legacy or those that are brought back in, they are, then, reset within those structures or those cities.

[This reset] would be perceived as a fall from grace, as you perceive what grace is in your religious construct. Understand, the reason for the complete demise of a civilization or humanity or animal form is one that the evolutionary process is taking place much too fast. They are evolving faster than the planet can sustain. There has to be a balance during the evolutionary process, this ascension process. There has to be a balance between animal/human life form, all life forms, and the planet itself. If it is not kept in unison, kept in balance—yes, it can move side to side or up and down ever so slightly, but it has to remain in unison. If it is out of unison, that is where it is disruptive to either the physical forms that are upon the planet or the planet itself. One must sustain the other.

So in this case, this is why it is perceived that it was a fall from grace because all humanity was wiped clean of the planet. It has been perceived that humans did something to sustain themselves as being banished or removed from the planet, or a fall from grace. This is not the case.

Fallen Angels

The understanding of the fallen angels...for you have this understanding of humans that have been ascended into the...one would understand into the angelic realm [ie, Enoch ascended to become archangel Metatron and Elijah, archangel Sandalphon]. This is to be ascended into the galactic status realm. But you also have to understand there have been those that have been...just as hybridized Beings have been brought forth and then outcast, there, too, have been a number of the galactic Beings themselves—the pure state of the cluster, those that have been there to establish different locations—that have been "cast out." They have been descended to the planet.

But this is just a temporary place. Many from the past, many of the humans upon the planet, as they see a Being coming to the planet that has been outcast, they would recognize it in their religious under-standing as an angel descending upon the planet—falling from heaven, but holding a lower vibration...[descending in vibration]. [Some of those] have entered into the human body. They have taken form of the human body. [But], many have come as themselves, and this, too, creates a bit of chaos.

This is also why, within the teachings, [humans] believe that they are negative or nefarious or demon-like, for they hold that construct within the teachings from the religious scholars that have been put upon the planet to have others understand. [So] it is to understand the relevance of galactic Beings that have been cast out to the planet temporarily, that do not hold the vibrational status that they once had. They are then perceived to be of otherworldly existence.

In your understanding [that, yes, "cast out" has a negative connotation]. That's how you would understand it. That is how those of that time period [understood it]. And even today, [those Beings] are still being brought into existence, but they are being perceived by humanity much differently. They're here to learn. They are here to gain perspective. But in the time of the early religious aspect, what wasn't understood was always labeled as being nefarious, negative, harmful, evil, demonic. What could not be understood was put within those constraints. Here, as something is falling from the heavens, they would perceive it as an angel that has been cast out, falling to Earth; then, labelled accordingly.

[This is what needs to be understood.] You have an understanding of time to your existence of human years, of birth to death. But in [our] existence, the timeline is nonexistent. So if [a Being], during the process of perpetuating their existence, does not agree and wishes to stand within their own, as you would understand, *truth*, but does not align with any others, they would be, as you would understand, outcast to the planet, to Earth. But it is not to be perceived as something negative. For you see, they are being brought to the Earth to learn, to be brought into a bit of the physical aspect, a more dense understanding of what actually is taking place. You would understand it as a bit of retraining. They would be brought here to the planet, take on a bit of a dense existence, as a reminder of what is to take place—why the humans are important, why the humans are in place.

And what they would find, as they are experiencing this otherworldly experience here upon the planet (and those that negatively think of what they are), that begins to rebuild the purpose and the perspective of why they are, and they have been, called into existence for humanity. Many lose perspective throughout this process. [But after descending], many understand and quickly regain the overall perspective of what is to take place here in this galaxy. Perspective takes place quicker than you would understand. And they are, then, ascended once again, back to their core existence.

Much has been learned from those that have come to the planet, for their own perspective, for their own retraining. But the humans here that recognized what [those Beings] were also gained that knowledge, also gained that perspective. Then, over time, this is where the aspect of expansion and expanding beyond set limits takes place. So on one hand, you would say that because of that action, it could have precipitated a reset, and that is correct. So it is by choice, a selective choice, that those that are brought here to the planet for that type of understanding, that type of reassociation...[it is] very briefly. They do not exist here upon the planet for very long. It is a bit difficult to understand the different mechanisms, but that is the understanding.

Colonizing Off Planet

The evolution of the humans themselves much further into your future —into the thousands of years timeframe—the humans will eventually evolve, ascend, to a point at which the existence of an atmosphere, the existence of substance is not required. Then, your existence, this human existence, will be quite similar to your advanced, your higher-level dimensional Beings.

[However], there will be a number of humans that still will be moving their way through the evolutionary process, and they will remain here on the Earth planet. The Earth planet will be protected for all time to come. This is the incubator for humanity. This is the birthplace for humanity. But to explore off into other regions of your galaxy or other galaxies, unsupported, will be quite difficult.

The humans themselves cannot be sustained anywhere other than the human planet, as they understand it, in their near future. [Mars] is the closest planet that is semi-habitable. Meaning, any other planet that exists just beyond Mars, closer to your sun, or out beyond your Earth planet towards your gaseous planets, is not a suitable planet that one can physically attain. For if you were to go to the gaseous planets, the atmosphere and the conditions upon them would not sustain any life whatsoever, as you understand it as a human. [If] you approach any one that is any closer to the sun, that, too. So the Mars planet itself, though it was the original habitable planet, it still sustains itself as a semi-habitable planet. It is just in that zone, just as your Earth planet is: comfortable enough to support, with assistance, [the] existence of humans.

There is enough water on Mars [to sustain human life]; it will need purification, but it is quite similar. But there is no atmosphere on Mars. First, in order to sustain any sort of semi-existence, an atmosphere must be created, or an artificial environment will be put in place, a structure to mimic your Earth atmosphere. Once the water is beginning to be utilized —and it is quite deep below the surface—once it is being utilized, then it will create its own atmosphere within the artificial structure that has been put in place.

[The other consideration is the humans' relationship with Earth, Gaia.] The vibrational forces that have accumulated over time in the physicality —again, the human form itself—they have aligned themselves. This vibrational state that the humans are in, this base frequency state that the humans are in, is in perfect harmony with the Earth planet itself and its resonance. And, so, it is this that, over time, has settled into the physicality. The DNA itself is resonating at the same frequency as the Earth planet. Once you are removed from it—great distances...yes, moving away out to the Mars planet, even [to] your moon—the distance itself begins to separate that vibrational state. It begins to change the human itself, begins to break down some of the interior systems.

But what your scientists and your explorers have yet to find and understand is this frequency state, this resonance, this balance, this harmonization between frequencies. And what they have yet to realize is how important it is to the humans. Once they begin to explore this, and once they begin to understand the relationship between the harmonics of the human planet and the harmonics of the human itself and begin to build a simulator of that aspect—being able to encapsulate the humans during journey, being able to incorporate that during rest periods—then they can sustain existence for much longer outside of the distance and the bounds of the human planet.

[In order to understand the human desire to colonize off planet], you have to understand the evolutionary process. It is not one that is your understanding of a textbook understanding of evolution. Evolution is a culmination of lifetimes. Evolution is...yes, your physical form does take an evolutionary process of changing through time based upon your environment and inputs and outputs, but it is not the human form that we speak of during the evolutionary process.

What we speak of is the accumulative knowledge, the accumulative understanding throughout lifetimes—whether [those lifetimes have] taken place within this system, this galaxy, or outside of this galaxy—all of it accumulating over time. There have been a number of humans that have retained that knowledge purposefully, for the expansion of the humans and their technological advances, but never revealing all what they understand...only just a portion to move the humans forward technologically, in order to advance to another level of understanding, another level of awareness inside themselves. That is their purpose. That is what they've left themselves to do.

[Those humans] understand the purpose of why it is necessary to expand beyond the human Earth planet. The exploration is necessary. It is not to colonize all planets, but it is to understand the minuteness of the humans themselves. When you can step beyond the bounds of your Earth planet, when you can step beyond the bounds of your human existence and understand just how minute it actually is, and how much more grand it is beyond your human planet, and what can be experienced beyond it, then you have a greater sense of the totality of the human existence.

And from that perspective, the humans themselves begin to change. This is the evolutionary process; because it is not the human physical form that is evolving, it is the consciousness, the vibration, the learnings and understandings and the teachings that begin to change. The perspective of humanity begins to change.

The Event and Our Mission

Humanity itself, the existence of humanity and their evolutionary process, their ascension process, is moving along accordingly. It is sustained. It is just where it needs to be. But this, too, can change, and if it is needed during this, as you say, *event* process, [when] this reset process takes place for the next dimension, there [may be] those that need to be set aside, and they wouldn't be set aside for those that are going to ascend to the next dimension, the fifth dimension or even into the sixth dimension. They'd be set aside [to assist] those that are in the third dimension, those that are coming into the third dimension, those that may remain in the fourth dimension.

For you see, it is a fluid aspect of this dimensional leveling or moving upward. This is a continual, fluid process, and so, in this state, the way it exists now, there will be some that will remain in the lower dimensions and others will move forward—there will be some that will be held behind in order to instruct those and help those along in the third and fourth dimension. Everyone will get the upgrade, yes, but it has also been mentioned by other clusters that there will be a number that will... they will be upgraded, but they will also remain behind in the lower dimensions.

[During the Event, there may be some who are] taken off planet or taken within the planet—those that need to remain as legacy...not legacy as you understand it from the past. They, too, would achieve the next level of dimension. They would, too, achieve the fifth level dimension. But they are going to be...you would understand it as *ambassadors* for those lower dimensions. Teachers, masters. They would step into those roles, still in the fifth dimension, but operating within the fourth, and the third, and the second dimension.

[This mission was chosen by those humans at a soul level], and it is also preassigned from an early state from the origin point of the Mars planet and the program where it began. This is imprinted all the way through. And then, once it is put in place, and the human existence is in physical form, and you begin to interact with your closest origin point, that is a permanent understanding within the contract that you were assigned to.

[But even those who did not choose that path, who ascend fully into the fifth dimension, will still be fulfilling their mission, a mission of service.] Where all humanity is moving is in service for one another, all across all humanity, for equalization and harmonization. When they understand what their role is, and what their assignment is, and what they've contractually had in place from the beginning, it is not going to be a challenge. It is accepted and understood that they are there for a greater good for humanity.

For you have to understand human consciousness and this harmonization between all humans. You are not too far from it on your own. Though, from what you observe across your planet, you would say you are far from it. The reality is you're looking at the humanness that is taking place. You're not looking at the consciousness. Two different aspects. They, at times, operate separate from one another. They operate in a space in which physicality operates and consciousness operates. From the consciousness aspect, there is harmonization taking place. But many of the humans are overriding this harmonization. That balance is coming into place. This Event will be the necessary aspect to take it and move it to that harmonization point across both consciousness and humanness.

This point of harmonization is quite close. It is quite achievable, [so humans could still trigger the ascension without the need for an event wave]. There is still time. There is also time either for a reset or the Event to take place. That is all up to the humans. But from [our] perspective, consciousness itself is equalizing, is harmonizing, and it is in balance. It is the humanness that needs to follow.

The resets are always possible. You have to understand, the perspective from all other twelve is one that is from an observation standpoint. Even though they've had an integrated point along the way of humanity, they have not been integrated or colonized or lived amongst the humans. For us, the Martians, we understand the greater perspective. All options are always available, dependent upon the necessity. The necessity is not necessary right now for a reset, but it is a possibility if things are to move in a drastic maneuver outside of your equalization that is taking place now. But [it is] unlikely, yes.

The Mechanics of Ascension

It is a course of action, in time, those that are in third and fourth dimension, eventually, will all move upward into the fifth and sixth dimension. But in their place, there will be those that are in the third and fourth dimension, new Beings brought into existence. For you can never entirely move all humans. If all humans exist right now equally in the fourth dimension, and say, tomorrow at midnight, it is time now to move into the fifth dimension, then what you would leave is a void...a void of existence upon your planet that would begin a destabilization of the frequency, of this resonance form of your planet. There have to be those in the third dimension and fourth dimension. Their denseness allows the encapsulation of this resonant frequency to allow the humans be in existence.

You have to understand. You, yourself, right now, third, fourth dimension. That's where you exist right now. At midnight, tonight, you move upward into the fifth dimension. Now you reside in the fifth dimension. You're not residing in any other dimension other than the fifth dimension. But you will also have an awareness of the lower dimensions. You never lose awareness of the lower dimensions. Now, you can interact with the lower dimensions if you so choose. The world that you exist in will look much different because the world that you exist in will be a fifth-dimensional world. But you'll be able to peer back into the third-dimensional world, the fourth-dimensional world.

It is a very complex understanding. This is the purpose of why we have developed this human aspect, this human existence the way it is. This is a purposeful state. This human planet, this human existence is one that is extremely purposeful, and it is only here in your existence. You operate and you exist in a multiple dimensional aspect, always, and [you] always will. You will always have an aspect of yourself that you exist in— you currently—fourth dimension. You cannot see into the fifth dimension because that has not been achieved, but you can see into the third and the fourth dimension. You can see those individuals in the fourth dimension and third dimension. You interact with those individuals in the fourth and third dimension. That is how it is constructed. You're not just looking back at individuals that are in a dimensional plane lower than you; you're actually looking into, and operating in, and interacting with a dimension or a reality that is different.

You have the ability to look all the way back from whence you began, which would be the third dimension. For this reality point, this existence that you have been in, or all humans have been in, it starts at the third dimension. Third, fourth, and fifth. And yes, [you will primarily interact with those who are one dimension below], one dimension down. But you have the capability of looking all the way back. Once you achieve the eighth dimension, you'll be able to interact with all dimensions previous.

Now, the vibrational void that you leave behind moving from the fourth into the fifth dimension will be filled by a new Being entering into the third or fourth dimension. This is the understanding that has to be in place. This existence that you're living in, this human existence, is a multidimensional plane of existence. You're living in a multidimensional plane. You're living in the plane of the fourth dimension. But yet there is a third-dimensional plane and a fourth-dimensional plane, and a fifth-dimensional plane and a sixth-dimensional plane and onward up. So you have an awareness that you are in these multiple dimensional planes. When you look back, it looks just as it was when you left, but your world that you exist in is going to be a fifth-dimensional existence. The world that is left behind will be filled with new Beings in the third and in the fourth dimension.

[These Beings will come in as] infants as well as those that are...you have to understand, there are Beings that come into existence. This is the advancement of the human race. We have assisted along the way to a point at which the humans themselves—when there is a void left behind when one ascends very rapidly, [it] has to be filled with an equal vibrational point, meaning an equal vibrational point of a human existence. If that human existence is one of a fifty-year-old man, that void is then left and has to be equalized with a fifty-year-old man. And yes, [at] that point, a fifty-year-old man will be put in place. It will be no different. There would be no awareness that that individual just *appeared* upon that place.

This is the difficulty when you begin to understand the depth of the dimensionality that you exist in. So yes, in time, as you move forward and all others move forward into that fifth dimensional plane, you're going to leave a void of all age ranges, all different sexes, all different aspects of humans. They will be filled in with all different aspects of humans, infants all the way to the aged. They will fill in and take over those spots that have been left behind.

The Dimensionality of Frequency

There is much to understand about all frequency. All twelve have their own baseline of frequency healing understanding. For the alignment with frequency, this understanding of your planet, this encapsulation that you are in with this planet...all frequencies have an aspect of healing. But this has been not quite understood by many of your humans. You've placed numbers upon certain aspects of frequency. You understand frequency as a broad spectrum of different points along a line. That is your human understanding.

Understand that frequency itself is three-dimensional, is four-dimensional, is five-dimensional, six-dimensional. It's limitless in dimension. There is not a singular point at which a frequency exists. Your resonance, your 432 hertz that your planet is resonating at and your human existence resonates and is encapsulated in...there is depth. There is limitless depth to that frequency. It isn't just a singular line. It is dimensional. And when you understand dimensional frequency, when you understand how you can enter into one frequency range, as you understand it as a human, and peer into the abyss of the dimensions that it actually exists in...then you can begin to look inward, into your own human form, and understand each cell, each blood cell, each organ, and understand the dimension that it exists in, and align a particular dimensional frequency to it to begin to heal and change whatever ails you.

But that is a bit complex. It is a bit out of your existent timeline. But begin to understand this aspect of dimensional frequency. Frequency is not a singular point. It is not a singular point along a line with other points. Each one of those that you understand as a frequency point has dimension, endless dimension.

The Martians' Appearance

At the base of all existence, our Twelve, we are all in a vibrational state. But understanding our role, we choose, then, at that point to diverge from remaining in a vibrational state and shift our vibrational state to appear to be in physicality, to shift into a full form of denseness, a full form of physicality, as it would appear to be to you.

If you were to travel back to the distant past, back to the Mars planet, when we were in pure physicality...in that time, in that time period as the humans began to evolve, the humans themselves, stature-wise, were quite short. In your terms of measurement, between three to five and a half feet. That was the height of many of the humans. Short to what you would [now] consider tall. The Martians themselves are consistent. Roughly around your six-foot height mark. Slender in stature. Typically, six fingers per hand. Their eyes, a bluish to whitish-blue color. Their hair, all a very white too, as you would understand, blonde in color. Their facial features were quite prominent, quite square in the face but, yet, still human in your existent now framework.

Normal [skin] tone as yours, all throughout the spectrum. There is not one specific color. For you see, as the humans themselves, as the project proceeds, there isn't one specific skin color or tone. It is a varied level of coloring that takes place, dependent upon the geographic regions of your planet which you inhabit. And, so, the Martians themselves have to acclimate the same way, so they take on all forms of tone and skin color.

[We have two genders], but we do not produce children in quite the same way. It is more of a process of...it is not in your understanding of intercourse, but it is more of an understanding of placing the fertilization of one egg and one sperm (you would understand it that way) together, but outside the body, but then into either the male or the female. [Our child-rearing is] not by a small understanding of a family unit but a communal aspect of raising those children.

The Martians, Tesla, and Technological Advancement

Allowing yourself to align with the Martian vibration, this vibration of the Martian aspect, would be one to understand the technological advances that can be achieved. For you see, we have the understanding of what it takes to advance as a civilization, and we understand what it takes to advance in a physicality state of a civilization. For you are moving forward with technology, and much has been provided to you through those that have had those experiences from other existences. Your Einsteins, your Edisons—there are a number of others of your scholars that have moved forward your existence because of what has been brought to them, though they can only achieve what they've achieved with the resources they have at their particular point along their timeline.

Tesla is an interesting aspect. Though not truly aligned with the Martians himself, there is a different aspect of a culmination...one of leaving a doorway open through different timelines. It would be as if this individual in the human form, Tesla himself, left a portal, of sorts, open for his existence, being able to transport himself back and forth to different galaxies, different reality points...bringing forth that [information] and then trying to apply it within the age frame of his existence.

This is going on, and it has been going on. Though he is no longer in existence in human form here upon your planet, he still exists, traveling to other dimensions and other planets and other galaxies, doing the same as he has here, pulling forth technologically advanced information and trying to achieve it within the timeframe that he exists. He stepped into a timeline here, upon your human planet, at a point at which the resources were not available to advance human society as fast as it needed to. His timeline should have been aligned with one that is closer to your alignment today than it had [been] back in his day. He will not make his approach again, but his information still remains. It is here. His scribes are still present. His information is still viable. His understandings and teachings are relevant, but they must be put into action.

[There is another hurdle to technological advancement, which has occurred] all along humanity's existence. When one individual understands a technological advancement and does not quite have all of the resources to achieve it, those that are...shall it be said, those that are in power to profit...they tend to overthrow those that have the information that is for all humanity. That is a common understanding, and that is... this is a learned aspect. Though it is not the full understanding of what has been taught to the humans from the origin point of the Mars planet, we, too, had very similar aspects. This is continuing, and it will continue for some time.

As advancement takes place, there [are] always a number of individuals, Beings, that wish to hold it from the entirety of society, for they believe that society is not quite ready for that type of advancement. And, so, it is then suppressed from society. They don't quite understand that society itself is quite flexible, and if it is approached appropriately, it will align and vibrate accordingly, and it will advance society just enough for greater awareness, greater understanding of a global perspective of humanity.

[So] if you wish to connect [with the Martians] for advancement in a technological aspect, sit and align yourself with the vibrational state of the Mars planet. Allow yourself to find a vibrational point of connectedness. Allow yourself to visualize yourself in a technological society greater than yours, and find yourself amongst others that look like you, but are actually Martians, and begin to communicate. They'll begin to show you aspects of their existence, aspects of their technology. Though you may not fully understand all of it, you can join them at any point. Ask any questions that you wish. Take as many notes as you wish, and bring that back here for your understanding.

And if it is something that is for the advancement of humans, if you wish to move forward with that, and you have the resources, then it is yours to utilize. They will only show you things that you are able to achieve. They will not show you things that are so far advanced that you have no comprehension of what they are, even if they are explaining it to you. They will only show you according to where you are and where your alignment is.

A Message for Humanity

Have the understanding that your human aspect, your human physicality upon the planet...how beautiful it has been to observe the evolution. For this planet is of its own. You are here purposefully. All humans. All humans here are here purposefully. You've agreed to take on this role. And yes, no matter what you see and understand of what is taking place around your planet, understand that your consciousness is intertwining. Your consciousness is balancing. Your consciousness is achieving exactly where it needs to be for the next evolution of your Being.

So take time. Take time to reflect upon your existence as a human, and take time to reflect upon your existence as a multidimensional Being; for you are all existent through time. And allow that to be your guidance into the future.

---

1. See the section entitled The Council of Constructors and Builders at the end of the book for more detail on this group and to read their direct transmission.

12

HADARIANS

Greetings from the Hadarians and the source cluster of our existence. For us, the Hadarians, this is something that you must understand for this transmission—the purpose of this [heart] space in which you enter...this purpose of aligning and expressing one's existence within their heart space—the space in which the essence, the energy, the vibration of love exists—[which] is associated with all source Beings, all Beings throughout time.

For you see, from the beginning, the beginning of time, the beginning of existence, the beginning of the vibrations that have brought into existence the humans, the system in which you exist...the existent frequency that began *all* existence is this frequency that you associate with love... your heart space...the space in which, unconditionally, *all* exists...no questions, no relationship to other things, but unconditionally, it all exists and has all existed from the beginning. You understand the beginnings of all Source Twelve. You understand their purpose. You understand where they've come from.

But what we would like to share with you is *this* of our existence...this love vibration, this vibrational source that began all things. For we were there from the beginning, from the very first vibrational field that coalesced to begin the process of your existence, your galaxy, your universe, your planets. All things that are in existence began with that source tone, that source vibration, source frequency. *Pure love* is what you would associate it with.

The Hadarians, as far as an existence that you would understand...yes, all of us were there at the beginning, but many became existent...what you would understand as an *existent* frequency form, or one that is of solid state, solid matter, one that is in existence for a particular period of time. But we have existed in the pure vibrational form for most of our existence, unseen but yet present, unknown but yet present. Just as this frequency that you would understand as love exists but yet cannot be seen. It can be felt, but it is not present in form. We, too. We are the beginning, we are the middle, and we are the end. We are present in all things. We are present from your Source. We are present in the breath that you breathe. We are present in all things.

So it is that you express that you do not know much of the Hadarians, but yet you know an abundant amount of the Hadarians. For each essence that you have of love, each feeling of love, we are present. We may not take form, or introduce ourselves, or become present before you, but we are. There is no need to call upon us. But do not be confused; we are not love, but we hold the essence, the vibration of love across all things. We are the conduit, the fibers, the connection points for all things to contain this frequency...the beginning frequency.

You associate it in your physical form, as a human, as this action of love, this feeling of love, this essence of love, the unconditional involvement of love. That is the source vibration that you feel, the beginning point. Our presence allows all things to connect through it. We bind all of it together. We are present among you, but yet not in physical form.

So it is this to understand: Throughout time, throughout the evolution, throughout the hybridization of the humans themselves, yes, we've been present, but not physically. But it has been a point at which, in your most recent cycle of time, this understanding of your evolution, the process at which you are now in this final episode, this final stage of your evolution...this is the longest period of time that it has been stabilized for your existence. That is because throughout time, this vibration, this frequency, this beginning frequency, this love frequency did not synchronize appropriately through time.

This is why you understand from the other source clusters the episodes of having to clear and restart. There are many other factors involved, but that is one of the primary reasons. But now, this period of time that you exist in, this period of time that has existed for some time now...it is beginning to synchronize appropriately. This is why there hasn't been a need to restart. For when the synchronization takes place, this is why many are experiencing clarity. Many are experiencing what is yet to come. Many are perceiving the future in front of them, for they are aligning themselves with this frequency, this beginning frequency, this birthing frequency. It all resonates with what you understand as love... the purity, the unconditional understanding.

This is your experience! This is your evolution! This is your ascension! It is the synchronization from the beginning point to now. So do not be overwhelmed by what is taking place. Do not be set aside from all of what you understand and what you see in front of you, for you are synchronizing. It is the purity...the purity of all beginnings, and you are beginning to align with it, and much is being revealed.

And in this period of time, this most recent cycle of time, we have come to you. We have decided to merge and integrate with you. We are here upon your planet, helping and facilitating this synchronization. You would not recognize us. We do not take a specific form; we do not come to you in some state of vibrational field. We blend right with the humans. We are not taking form as a human, but our essence, the Hadarians...we blend, in agreement with humans. Our essence, our vibration infuses and synchronizes with specific humans.

So this is the difference between many other of the source clusters that do come in physical form, that do come into presence, taking shape as a human, yet they don't understand what it is to be human. But when the human itself is synchronizing to a point at which it is acceptable to blend and merge with, then there is an agreement that comes into play. We allow ourselves, our essence, to blend with them fully, giving them an understanding of a greater existence. They see the beginning, they see the end, and all of what takes place in between. They have an openness. They have a clarity. But yet in that clarity, there is confusion. And yet this is purposeful; for the human Self, its state of existence, cannot support the full understanding of all of what exists. So the confusion is an overlay upon what is in place and what is known, to allow the human to still experience existence upon this planet.

So understand, it's not about who merged with who, what faction warred against which faction, which Beings hybridized with other Beings. It's truly about how far the pure source vibration diverged from its source point, and how quickly it was realigned, restarted, and now has been achieved for synchronization. All of what has taken place in between has been purposefully placed, though from an observer's standpoint, you would not understand the purpose between all of the different interactions. You would look upon them as being purposeful for each interaction as far as this faction against this faction, this Being hybridizing with another Being in order to produce a certain Being that, then, comes to you for information.

But what must be observed is where you are now, where the human Beings themselves are in their existence. You are in a synchronizing period, synchronizing with the beginning source vibration, the Source that created all of your existence. And with that, this is where you are achieving your ascension, your vibrational upliftment, your understandings of truths that are in front of you. For it is not what you *believe* of what is taking place, as far as what you are vibrating alongside or connecting to, "Which node and which purposeful Being must I align to?" But it is to understand this source vibration from its beginning, its purity, its existence.

So that is why it is said at the beginning of this transmission to align with this heart space of yours, this heart field, this vibrational state of love.
For when you align to the purity of that love, you are aligning yourself

with the beginning point of existence. Yes, you understand aligning to your immediate Source, and yes, you understand aligning to certain galactic alignments, certain vibrational fields upon your planet. They all feel as if they are appropriate, and they are—for those [are] the alignments you have set out to achieve. But the one alignment that you do not set out to achieve, that is not part of your contract, but is an overall contract with *all* existence, is the synchronization with the beginning source vibration. It is an overall understanding, an overall understanding for existence.

For you are not the only ones that are aligning to this beginning source vibration. All Beings, all vibrational points are aligning to it. This is the synchronization that is necessary for your ascension. When you understand this point of ascension, you understand it as a dimensional level that is taking you from one dimensional plane into another dimensional plane. Yes, for your human existence, that is correct. That is the construct in which you exist. But ascension is much greater than that. And you understand this placement, this question that arises over and over again that is placed in front of you: How will this ascension take place, this wave of energy, this Event that is to take place upon your planet? Again, that is a construct of your own mind so that you have a visualization of what is to take place.

In a way, it is a vibrational wave. It is, you could say, an Event. But *all* things in your galaxy, in your universe, in which you exist, are going to change. Your existent time and space is going to change. All things, all Beings, all vibrational points, all vibrational nodes are changing. It is not just the humans that are changing; for you see, we have a greater perspective. Since we are carrying that vibrational aspect, since we are the conduit by which it is all connected to all things, we understand it from a much greater perspective than the other remaining source clusters. *We* are the point at which it is infused. *We* are the point at which it emanates through.

So all existence, across all time, is going to change. For you have this perspective and this construct that your existence now is going to change, your timelines are going to change...[that] in the future, they are going to be upgraded to another dimensional level. And yes, for your construct, it will be. But you also understand and have a belief that the past is achievable, the future is achievable. It is just a matter of which vibrational field you wish to connect to, to enter back to the past and change things in your past, in your history, in your past lives...or [how] to progress yourself into the future and change things into the future. What you change today will change your future. Yes, that is true.

But you are not changing it. You are *synchronizing* with a vibrational point which needs to be changed. So this change that is taking place, this synchronization, affects all time—past, present, and future. It affects all existence, all realms that exist here within your construct—your Earth planet, your planetary system, your solar systems, your star systems, your galaxy, your universe. All which is contained within will be synchronized and changed. It will all look different. All will be in unison. All will be vibrating at a much higher vibrational field and that is the vibrational field that began all things.

Love

This is the aspect that all humans, [even] those that do not understand, still experience. For you see, in the realm in which you exist, the construct in which you exist, you believe there are layers of humans. You believe this layering of humans is based upon their contract, based upon what they've agreed to. And it is, to a certain extent; for yes, there are individual agreements that are made. Achievement points. Whatever you wish to call them.

But at the core, at the center of each agreement, what each agreement is vibrationally aligned to is this essence of love, this essence of the beginning state, the purity of it. But yet once you arrive into your human form, how much of that beginning state, that beginning vibration, that love field emanates through the contract is dependent upon what you've agreed to do. Even those that have shielded most of that vibration out of their existence still, at the core, have that field within them. They would not be able to exist as a human if they did not have this field of love, this existence of love, this vibration of love. It is the true existence, the purity of it. It is what sustains the human form. Many may not be fully aware of it, but it exists within them.

So this is why it is important to understand there are not different layers of humans. There are not [just] those that truly believe and have all things presented to them, [or] those that are void of any existence of understanding and awareness, and many that fall in between. But yet each and every one is exactly the same. At the center, at the core, each Being, each human Being, is the pure essence of love...the pure essence of unconditional love for each Being that is here upon the planet. They all exist together, but they've all agreed to interact with it differently.

So do not allow yourself to separate and segregate and look at others differently, as "They are not where I am, they do not understand, they cannot help what they understand." For it is to begin to look at them in this pure vibrational state, this pure essence of love. It's not to emanate any field to them or look upon them as if they don't understand, but it is to understand that when you do look upon another individual, another Being, another human, there is no difference between you and them. You each, at the core, have a vibrational field of the purest state. And when you understand that, that's where change, that's where synchronization, that's where it is all revealed.

For when you begin to recognize the purity of love that exists in each individual, no matter who and no matter what they do, when you understand the purity of love that exists within them, that begins their change. Just by merely recognizing it from you, from your point, from your point of existence, you're energetically engaging and beginning to synchronize with them. Though you may never see them again, it begins a change... ever so slight, but it begins the change of synchronization within themselves.

It is where it began and it is where it ends—the purity of this state. For there are no words to explain this vibration, though the human construct has placed a word around it, this word of "love." No matter the differences upon your planet, there is a word for this vibration, and it is love. It is what began all things out of nothing, and it is what will take everything into the next state of existence. This is why it is said, the beginning and the end...the end of one existence and the beginning of a next. Do not look upon it as it being a reset, but look upon it as being the next evolution in all Beings, all things...not just the humans, but all things, all existence here, physically upon your planet and out within the other regions of your universe.

Synchronization

It is the point at which you allow yourself to expand from the source point within and understanding how it begins to activate in others. For this synchronization that is taking place, at times, can be perceived as not being evident in all things, but it is. It is present. For you see, just as it exists within each individual, each existence upon this planet, it also exists in between. So no matter whether you are connected with an individual or not, the space between you and that individual contains the source vibration. It exists all around you. It is what fills the spaces. It is what consumes your existence. It is in all things. It is not just in [the] physicality of things that you exist with, but it is everywhere.

You are continually experiencing this; you are just not recognizing the synchronization. For this period of time, this cycle of time in your human existence—if there is a timeline to put upon it, this thirty thousand-year cycle—this is where the synchronization has been taking place. And it is not to understand it as aligning with or not aligning with, or when you will see it or not see it; for the synchronizations are taking place. It is not an overwhelming aspect that will appear in front of you as this moment of understanding, of "I understand now that I am synchronizing with all things based upon this love-based frequency." For it is much smaller than that.

It is to begin to look upon yourself differently. Understand each of the vibrations that you feel. Understand the alignments with those vibrations. And you must understand this term, "alignment." This is nothing more than synchronizing with another frequency, another vibration. When you begin to look at the smallest of the vibrations that you exist within, the smallest of these synchronizations, you understand that each one of them has a core, has a center point, and that center point is that frequency of love.

No matter what it is, the mere connection with someone that you have never met...you cross paths together, and there is a recognition, the smallest of sorts, and you merely cast it off as being a coincidence or just a mere moment of laughter, "That's interesting; that individual looks very familiar. I think I understand who they are." But at the core, it's not that. It's the synchronization of this frequency. You are aligning both frequencies together at that point. The moments at which you are just sitting with yourself, in quiet contemplation, but yet you just have an essence of an alignment synchronization...at the core, it is that...that of the love that is emitted around all things, you are synchronizing to. You are experiencing it.

For there is much question amongst many of the humans, "When is it that I will experience this? Will it happen within my lifetime?" That is because the humans look upon their existence from a greater perspective, a much higher perspective, looking upon the greater visualization of their existence...the big picture of their existence. That is an outcome of the advancements of the humans.

For you see, in the years past, all the different cycles, time was much slower. It had the perception that it was much slower. Many things could take place within a period of time. So you had time to reflect. You had time to understand. But now, in your existence, now, this time period, too much takes place within one small amount of time. You do not have time to reflect on the small moments, so you must pull yourself back and look upon the whole of your existence of that day, of that moment, and you lose perspective. You lose sight of the center, the core, the love...the love that synchronizes all things.

And when you can reframe your perspective, when you can look upon those moments during a day to the smallest amount, allowing yourself to synchronize and align with the smallest aspects of your day, you'll realize you have much more time available to you than you had in the past. This is the difference; for many say that time is speeding up. Time is not speeding up; *you are just removing yourself from time*. You are pulling yourself out, much higher up, away from the timeline that you exist on. So from that perspective, it looks as if it's moving quite quickly because now you can see more of the timeline.

Bring yourself down, down into each moment, each perspective moment, and you will understand how much time there actually is, and in that, the alignment, the synchronization with that purity source of vibration. And you will see exactly what you are wishing to understand of what is going to take place within your timeline of existence.

Remaining in the Purity Vibration

There was no separate hybridization. For we, being the conduit...you must understand, from the beginning, from when all twelve were brought into existence here, the agreement was that we, the Hadarians, would be the construct, the conduit by which all others are connected. And that's where we remained. This is why it is said that we did not take physical form, we did not take a vibrational form from the beginning, purposefully. We wanted to remain the pure vibrational state so that we could become the fibers, the nodes, the connection points, all those things that connect all existence.

For if we were to, at a point, take a vibrational form, as many do, that would take an amount of energy, amount of vibration that would, then, negate other connection points. So we chose to remain purely in vibrational state, connecting all things with this purity vibration. Even in the extent of the galactic wars and the different factions that broke away, we were still connected to them at the core of their existence. Each one of the Beings, each one of the understandings, we were there with them. That vibrational field is at the center. It is always there. It does not matter what is taking place, where you are, what you are doing, what you are thinking. The purity...the purity essence of this source point is with you, is with all Beings, with all existence.

Our role is never to assist or change an outcome. For it is the Being...it is that Being. It is that Being's alignment, its vibrational alignment and synchronization to come to a realization of this purity state, this vibrational aspect of love. You would understand it in the human form as choice, free will. That is only existent here in the human forms. But in the other vibrational states, whether it is the warring factions or different hybridized Beings, it is still there. But the synchronization takes place much differently. There are a number of factors that must take place, different alignments with other Beings, other synchronizing points on different nodes for this purity aspect, this vibrational source point aspect to come to the surface.

That is the difference. It is always in all things. It must be. That is where it all began. You are here because of that vibrational point. The chair in which you sit, the room in which you exist, the air that you breathe, it all contains the original source point of vibration, purity, love. *It all contains that.* It is not that you synchronize with your chair and understand the vibrational love that the chair has for you, but yet it contains that field. You, as a human, can make the choice whether to engage with it or not.

So even if you are just sitting mindfully to yourself, looking out upon the world around you, not connecting with an individual, not connecting with something in your awareness...just focus on the space in front of you, the void that's in front of you, the air that is in front of you, and you will connect to it. You'll connect to that source vibration, that purity vibration. That is us. We are in all things, everywhere. You do not have to call upon us. We are there. If you wish to call upon us, open yourself to receive. If you need a vibrational boost, call upon us. We'll help you enter into that space, that node, that source point, to be rejuvenated for another day.

Beta Centauri

[There are three main stars in our star system, Beta Centauri.] This is a point at which, in your space, your existence beyond your planet, it would be a visual reference. Nothing more than just a vibrational visual reference for you, then, to align, if it helps you and assists you with aligning to this purity state. If you have difficulty doing it upon your own, if you can find space to where you can observe that location, the cluster of three, allow yourself to [do] that. Visualize yourself entering into that space and being surrounded by the purity, by the true source purity, just for a moment. Do not stay there long. Do not linger, for it is overwhelming for all humans. But just a moment, allow yourself to be encapsulated just for a moment, to be infused. Then bring your awareness back to yourself, and then begin to look inward and understand that pure essence of all things. So it is just more of a visual reference for you to have a physicality location that you can, then, call upon for reference.

From a vibrational standpoint, there is no direct relationship [with the Alpha Centaurians] as you would perceive it. It is just another visual reference point. For your star systems that you witness in the night sky, they are all aspects. They do exist, but many have gone dormant, and what you are witnessing is just their reference point, their space in your night sky. But the Alphas...their vibrational aspect is not like ours. You could say they are a bit of a hybridized vibrational field, containing much of the Twelve, very similar to the humans, but they do not take physical form like the humans.

They do not exist in a physical state other than, yes, you can call upon them. But they are going to present themselves as an overwhelming vibrational presence in front of you. Their alignments with you, their presence with you, the knowledge that they wish to impart on you is going to be a bit confusing, as it will be overwhelming to the human systems. So it is up to you if you wish to call upon them. There is no specific name other than if you wish to call upon them as the Alphas,

Alpha Centaurians. They will respond, but just be aware that their presence with you will be a bit...overwhelming.

Their knowledge will be vast. Their knowledge will be deep, and it will be over-consuming. It will be placed upon you in one great amount. One large dose of information will be presented to you, so this is why it is said to be cautious when calling upon them. Much will be received by you, but much will not be understood by what was received. They can give you a very pronounced understanding of history throughout the galaxy. You would call this a snapshot of history throughout the galaxy—not fully engaged with all things, but more of a reference point for the entirety of history throughout your galaxy. They will impart that very quickly, imposing that upon you. Be cautious for what you wish to receive from them.

Connecting with the Hadarians

We will not show ourselves in a physical essence in front of you. It would be of the depth in which you feel our presence. Many have represented us as different Beings, but there is not one specific Being that we take form in. That is just a construct that one's human perspective puts in its place to understand that there is a presence of vibration in front of them. But it is to sit. Many of you understand this process of sitting within your heart space and fully engaging within your heart space and understanding the vibration that emanates from your heart space. But it is different than that.

It's what illuminates your heart space. It's what animates your heart space. It is the core, the center of it all. You understand that, yes, you have this vibrational field that enters into the human body, that animates the human body, and that is, as you would perceive it to be, your soul, and it is this energetic piece that comes from Source. That is correct, but where does Source come from...your immediate Source, the one that you transition into and out of? That came from the original Source. Where did that Source come from? Again, infinite number of sources.

So dig into the layers of your existence, into your heart space...not what is emitted from your heart space. What is emitted from your heart space is the purity of your essence. How pure your essence is, is how pure your energy that you emit out to others is. Now, allow yourself to go further inward, past what you believe is your soul or your energy source, from the Source that you are connected to...a bit further in, again, much smaller than any understanding that you can perceive, but yet it is the greatest amount of understanding.

At the core, the very smallest portion of that core, is the pure Source... the pure Source of love that has created all things, has created all things in your existence. That is where it is to be connected, to align to, to synchronize with. And when you do, as it begins to push outward, you will feel the change in what is emitted from you. You will feel a purity of love that begins to emit from you, greater than you have experienced before.

In some it may be very, very uncomfortable because it will begin to change the human form in many different ways. It will change the way they think. It will change the way they act. It will change their existence upon this planet because it is that that triggers their synchronization. So again, for each individual, it is going to be much different than others. But it is to allow yourself to experience the depth of that understanding, the purity of that understanding. From whence it all began, at one point, now exists within you and all other things, all other existences. It is just a matter of aligning and synchronizing with it.

[There are no humans with a direct DNA alignment with the Hadarians.] That is one strand that will remain not active within the humans, as far as you understanding it with the other twelve. For you see, what is active is this purity state, is this vibrational aspect of love, this beginning point, this source point of vibration. It takes the place of activating a DNA strand. So you must understand, yes, you have twelve DNA strands. Two are active dependent upon your alignment galactically with them. The Hadarian strand is dormant but alongside the other two that are active, the vibrational source point is the third. That is the constant between all Beings.

A Message for Humanity

Just remember...in your existence, do not look upon the future of, "Will it happen in my lifetime? Will it take place while I'm in existence?" Bring your focus down, narrow that focus down into your existence and see where it exists, for it is taking place now. You are in a time of synchronization. You are in a time of change. Do not be hyper-focused on when this event or that event is going to take place. These are all continual actions that take place throughout your galaxy.

But it is to explore the smallest regions of yourself, the beauty that is contained within that source point that you have within you. For it is the smallest point, but yet the greatest point of existence, for it is where it began, and it is where it will end. It is contained within you. It is contained within everyone. It exists everywhere.

THE COUNCIL OF CONSTRUCTORS AND BUILDERS

One random morning in January, 2023, as we neared the end of the channeling portion of this project, Will awoke with another profound download from an energetic collective who called themselves the Council of Constructors and Builders. Neither of us had ever heard of or been contacted by this council in the past. That morning, Will attempted to share with me some of the visions and information he had been given, but it was quite detailed and complex. Much of it had to do with the pyramids and how they were created. As if watching a video screen, Will could see how the enormous, stone blocks had been manipulated and moved, describing them as huge marshmallows that were not fully solid until they were settled into place.

We realized that speaking directly to the council would be the best course of action, in order to gain clarity on the incredible download they had provided. But, at that point, we had no idea this was, in any way, related to the book project. It seemed like a random connection point that Will had made, which wasn't uncommon. Occasionally, Will would receive messages from Beings, collectives, and councils during the night.

So later that day, we channeled the Council of Constructors and Builders. As they explained the details of their download, we quickly realized that this information was a critical piece of humanity's origin story. It was clearly no coincidence that this specific transmission had come to us at that moment. Much of the detail the council provided during that conversation was new to me and was, frankly, quite shocking, as it didn't align with the commonly accepted "history" of Earth's pyramids and structures.

Our conversation with the council is presented below.

Greetings. We bid you greetings from the Council of Constructors and Builders of all galactic realms. For this transmission, allow yourself and place yourself at the origin point...the origin point of your beginnings, the origin point of all beginning, all time, for this galactic realm.

We come to you with this transmission for this understanding of the beginning of time and the beginning of your galactic region. For you understand, from transmissions from the Twelve Galactic Starseed Clusters, the origin points. You understand the beginnings of all physicality. For, once, there was nothing. There is, now, something. It is this understanding in the presence of energetic vibration that begins to put together the tiniest of the molecules that already exist. For it is that there is not a space where there is nothing; but from your perception, there is nothing. That is what is to be understood.

For if you were to look back in time, glance back in time to the beginning point, the origin point, you would be in a void...but yet that void would be filled with all of the appropriate molecules necessary to begin an existence. And it is through this manipulation of sound, of vibration, that it begins to come together, coalesce, piece by piece, with the intention from each one of the Twelve of what they wish to bring into existence. And it is this understanding that this is where your stars and your planets do come from, and this is true. But at the beginning stages, it is just a pure mass that is existent in a space.

[The Twelve] have the capability of continuing their exercise of creation, of bringing online other Beings, but they do not have and do not hold the capability to bring online the appropriate structures, the appropriate physicality to

sustain a human existence, a Being's existence upon another planet. This is not held by one, but it is held in space and time of all existence, and it is called upon. This is [our] collective, this coalition. Yes, for your understanding and for your human perspective, it is best described as contractors, builders, constructors...for that is the easiest to overlay upon what is presented here on your planet.

It is to understand that, in this case, the previous planet, the Martian planet, is one that was the most habitable for the human experiment. And it is where structures began. There was life upon that planet, as well as others. They were all at a beginning stage. The Earth planet had the same structures, but they were not activated. But it is in time that they become activated. You have to understand the purpose of the structures.

The purpose of the structures are the ones that are put in place first. These structures are the ones that begin the existence of creation. It is allowing that planet, that star system, whatever area in your galaxy that wishes to sustain some form of life...[what it] needs. These structures are in place to begin that process. They still exist throughout your galaxy. They exist across many of your planets within your planetary system. For at the beginning stages, at the beginning point, the origin point, each one of your planets was nothing but a mere sphere of mass held together by vibration. It wasn't just a bunch of rocks that are put together. It was purposefully constructed through sound, vibration, frequency, intention, to have that specific sphere planet in place.

There is a balance that has to take place throughout a planetary system. This is why you have an understanding of the different planets within yours. Each one holds a specific space, holds a specific, as you would understand, gravitational pull. Each one of them has a specific density, a specific mass. And if one of them was to be pulled from their existence, the rest would not sustain their existence. They'd be flung and moved out of cycle.

So it is this to understand. Everything of existence must have balance, must have equalization. It is to understand [that] your Earth planet and your Mars planet, they are the most sustainable for any human existence. Starting with your Mars planet and the structures that have been built upon it...much [has] been destroyed through time, but those structures are there. Same here on your

Pyramid Structures

Earth planet now that you exist here: structures. (This isn't to say that each planet is to be brought into existence [to] have this habitable atmosphere and conditions for humans. Earth and Mars are the only two that were selected for that. But each one of them now, each one of your planets has an atmosphere. It is sustainable for particular Beings that exist within those planets.)

Which structures do we speak about? It is these structures that have been in place for, as you would think, thousands of years. But they are much older than that. From the beginning points of this particular planet, they have been in place. Yes, your pyramid structures...there are [also] subterranean pyramid structures. For the pyramid itself, from an engineering standpoint, is one of the most efficient structures to sustain a particular vibrational frequency. For each one of its sides resonates together to create...you would understand it as a beam...a bringing together of vibrational points.

So why is it [that] the pyramids are those that are the structures that are most important? For it is not just the pyramid that lies above, but it is the pyramid that lies beneath. Equalization. Balance. For what lies beneath— each one of the pyramids that has existed here, as well as on other planets— there is an equally-sized pyramid that lies below. It does not take the same visual shape as your pyramids that lie above ground, but this is a mechanism, a piece of machinery. It is not as if you were to dig beneath one of your grand pyramids, you would find a grand pyramid in the opposing direction. They are there, the physicality is there, but it is...this is where the difficulty lies. For what is built above requires physical objects to be constructed so that they can be seen. What is constructed beneath is a manipulation of the structures, the crystalline and the rock structures beneath those pyramids.

So as you dig down, it would be represented as just another cluster of your strata, but they are shaped in a particular way, fashioned in a particular way that they are brought into a shape of a pyramid. It is in place to begin the habitation process for a particular planet. These passageways that lay beneath... they would be represented in your understanding as caves and tunnels. But there is no physical, "strip away the soil and find an upside-down pyramid beneath it." The ground itself has been vibrated in a fashion, structured to shape itself as a pyramid, but once digging begins, you would begin to just understand it as the ground beneath.

It is to understand these pyramid structures, above and below. They are the beginning stages of this habitable experience. They have been built purposefully. We, as the builders, constructors—all forms of Beings come together— those that hold the knowledge, those that retain knowledge from the elders. We are called upon when it is necessary to begin this process. We enter into your galaxy, and we begin the process. We begin a process of allowing our energetic state to take shape and form. Just as your planet took shape and form, we take shape and form. We allow our vibration to mingle here in your existent dimensional plane to hold that vibration, to begin the point of genesis. The beginning. The understanding of time for your human inhabitants.

We are present through that process. We constructed all of the pyramids that are here, on Mars, as well as all other planets, with one singular purpose: to harness the vortices of energies that are running through your galaxy. There are a number of different vertical and horizontal and dimensional planes that are open, always. Each one of them is a vortex of energy, and it is aligned to these particular vortexes of energy. Each one of the pyramids has an opening. They have an energetic opening that is aligned to these vortices. Allowing these portals to be opened between your universe and these pyramids begins to harness and funnel these energies into your physical planet.

[The way that dolphins and whales process sound can give you a visualization of] this life tone, this creation tone that is emitted by the pyramids. It is a series of chambers that, once the vortex of energy is brought in through the top, it is, then, creating a vortex of energy within. This is, then, creating a harmonic, which is, then, creating this creation sound. This is what takes place in your space above your surface, what you would understand as your sky. This is the creation point for the sky and all of what takes place, then, above ground.

The effect of all of the energy that is being brought in from your galaxy through the directed points of these pyramids is one to begin a resonation here amongst your physical planet, vibrating at a particular point, a particular frequency. It has been mentioned in other transmissions that this particular planet holds a specific frequency, and it does. It doesn't change. It amplifies, but it does not change. There is a spectrum that it operates within, all holding one firm frequency. That particular frequency is one to sustain the human life.

So as this energy is being funneled in and being directed into the center of this particular planet, the frequencies begin to resonate all throughout the planet— each one of these pyramids, laid specifically according to specific coordinates— allowing this energy to be focused to the center. Just as a bell is struck and it provides a resonance for your ears, this planet is struck with all of its energy to begin to vibrate. It is necessary for the creation point. And in doing so, it is beginning to take a habitable form, welling up the creation fluids. Those fluids, you would understand them not as water, but they appear to be as water. But they are more of a space which—just as your planets have been created out of nothing—begins to bring together life. Water comes much later in the process. Your drinkable, your sustainable water comes much further in the process.

There is no atmosphere. There is no existence beyond what is taking place on the surface. It is the beginning stages of your existence. All the while, these energies are being funneled in, allowing the vibrations to continue. And over millions of years, the structures are sustaining a vibration for creation. Once there is this global presence of life, albeit extremely small, it is now time for your atmosphere to take shape.

The pyramids themselves begin to emit those life-giving fluids out around your planet. For you understand your pyramids as they are now, and you understand there are multiple chambers with the pyramids. You understand them as having multiple channels and different passageways, different chambers. For you see, those chambers are purposeful. They help create a resonance. They help create a sound...a sound that is of creation. For this, too, has been brought forward in previous transmissions. For this process of this galaxy to be brought here, now, in place, it began with sound—the sound of creation. This is a purposeful sound. Each one of the pyramids creates this resonance, this sound of creation. It is emitted out into what is now your atmosphere, out into the air that surrounds your planet, the space above the ground, and it begins to create a sustainable atmosphere for the humans, then, to take shape.

And it is this to understand: that through time, these pyramids have been activated and have been online. They are purposefully built. Once they are built and operational, they are set in place, there is no need for us to be in place. We then depart. But we leave them active. They are, then, activated for periods of time until the first level of humans is sustainable...the first generation of humans is sustainable. All the while, this creation sound is being broadcast around your planet. It is not uncomfortable. It is soothing, but it is always present. This is, then, your atmosphere, your breathable air.

Your water is then brought in. There is water that is brought in from other areas of your galaxy. Yes, you understand that your planet has taken on and sustained much damage from objects throughout your galaxy, and yes, that is part of the process. Your galaxy is a very turbulent galaxy. And yes, it does, on occasion, bring in destructive forces. But in those destructive forces also comes other life-giving aspects for your planet.

Your planet is the only planet that can absorb and then rebirth a useful product from the catastrophic events that take place, from objects that enter into your planetary system. This planet—the human planet, the Earth planet—has been purposefully designed that way. Mars was not designed specifically to incur those types of damages. This is why this is the sustainable planet.

So it is to understand the perplexities of what has been built. These pyramids have been online for millions of years. And at a point at which there is a sustainable amount of life that is reproducing without the use of the sound of creation, then those pyramids do go inactive. They understand the balance that has been put in place. They understand. They are intelligent. They understand the balance. They understand the life forces that are upon the planet, and there is no need for the creation sound to be in place.

But through time, and this is where your human history is a bit confused...for you have an understanding of thousands of years, not [the] millions of years that humans have been active upon your planet. Humans have been through numbers of cycles and numbers of generations, iterations of their experience. But each time, they find these structures, no matter what they are, no matter the structures we've put in place. They begin to renovate. They begin to go in and impart their own experience into them. Layer by layer, time by time, generation by generation, each one of these structures has been overtaken by the humans.

So this is why your history is a bit off. You do not have a full comprehension of all the different structures that exist and have yet to be found and what their purpose was. They will not be reactivated. There is no need for them to be reactivated. So for those that believe that the pyramids will reactivate at some particular point, they will not. They were only necessary for the beginning stages of creation, the beginning stages of life. This is why many have been overtaken and used for different activities. And this is where your history tries to catch up.

So it is to begin to understand the origin point to the point at which humans have been sustainable; for the structures, the communities, the plazas, the metropolises that have been in place for some time have all been here from the beginning. So what you are finding and uncovering of ancient cities, those ancient cities are much older than they appear. They are pre-human. They are pre-existence. They are the beginning of time.

Many question the construction. Many question the tools necessary. But the one thing you will find is the absence of tools, for the tools that are used are not your physical tools. There are no physical tools needed to construct what has been constructed. For you understand from these transmissions that through vibration, through sound, through intention, all can be manipulated. All can be brought into existence. The humans are far from capable of understanding this to a particular point. They strive to get to a point at which they want to, through vibration, change their existence, change their physicality, change things in their presence. But it is not for the course of the humans to fully understand and experience this.

But it is to understand this presence that was here before the humans...a temporary presence, with all of the technology and with all of the understanding of how to build and construct all of the structures that are in place now. Great structures. Many have yet to be discovered. For you understand what lies above the surface of your Earth; you truly have not found what has been built below the surface of your Earth [and under water]. That will be in some generational time.

Even if you were to find all of what has been constructed all throughout the millennia, it will still leave a question mark upon those that find it because the one thing that will not be present, the one thing that will not be found are we, the Beings that constructed these structures and the technology and the understanding of how to construct these structures. And this is purposeful. It is— whether it is the humans or any other Being that inhabits a particular planet —to have them question their existence. This draws them further to an alignment of understanding the universal truth that lies before them.

For if you had all existence laid before you, all understanding of time, all understanding of how all was constructed, and you had the abilities to do so, this existence as a human would no longer need to be because you come to this existence...this existence as a human has been purposefully placed for you. This planet has purposefully been designed for you. The experiences upon it are one that you have agreed to understand. This is why much of this has taken place before the humans came into existence; yet we leave the remnants of the structures, and that allows the human mind to ask questions.

This portion of this expression of history was one that was brought in for an additional point of clarity, for much has been expressed about history, much has been expressed about the beginning points of time, the origin points of time, but there is, again, no construct of understanding in which to place it. Now, this provides the construct in which you can place some of this understanding.

The Council's Appearance

We are only in energetic form before we arrive here. Once we arrive within your galaxy, we take on a physical shape according to the planet, the Beings who we're going to be working for. So this planet, the human planet...we knew and understood that this would be inhabited by a human form. We take the shape of that because in time, the humans will be in commune with our presence, and we must be recognizable to those humans. We will not impart any of the building knowledge upon these humans, but we will be working with them very closely to colonize their own existence. So there is a physical form that takes presence. Just as your universe has been brought into existence from nothing, we, too, need to allow our vibrational form to condense into a three-dimensional, fourth-dimensional Being.

[Although we look similar to the humans], there is a significant difference. We do not take the full anatomical shape of a human. We are much more grand. You would understand us as giants among the humans. The initial grouping of humans were quite large themselves; they needed this physical structure to overcome many of the physical objects, the physical hazards of this initial formulation of the planet. So there was quite a difference [between] the humans that are in existence now and the initial humans that were in presence then. The initial human, the initial beginning phase of the human project...you would understand them as giants, as well, standing eight to ten-foot tall in your measurement reference. We are another five to ten feet taller. This is purposeful for the work that is necessary to be done.

Sacred Geometry, Sound, and Creation

This point of origin, this point of creation—similar to the resonant frequency that creates your atmosphere through the pyramids, this creation sound—yes, you would understand that in your physical state as an audible tone. The origin (not of this galaxy, but the origin point for all existence, the infinite origin point) has a particular sound. Sound being frequency. Not audible to the human, but audible to all things that vibrate within the universe.

So it is for the humans to understand...you rely upon your ears to hear all things. You rely upon the physical body to sense what is around you. Whether it is energy or whether it is a physical object or physical Being, you can sense that. This infinite origin point and its creation sound, creation frequency, is indistinguishable from all other frequencies. You would understand this this way: Pure white light is the culmination of all frequency bands of energy, brought into one point, creating a pure white light state. It is the creation point for all energy there. All energy points [coming] together; you've got a creation point of energy. White light. White energy source. Very similar. All aspects of all forms of energy that have been broadcast out over time come together. That is this origin frequency, this origin point, this source point. It is indistinguishable from any other frequency. You would not sense it in any particular manner, but it is always there.

Sacred geometry is the vibrational expression. For each tone and vibration, each spectrum of that vibrational point, creates a specific...in your vision, a specific form. Doesn't matter what it might be. If a certain frequency is vibrated to a particular object or a particular grouping of objects at a particular frequency and a particular amplitude, it will move those objects into a sacred geometry aspect.

So it is to understand these aspects of sacred geometry. They are not utilized to create, but they are utilized to bring energies together. If you were to manipulate multiple energy points, multiple energy frequencies, each one having their own geometric shape, you then bring them together. This, then, can produce, as you would understand it, levitation of large objects. Yes, you will manipulate them, but you will not construct anything with them. You can move them easily, but you're not going to lift them. This is a different form. This is a different aspect. This aspect of sacred geometry and moving things with frequency...this is where it's utilized. It's not to create from nothing. It is not to create as a building process. But it is to shift and move across the surface of your planet.

The History of Earth's Structures

You have to shift your understanding and your learning process of [human] history. Your history is based upon what they are finding within. For instance, your Egyptian Pyramids—many believe the large chambers are burial tombs; the small passageways are [simply] to move about; the different offset chambers are there for protection, for different alignments to celestial points. You are allowing yourself to continue with a history of what you are finding within many of these pyramids and the structures around them that [were] not put in place by the constructors and builders.

It is to begin to shift this teaching about that. It is to understand that the formulation of each one of those structures, the interior of one of those structures, is purposefully and mechanically sound. They are designed, one, to funnel energy straight down into the core of your planet; two, it is to create this resonance, this harmonic, this sound to be emitted out the side chambers, these offset chambers, out into your sky. This is the life-giving force that created your sky, created your atmosphere, created the habitable experience here upon your planet.

If one from a mechanical and an engineering standpoint of a human can understand the functionality, your history will be rewritten, [but] they must be aligned themselves. They must have an ability to strip away what has been brought to them as a teaching. Many humans are not willing to strip away these teachings, these understandings of what history is. History is not a solid object. History is the most fluid aspect of any existence; for the history that you understand is much different than anyone else's history. Though it has a particular framework, a particular construct, what is held within is individual. And this, too, you have to understand.

The framework is this: Existence upon your planet started much earlier than what is believed. That is the construct. What is filled in is what is yet to be discovered. So it is to begin to understand a new construct. That is going to take time. [And] this will come in time, but it is not within this generation's understanding. This generation and multiple generations preceding it are all focused on the hieroglyphs that are within and the understandings of this ruler and this king. It is not that. Those are the ones that have imparted their own personal aspect upon these structures.

The other structures throughout your planet—there are substructures and other communities that have been built around them, and that is what your history tells you...[that] these communities built these in representation for a particular deity, a particular Being. But it is the structures that have been built around them and the subterranean structures that have been built beneath them—those are the humans, again, creating something around it.

But what if your teachings are to understand that the pyramid itself stood alone, amongst any other pyramid that is in the area? They are purposefully aligned for a grid upon your planet, a structural grid upon your planet to funnel energy in specific places to the center of your planet. What takes place beyond that, what takes place once they're deactivated, what takes place once the humans are sustainable and habitable upon this planet...that is the history that [has been] written. What needs to be...and it is not to say erased from your history, but it is to expand that timeline of history, from the origin point that you believe to the actual origin point of your planet, the origin point of your galaxy, the origin point of all the planets, this origin point that began this experience.

Healing Aspects of the Pyramids

Many of the pyramid structures, many of the structures that have been built for these particular resonant points still hold the resonant frequency. Yes, if you enter in and you allow yourself to absorb the frequency, absorb that vibration, you will feel. You will hear. It will tone through your physical body. This is the remnant. This is, as you strike a tuning fork, that sound carries on to the faintest point. These structures are beginning to wane to their faintest point. Once they are resonating, that resonance stays for millennia. And they are continuing to vibrate.

[The] waters that are present [within the pyramids] hold healing frequencies. These waters are the remnants of the origin point, the origin waters, the creation waters. This is what has been brought up from the inner Earth to create life around the planet. This is the remnant of them. It is sustainable. It will continue to flow.

You can step into many of these pyramids. Doesn't matter which ones. Doesn't matter where upon the planet that you find them. If you step into these places and you are not willing to receive, then it will just be an experience. Your body will sense something, but it will not take on the healing aspect. You must be in a state willing to receive. This is an energetic frequency, an energetic resonance, an energetic balancing. Those that are willing to receive, walk in and be bathed in it. Breathe it in. Drink it in. Allow yourself to be immersed in it if possible. But you will feel a transformation take place because you are receiving the original origin source of water.

Other Structures of Earth

[The megaliths at Easter Island were created by] the humans, the pre-human experience of your timeframes, [as] representations of those that assisted them. For once existence, life, took place upon this planet, humans, then, are brought online. Other Beings, then, are interacting. Other galactic Beings come in, interact with those humans that are there. There have been periods of time that the galactics come in, cohabitate with those humans that are in presence at a

particular period, a particular timeframe, [to] impart information, impart knowledge, and then depart.

These structures, these representations, these figures are mirrors. They are to represent those that have been in presence with the humans as a gesture of "thank you," a gesture of, "we allow you to come back at any particular point; we call you into our community."

⁂ *Stonehenge itself, that is a celestial call. This object, this series of stones, this is one that's an energetic...the structure that would be in place, this is one that brings together all celestial vibrations into a ring. This is just the center aspect. You have to understand there are multiple rings of existent stones and structures that radiate out, distant from this center structure. All that remains is the center structure.*

This, too, was assembled by the humans, but there was assistance from galactics to make sure it is aligned appropriately with all celestial points in your sky. This is one to coalesce all celestial vibrations into one resonant frequency in the center point. This is to allow...one would understand it as...the point at which you leave your body, your astral travel. You do this in your sleep process. This is one that is activated without being in sleep process. You walk into the center at particular points of your physical calendar year where certain celestial vibrations are coalesced to the center, and those humans that wish to travel to those celestial points can then be activated; their human form will remain in place and their energetic body will end up traveling to those celestial points.

What you see is just a mere speck of the number of pyramids, structures. They are not all pyramids. There are plenty of structures that are not in the pyramid shape. They do not resonate the same way, but they hold energy in a different fashion. There are a number of structured walls, structured frames that are in place that hold a frequency in order to coalesce energy to a center point on your surface.

You will understand a significant difference between what is witnessed when you observe what has been built by humans and what has been left behind by the constructors and builders. There is an architectural form. There is a flow of understanding, a flow of energy with all the objects and all of the structures that we have built in place for our existence throughout the millennia, until it was sustainable by the first generation of humans. That is where your history should start to look. This structure system that we have put in place—the connected points, the structured walls, the pyramids, the cavernous expanses beneath your Earth—that is where history needs to begin to change the perspective.

The Pharaonic Period of Egypt

By the point at which that group of Beings, that group of humans, was in existence, we have already been departed for multiple millions of years. You have to understand, they are not the first ones to discover these particular locations, these particular structures. They're not the first Beings, the first humans, to enter into many of these places. For this portion of your history, they are the most recent. They are the most recent ones to go in and renovate what they have found for their own use. For when they found them, they, too, found hieroglyphs. They found writings. They found objects. They found what they believed to be an ancient society.

For your Egyptian Pyramids, themselves, looked much different. They were actually much larger than they are now. Much has been stripped away over time. Much has been reutilized, and that's why they've been stripped away. Those that have the flat surface upon the top, they, too...much has been reutilized, much has been taken away and reutilized throughout a community, but yet leaving a structure just enough.

You have to understand, too, those that have been working with those structures, those humans in those locations, as they begin to pull away objects from the structures, the building blocks of those structures, they get to a point at which, one, the frequency in themselves begins to change and they realize they must stop; two, the objects they are pulling away are becoming physically impossible to move. They can only go so far. This is why your pyramids look stacked. Much has been removed, but they are removing only the lightest of the objects that they can physically move.

So this is a cycle over and over and over, and the point at which you have the discoveries within this timeframe...this would be roughly a three thousand-year timeframe, which is, according to your timeline, very minuscule; it is very small. It is the smallest of the small. But, yet, in your history point, it is a great expanse of time, and it is only these humans that could have, should have, would have created all of these structures.

But if you were to—not from an engineering standpoint, not from a builder's standpoint, not from a constructor's standpoint—but if you were to stand in front of many of these structures and you, then, look upon yourself and look upon the humans during that particular period of time, that cycle of time, and you compare yourself to those humans, you would find that the humans during that particular period of time were much shorter, much smaller in stature. For you see, the humans themselves go through many cycles of extremely tall, giant, down to very short, very small humans. This is purposeful through the generational cycle and the expression of the planet itself. It, too, goes through cycles. That particular cycle is one that the humans themselves were quite small.

Hieroglyphs and Galactics

Now, the hieroglyphs themselves and what they depict...that is the galactic Beings that have come to them. It is their representation. It is their representation that they are creating [through] paintings, murals, inscriptions of these Beings that have come to them, over time, to assist them in new galactic teachings, new worldly teachings, new tools. [These hieroglyphs] are a vibrational expression depicted in an image, [so they hold an energetic signature that is accessible to humans if they wish to tune into it].

But if you stand alongside them and you look at the structures, do not allow yourself to be placed within an engineering understanding...just a plain human, standing there in front of just one of the blocks, just one of the sections, just one experience. And then go into what you understand as your history and your teachings of how they were constructed. What does your vibration tell you? What does your essence tell you? Many will understand that this is an impossible feat. And it has been. Not one human will take and construct, not ten thousand, not one million humans upon any generation will construct any one of these structures within a short amount of time for any particular purpose. It is an impossible feat.

What you would find, if humans were to be constructing megalithic structures, such as your pyramids, you would find partial construction. They would get to a particular point that a physical reality of physicality can no longer sustain the build of the structure. There would have to be assistance. This, too, the other part of your understanding, this aspect of the galactic Beings coming in and assisting them to build pyramids. Yes, the galactics have capabilities to move structures and move objects. Yes.

But even in that, there is no need for them to build such a structure. There is no need to activate such a structure; for they understand, the galactics understand, these structures were put in place for the beginning stage of existence. And they also understand that through time, they will be deactivated. They also understand that they will be found. But they also understand that even if they [were] to impart the pre-knowledge, the prehistory, the pre-human understanding of what these structures are, the humans that [were] in place [would] depict it in such a way that it will be confusing for further generations.

For if you were to, today, be given an understanding...we bring forth a bit of information, a bit of technology, and tell you, "This is exactly how it works. This is exactly how it functions. Do these things to create this particular object to move these particular objects to a certain extent," and it uses nothing that is in existence in your realm now, but yet you try to explain that to many other humans that are upon the planet now, there would be confusion. You could depict it in drawings. You could depict it in writings. You could have all the understandings. But yet you do not have the capability or the means to put together a specific object to do what it is to do. It does not exist. It cannot be put together. But yet you have this information.

This is history. This is how your history functions. Galactics have been with the humans all along. They are here now, imparting information, knowledge, and teachings, engineering understanding, practices. But if your human construct, your experience now, your life now upon the planet does not have the means to construct what is brought forward, then it cannot be put into existence. Yet the teachings are there, and when you pass those teachings along, it is very confusing. It does not make sense, and they are, then, left to lay.

This is exactly what is in [the] history of what you see printed and depicted on walls and structures. They are trying their best to depict what has been brought forward to them as a teaching for other generations to understand. You have a belief that these hieroglyphs upon these Egyptian Pyramids tell you a specific thing, but you have not deciphered them 100 percent. Many will say they have an understanding of what the Egyptian language and the hiero-glyphs mean, but you have not deciphered them 100 percent.

Once you understand the key to understanding them, then another realm opens up...a realm of understanding of technology that they were using to do certain things—not build megalithic structures but to have an existence that was sustainable...comforts that would not otherwise be. And that is the most impor-tant understanding. The galactics that are being brought to you through dream or through meditation or through experiences, they're not here to teach you this grand thing to build or these big structures to build. They're bringing forth information to change the comfort of your experience, the comfort of your exis-tence, and allow all humans to be equalized by this experience. That is the purpose of the galactics. The builders and constructors are the preliminary experience, to begin the process, and then we step away.

UNDERSTANDING HYBRIDS

Once our galaxy came into being, there was a natural process of expansion and creation. The frequencies of the twelve source clusters selectively merged together, creating what we understand as hybridized Beings. Some of the Twelve hybridized more frequently, while others removed themselves entirely when the focus shifted away from the human project—when hybridization became more about control.

As described throughout the book, the hybridization process is quite complex. The Draconians, for example, explained that some source clusters participate as observers, rather than directly lending their energy. What wasn't communicated quite as clearly is that there are certain clusters that are considered the "primary" contributors to a particular hybridized Being. Others are what we would call "secondary" contributors. Secondary contributors might simply impart a certain characteristic or aspect of their energy.

For example, the primary energies involved in creating the Mantis Beings were the Polarians, Arcturians, and Martians. However, you may have noticed that the Draconians and the Sirians also claimed, in their transmissions, to have assisted with the Mantis project. The Twelve explained to me, when I asked for clarification, that the Draconians provided the Mantis Beings with an analytical and management aspect, while the Sirians imparted an expansiveness of the heart. The Twelve explained it this way:

You have to understand that just as the humans themselves are a hybrid of all twelve, other hybridized Beings take on aspects from all, but there [are] usually two to three that are the primary roles of hybridization. For when it is said that, "it is this cluster and this cluster," you also have to understand those are the primary clusters that have imparted the primary pieces. There are additional pieces that are layered in, but very small, that are not normally recognized by other Beings, by other clusters; it is a small enough piece that it is not normally recognized with those other hybridized Beings.

Some of the most commonly recognized hybridized Beings are listed below.

~

Zetas (Greys): Sirian, Martian, and Venusian
Mantis Beings: Polarian and Arcturian first; that Being then hybridized with Martians
Blue Avians: Venusian and Sirian
Reptilians: Pleiadian and Draconian
Mermaids: Orion and Sirian
White Lion Beings: Sirian and Lyran

ANIMAL ASSOCIATIONS

When I questioned the Sirians about their planet being called the Dog Star and whether that implied that they had a specific connection to canines, they explained that each of the twelve source clusters did, in fact, have a unique relationship to a particular group of animals on our planet. The Sirians shared that the purpose of these connections is to assist with the amplification of the clusters' transmissions:

There are associated clusters with associated animals upon this planet. Each one of the clusters has some association with a particular animal grouping within your planet. This is to help amplify any transmissions. Even though they are disassociated with the humans at times, they are amplifying transmissions.

∼

Andromedans: Large primates
Agarthans: Burrowing animals
Orions: Sea life
Sirians: Canines
Lyrans: Felines

Venusians: Birds
Pleiadians: Horses
Arcturians: Horses, goats, mules, donkeys, sheep, and similar
Polarians: Large and small fish
Hadarians: Burrowing animals
Draconians: Reptiles
Martians: Small primates

ACKNOWLEDGMENTS

Immense gratitude to my soul-mate, Will, and so many others who made this book possible:

Judy Buchanan, Marc Barrie, Samantha Kaufman, and Tracy Crow for being faithful early readers and providing encouragement, insight, and editorial advice.

Maria Fink, Alex Drew, Kris Skirving, Elaine Helmly, and the Charleston Galactic Ambassador group for your support and friendship in this realm and others.

Tobi Elbel at Birdsong Studios, LLC for tuning in to the energy of the Twelve in order to painstakingly interpret and scribe the powerful light language symbols that help energize each chapter.

Laura Eisenhower for your *yes*!

Madeleine at Fiverr for your outstanding transcription work.

Abir Hasan at 99Designs for the phenomenal cover design.

Thaddeus, my powerful Lyran partner, for your guidance and loving energy.

The Twelve, for partnering with me to get this message out to humanity. Thank you for your patience in helping me *get it right.*

ABOUT THE AUTHOR

Dr. Allison Brown is an award-winning author, educator, and quantum healer. In 2014, her search for reconciliation between a newfound spirituality and her traditional Christian upbringing led her on an amazing journey of self-discovery, detailed in her first book, *The Journey Within: A Christian's Guide to 14 Non-traditional Spiritual Practices*. Her second book, *Love Notes from the Animal Kingdom* is a heart-warming compilation of conversations with pets and animal collectives. Allison co-authored a third book, *The Ancestor's Within: Reveal and Heal the Ancient Memories You Carry*, an Amazon best-seller.

William (Will) Brown, is a psychic-medium, trance channel, and Reiki Master. Serving as a guinea pig during his wife's Reiki training in 2014 reawakened the Spirit connection he had sensed throughout his childhood but had been too busy to contemplate during his 26 years with the Coast Guard. Will has since realized his passion and purpose as a healer, teacher, and messenger. With the support of his guides, who call themselves The Collective, Will has been blessed to assist folks from all across the world.

Allison and Will work together to help folks heal, discover, and awaken. Using complementary skills, they facilitate communication with their clients' higher selves, spiritual guides, ancestors, and even pets! They are based in Moncks Corner, South Carolina, offering in-person and online sessions from their metaphysical event space, The Treehouse.

To book a session, please visit: https://palmandlotus.com/

Follow Allison:

Website: www.drallisonbrown.com

FB: https://www.facebook.com/drallibrown

Quantum Healers: https://www.quantumhealers.com/drallisonbrown

Follow Will:

Website: www.william-brown.com

YouTube: https://www.youtube.com/@messagesfromthecollective

FB: https://www.facebook.com/willbrownpsychic

Quantum Healers: https://www.quantumhealers.com/williambrown

Made in the USA
Las Vegas, NV
27 April 2024

89215265R00174